LOST VOICES FROM THE TITANIC

LOST VOICES FROM THE TITANIC

The Definitive Oral History

Nick Barratt

preface
publishing

Published by Preface 2009

10 9 8 7 6 5 4 3 2 1

First published in Great Britain in 2009 by Preface Publishing
20 Vauxhall Bridge Road
London SW1V 2SA

An imprint of The Random House Group Limited

www.rbooks.co.uk
www.prefacepublishing.co.uk

Addresses for companies within The Random House Group Limited
can be found at www.randomhouse.co.uk

The Random House Group Limited Reg. No. 954009

A CIP catalogue record for this book is available from the British Library

Hardback ISBN 978 1 84809 149 8
Trade Paperback ISBN 978 1 84809 150 4

The Random House Group Limited supports The Forest Stewardship
Council (FSC), the leading international forest certification organisation. All
our titles that are printed on Greenpeace approved FSC certified paper carry
the FSC logo. Our paper procurement policy can be found at
www.rbooks.co.uk/environment

Mixed Sources
Product group from well-managed
forests and other controlled sources
www.fsc.org Cert no. TT-COC-2139
© 1996 Forest Stewardship Council
FSC

Typeset in AGaramond by Palimpsest Book Production Limited,
Grangemouth, Stirlingshire

Printed and bound in Great Britain by Clays Ltd, St Ives plc

Contents

Preface

Outline

If you were to ask someone to name a famous ship from any period of history, you would almost certainly receive the instantaneous response '*Titanic.*' And if you then asked why they chose that particular ship, the words 'iceberg' and 'sunk' would not be far behind. There have been bigger, faster and more beautiful ships, but the story of the *Titanic* has been etched in our collective memory ever since Sunday 14 April 1912, when it collided with an iceberg en route to New York during its maiden voyage. The ship originally described as 'unsinkable' by its owners and designers took just over two hours to fill with water, breaking in two and dragging over 1,500 souls to a watery tomb at the bottom of the Atlantic Ocean. What is perhaps most remarkable of all is not that so many died that night, but that over 700 people survived the sub-zero water and lived to tell the tale.

Lost Voices From the Titanic provides a definitive narrative of the disaster in the words of those who designed, built and sailed on the ship, as well as contemporary accounts from the resulting inquiry. Also included are articles from newspapers and journals, which took a morbid interest in the tragedy and its aftermath. It is a harrowing tale, combining incredible folly and unimaginable courage in equal measure, where eyewitness accounts from those lucky enough to survive will transport you back to those heartbreaking moments on that fateful Sunday night when families were separated for ever, and those left behind were forced to deal with the reality of their approaching death.

Historiography

The *Titanic* has been extensively written about over the years – there are literally thousands of titles available, ranging from Walter Lord's widely regarded *A Night to Remember,* published in 1955 and made into a film of the same name three years later, to the more recent *Titanic Voices: Memories from the Fateful Voyage* (1997), which focused on oral testimony and contemporary accounts centred mainly on the experiences of people from Southampton and its environs who were affected by the tragedy, and another anthology of archival material, *The Titanic: Lost Words* (2005). Public perception of the disaster in recent years has been primarily shaped by dramatisations, such as James Cameron's blockbuster film *Titanic,* released in 1997 and breaking box-office records at the time – further proof of the ship's continued allure down the ages. The defining image of the *Titanic* is now Kate Winslet and Leonardo DiCaprio standing on the prow of the vessel as it ploughs through the waves. Yet there is danger in combining historical fact with fictional characters to create drama, as it becomes much harder to separate myth from reality in the public mind, a feeling succinctly expressed in David Mitchell's novel *Cloud Atlas*:

> The workings of the actual past and the *virtual* past may be illustrated by an event well known to collective history such as the sinking of the *Titanic.* The disaster as it *actually* occurred descends into obscurity as its eyewitnesses die off, documents perish and the wreck of the ship dissolves in its Atlantic grave. Yet a *virtual* sinking of the *Titanic,* created from reworked memories, papers, hearsay, fiction – in short, belief – grows ever 'truer'. The actual past is brittle, ever-dimming and ever more problematic to access and reconstruct: in contrast, the virtual past is malleable, ever-brightening and ever more difficult to circumvent / expose as fraudulent.

The role of the academic historian is to sift through evidence and compile a narrative, timeline or thesis. However, an attempt to produce an account as close as possible to what actually happened, no matter how well intentioned, not only becomes harder to achieve as time passes and eyewitnesses either change their views – coloured by subsequent media coverage or influenced by reflecting on other accounts of the event – or die out, but is also affected and shaped by what the historian considered happened: a type of natural bias. On the other hand, when dealing with a topic that is as famous as the *Titanic* it is important to recognise that certain sections of the story are already well known because of previous media attention, and not only retell these passages but also challenge preconceived ideas. Furthermore, the standard narrative account of the *Titanic* starts and ends with the maiden voyage, the iceberg and the rescue operation by the *Carpathia* – because these are the dramatic events that people remember. This is reflected in many of the publications on offer in bookstores, and increasingly online, which focus on April 1912 and the following months – combining pictures and eyewitness accounts of that fateful night. As Walter Lord explained, when writing on 26 June 1955 to Mrs Helen Melville 'Mel' Cooke, daughter of the *Titanic*'s Captain Edward John Smith, he saw his role when compiling *A Night To Remember* almost as a that of tour guide to the past: 'I just want to recreate the night the *Titanic* went down so that anybody can picture exactly what it was like. I want to re-capture all the little incidents and details. I want to preserve all the drama, excitement and courage that blended with the ice and the stars to make this night so utterly unforgettable. People are growing old now, and I want to do all this before the story fades away.' (LMQ/7/1/18, National Maritime Museum) Yet the legend of the *Titanic* is equally shaped by public expectations of the ship before it set sail. These were based on context and circumstance that needs to be explored to fully understand why the news of its demise created such a reaction; and why the consequences of the disaster were so far-reaching.

Aims and structure

In many ways this book aims to bridge the gap between yet another forensic examination of how the ship sank – a topic that was tackled on television in a recent Channel 4 documentary *The Unsinkable Titanic* (2008) – and a simple regurgitation of familiar stories of heroism and tragedy from literature in the public domain to provide the human story behind the disaster. It is easy to list the eight or so key factors that combined to create the unique circumstances behind the tragedy, but this is too clinical for a book of this nature. Instead, the people linked to the *Titanic* need to be given prominence when retelling the story, and this approach has largely determined the structure of the book, with the division of the narrative into three main sections.

The context of the conception and construction of the *Titanic* is given real prominence and forms the first section of the book, because it helps to explain just why the tragedy was greeted with such shock at the time. It contains commentary from sources such as newspapers and the people concerned with the project, who went about their business blissfully unaware of the fate of the *Titanic* and the infamy that would carve its place in history. Therefore, the accounts of the construction process from the workers involved and the reports of the events that marked the conclusion of each successful phase of construction, testing and fitting out were written primarily from the perspective of how impressive the *Titanic* was from a technical point of view. Similarly, the third section of the book examines how the disaster had a profound effect on maritime safety that is often overlooked. So official sources and newspaper accounts once again sit alongside more personal testimonies that trace how the disaster affected the survivors, perhaps none more deeply than J. Bruce Ismay – the driving force behind the *Titanic*, on board when the ship struck the iceberg and vilified afterwards for a variety of reasons. These two sections act as bookends to the main narrative of the maiden voyage, which features the accounts of those who were lucky enough to escape with their lives and give equal prominence to emphasise the personal trauma suffered by the survivors. The study of contemporary versions of events prior to the sinking is crucial to understanding the *Titanic* story, for the very reason that they are untainted by hindsight and prior knowledge of the ship's fate. However, one problem is that such accounts are rare, and a large amount of information was gathered by the American and British investigative teams for the official inquiry into the sinking when key players were either dead or naturally reticent about some aspects of their role in the tragedy. These official reports still play an important part but in a slightly different way, which is addressed below.

For similar reasons, it is just as vital that a sense of the confusion surrounding the actual sinking is conveyed. The very nature of the disaster meant that events unfolded at great speed, giving rise to conflicting accounts and often irreconcilable narratives of key moments that have led to historical controversy. Free from the judgements of historians, who often seek the 'absolute' truth in any incident such as the sinking of the *Titanic*, you can make up your own mind about some of the mysteries that still remain: the cause of the tragedy, who was to blame for the events of the night of 14 April; whether a member of the crew committed suicide after being forced to shoot men trying to clamber into the overcrowded lifeboats. The eyewitnesses, and boards of inquiry, certainly had their strong opinions.

The cast

Given that over 1,500 of those on board the ship were unable to give their view of the disaster because they died in the icy waters, the accounts featured in this book provide a version of events dictated by the scars and prejudices of the survivors. However, some of the voices of the lost are also included in the book – letters written about the ship as it was sailing from Southampton to Queenstown, memorabilia handed to loved ones as the ship was sinking, for example. However, the journey begins, and as you will see also ends, with the Ismay family who founded the White Star Line shipping company that owned and influenced the design and construction of the *Titanic*. It was their drive and determination, as well as their rivalry with Cunard, which created the circumstances in which a fleet of super-ships could first be imagined, and then with the help of Harland and Wolff, their long-term business partners in Ireland, turned from a dream into reality.

Yet a book of this nature would be incomplete without hearing from the people who not only designed the ship, but actually built and tested it. The dangers of constructing a vessel the size of the *Titanic* are recounted in newspaper reports of accidents, but the pride that the riveters, plate layers and outfitters felt on completion suggests that working on the *Titanic* was more than just another job. Some of the excitement and anticipation that accompanied both the construction process and sea trials can also be recaptured from documents of the time.

Naturally, the most poignant voices are those recounting the events of 14–15 April 1912. One of the most vivid accounts was provided just days after the disaster by Mrs Charlotte Collyer, who was on board the *Titanic* emigrating to America to start a new life with her husband Harvey and young daughter Marjorie. Although Charlotte managed to scramble aboard a lifeboat clutching her daughter, Harvey was forced to stay behind on the sinking ship and drowned. After rescue by the *Carpathia* and safe arrival in New York, she was left destitute – all their worldly possessions and money were lost with the ship. Despite drawing funds from the charities established to help the victims of the disaster, she decided to sell an account of her story for $300 to the *Semi-Monthly Magazine*, and used the proceeds to eventually return home to England. Her story is one of a number of accounts; each adds a different perspective to the chaos and growing terror as the realisation dawned that the ship was in serious trouble, transporting the reader to the heart of the unfolding tragedy.

One potentially significant voice that remains silent in this book is that of the man who had ultimate responsibility for the *Titanic's* safety throughout its maiden voyage, Captain Edward John Smith. His conduct during the hours before the collision and once the ship started to sink attracted a great deal of criticism from both the popular press and the official boards of inquiry convened to investigate the disaster, yet because he perished with his ship, he was unable to defend himself. Much of the controversy surrounding his role is simply due to the confusion which ensued that night, and he remains one of the lost voices who took his thoughts and feelings with him to a watery grave.

The sources

As indicated earlier, there is so much secondary literature about the *Titanic* that it can be daunting trying to piece together what happened. These days, however, there are online resources to help you through this maze of information that also contain new data and research. Perhaps one of the best is www.encyclopedia-titanica.org, which includes online access to the passenger lists, biographies of the crew and passengers, and articles written by leading experts in the field.

For the preparation of this book, several key record offices and document collections were consulted. First and foremost, the National Maritime Museum in Greenwich has a massive *Titanic* archive, including the business papers of the Ismay family and the Lord McQuitty collection papers used by Walter Lord to create his book *A Night To Remember* published in 1955. These were in turn based largely on the research of and correspondence to and from Walter Lord for his 1955 book. The National Archives in Kew contain official paperwork relating to the British inquiry, which has been placed online alongside the corresponding US material on www.titanicinquiry.org. The final reports of the inquiries form an important narrative within the book, as both provide key technical data relating to the *Titanic's* construction as well as a running commentary on how the disaster unfolded. It's amazing to consider how quickly the inquiries were convened – the announcement that a US investigation into the disaster would take place was made even before the survivors arrived in New York on board the *Carpathia*. The speed reflects the shock felt when news of the *Titanic's* fate started to reverberate around the globe.

Newspaper reports on the construction, sinking and aftermath are held primarily at the British Newspaper Library at Colindale, while regional archives hold their own collections, such as the Public Record Office of Northern Ireland, where much of the Harland and Wolff archives have been deposited, along with specialist material in the archives of the University of Glasgow, for example. Resources are not restricted to contemporary paperwork; the BBC created its own archive based on oral testimonies recorded and broadcast over the years, which can be viewed and heard online at www.bbc.co.uk/archive. And the last survivor, Elizabeth Gladys 'Millvina' Dean, kindly granted an interview during the preparation of this volume; some of her comments made nearly a century after the *Titanic* sank are included here. Sadly, she passed away on 31 May 2009, and it is a great regret that she did not see the publication of this volume.

The location of each source quoted in this book is provided at the end of the transcript. Where possible, contemporary spelling and phrases are used, but where time has rendered meaning slightly harder to comprehend, a note has been added to help with interpretation.

Acknowledgements

Although I wrote the text and selected the passages, extracts and key characters that feature in the following pages, the book simply could not have been written without the help and support of some very special people. First, thanks must go to my agent Heather Holden Brown and her assistant Elly James, who worked tirelessly to secure the contract and – as always – showed great faith in my ability to deliver the finished product. Second, I'd like to acknowledge Trevor Dolby, Nicola Taplin and the publication team at Preface Publishing, who were incredibly encouraging, patient and supportive from the development of the initial concept through to the writing and editing of the manuscript. Without their professionalism, which shines through all these pages, it would not have been possible to produce the book you're now reading. Also, I'm very grateful to Charlotte Young, who helped with the transcription process of all the many documents selected for this book.

I must also comment on the role played by the aforementioned Millvina in shaping the final draft of this volume. As a historian, it is always a thrill to meet someone who was an eyewitness to a major historical event, and Millvina Dean kindly permitted me to film her recollections in February 2009. In preparing for the interview, it was impossible not to view her as almost a piece of living history, the final link with an event that for everyone else on the planet is something they have only read about or seen depicted on screen. Yet when I visited her in Hampshire, she was quick to point out that she was an ordinary person made extraordinary by the event that had made her famous, even more so as the number of remaining survivors diminished until only she remained. Millvina was also keen to stress that she was only a few months old when the ship sank, so had no actual memories of the occasion – indeed, she only found out she had been present when her mother, Eva Georgette Dean, who also survived with Millvina's older brother Bertram Vere Dean, remarried and told her the story. Eva's first husband, Bertram Frank Dean, had perished in the disaster. Yet, despite the second-hand nature of the account told to her by her mother, it was still an electrifying moment when she described how she had been lowered into the lifeboat in a mail sack and about the momentary fear her mother had felt when she lost sight of Vere and thought he'd been drowned too before discovering that he was being looked after by another passenger in the lifeboat. The matter-of-fact tone of her account and the clear sense of loss she still felt about her father – 'such a handsome man, the love of her [mother's] life' – means that you see the tragedy through her eyes and realise that every account contained in this volume was related by real people whose lives were dramatically affected by the events of 14–15 April 1912.

The biggest vote of thanks must go to Laura Berry, senior researcher at Sticks Research Agency, who undertook the vast majority of archival and picture research for this volume and set up the interview with Millvina Dean. Her ability to unearth highly poignant yet little-known contemporary testimony never ceases to amaze, as did her patient and philosophical responses to my demands for more information as the deadline for the delivery of the manuscript for this book loomed on the horizon. It is therefore to her that this book is dedicated.

Part One

The Background and Construction of the *Titanic*

1

Historical Background

The World in 1912

I think it is not untrue to say that in these years we are passing
through a decisive period in the history of our country. The
wonderful century, which followed the battle of Waterloo and
the downfall of the Napoleonic domination, which secured to
this small island so long and so resplendent a reign, has come to
an end. We have arrived at a new time. Let us realize it. And
with that new time strange methods, huge forces, larger combinations – a Titanic world – have sprung up around us.

The Times, 24 May 1909

Before the story of the *Titanic* can be told, it is important to consider
the period of history in which this iconic ship was conceived, simply
because the world was so different to the one we know today. What
life was like for everyday folk in the year of the disaster, 1912, is very
difficult to imagine, especially from a technological point of view given
our familiarity with instant means of communicating with one another,
access to information at our fingertips via the Internet, and the ability
to travel to the other side of the planet in 24 hours. Plans to design
a giant, luxury vessel that would transport its passengers across the
Atlantic in comfort and record time – the *Titanic*'s theoretical top
speed was 23 knots, little more than 26 miles an hour, and it would
have taken 7 days to travel from Southampton to New York via
Cherbourg and Queenstown (now Cobh), Ireland – may appear quaint

to someone used to the concept of space tourism in the twenty-first century, but it is easy to forget that in the first few decades of the twentieth century long-distance affordable travel was limited to rail or sea, and was not something to be rushed. Motor cars were still very much a novelty on city streets, as large-scale production had only got under way in 1902; and mechanised flight, while a reality by 1912, was still very much in its infancy and largely restricted to air shows and military applications – the Royal Flying Corps was formed in this year, and a commercial application for airline travel was still a distant dream.

In short, this was a very different age to the one we are used to. Queen Victoria had only been in her grave eleven years and her grandson, George V, was on the throne; Herbert Asquith was the Liberal prime minister; women were not allowed to vote unless they were property owners (indeed many men were also excluded from the democratic process), although the movement to extend the suffrage was gradually gathering pace; and strict class divisions still existed in British society. The Labour party had only been formed in 1900, the result of decades of struggle by working people and trade unions to gain representation in the electoral system. Strikes and riots featured prominently during this period, with coal miners and dockers protesting on the streets. Tensions were also growing in Ireland, with nearly a quarter of a million loyalist men signing the Ulster Covenant (and a similar number of women signing the parallel Declaration) to reject the idea of Irish home rule and a separate Irish parliament. This was also the year in which Captain Robert F. Scott and his team narrowly failed to become the first men to reach the South Pole, only to find posthumous fame when they perished in their attempt to return to safety. Shadows of the forth-coming global conflict were already being cast across Europe with the outbreak of war in the Balkans in October, with rumblings of dis-content being voiced in embassies across the continent and politicians casting worried glances at the texts of a complicated network of inter-national treaties and the perceived implications of maintaining them. In so many ways, 1912 was to prove a monumental year in history.

For ordinary folk living in Britain at the start of the twentieth century, a real sense of change and modernity could be perceived sweeping across the nation. Concerns about the political situation in Europe and the escalating arms race fuelled by the German empire's plan to create an Atlantic fleet to challenge British naval power were felt by all levels of society, but increasingly those outside the political and industrial elite were concerned with the acquisition of wealth and reaping the rewards of Britain's economic success over the previous half-century. Public health reforms, slum clearance and the creation of institutions to care for vulnerable members of society had improved living conditions for thousands of hitherto poor or lower-working-class families, while the regulation of child labour, improving health and safety standards and rising pay had ameliorated some of the worst features of the Industrial Revolution and brought a measure of disposable income to the workers, as well as the captains of industry. Consequently, there was a new market for consumer goods, and spare money was often spent on trips away – the birth of the holiday. An integral part of this process of material aspiration and economic growth was Britain's status as an island nation, reliant on the ocean as a means of communication with the rest of the world free from borders and other physical barriers to trade.

Britannia Rules the Waves

In 1877, Mr. Ismay offered to place the whole of the White Star fleet of steamships, then – as now – among the swiftest in existence, at the disposal of Her Majesty's Government for service as cruisers or transports in event of war.

Liverpool Daily Post, 1 December 1899

By the start of the twentieth century the British empire stretched around the world, and maritime trade was at the heart of its success. Traditionally, London had dominated trade and continued to play a major role, but the increasing size of vessels required to carry goods to places such as India, the Far East and Africa and the sheer volume of trade meant that the Pool of London and its associated dock were near to capacity. Western provincial ports such as Liverpool enjoyed a boom during the late nineteenth and the early twentieth centuries, based predominantly on transatlantic trade; in 1906, for example, the main goods being traded in and out of Liverpool were raw cotton, meat, corn and cereals, India rubber, wool, live animals, copper and timber. Tobacco was the tenth-largest import in this year, worth only a fraction of the value of the raw cotton that came into the docks for distribution to the hungry mills of Lancashire and beyond, and the resultant cotton-based manufactured products that were then exported around the world. Make no mistake, this was big business: imports in 1906 accounted for just under £147 million, and exports £150 million, making the value of all goods flowing through the port £297 million.

Transatlantic sea freight was not restricted to cargo and goods – it's easy to forget in our age of mobile phones, text messages and emails that written correspondence was the main means of communication, with letters, parcels and packages carried around the world in steamships. Long-distance messages could be communicated by telegraph, with cables connecting Britain and America since the mid-nineteenth century – ironically, the *Great Eastern*, a predecessor of the *Titanic* for the title of world's greatest steamer and famous for its own construction problems, laid the first successful transatlantic cable in 1865 and 1866 – and telephone technology was still in its infancy. Most people with relatives abroad, or whose business relied upon the transportation of packaged items, were therefore reliant on written communication, and mail packets, as they were known, formed a regular and intricate network of sailing routes across the globe.

Yet not only messages found their way around the world on a regular basis. Transatlantic shipping catered for a burgeoning passenger market, one that had existed since Britain had founded its North American colonies and then repaired its relationship with the United States of America after the War of Independence (1775–1783). Crucial was the formation of companies – such as Cunard in the mid-nineteenth century – that ran regular steamship services across the Atlantic from western and southern ports in Britain and Ireland to America's east coast. Speeds across the ocean gradually increased, cutting the journey time from months to weeks, so that by the end of the century it was possible to reach America in under a fortnight. Many people sought to leave Britain's shores permanently, to start a new life in the land of opportunity. Some were being squeezed out of traditional lines of work – agriculture, for example – while others were more opportunistic, seizing upon the expansion of America into its western states via the growing railroad network to travel to the California goldfields to find their fortune, or simply signing up to one of the construction gangs building the railways, cities and heavy industrial plants springing up all over the continent.

America was also seen as a place to escape hardship and persecution. In the 1840s many thousands of Irish fled the ravages of the Potato Famine in 'coffin ships', so called because of the very real chance they would die during their voyage from disease – cholera and typhus were rife on sailing vessels and steamships – or from drowning when overcrowded ships were lost in storms at sea. Other dangers included fire, starvation and even murder. Many families held 'living wakes' before the ships set sail, certain that they would never see their loved ones again even if they did make it across the ocean to a new life.

By the end of the century, other waves of immigrants were heading for America via British ports. East European Jews, fleeing the pogroms in the Russian empire in the 1880s, often stopped off in Britain, joining the growing transatlantic passenger trade with their few remaining possessions grabbed at the start of their flight months or even years before. The numbers heading to America from Britain and Europe grew so large that in 1892 an immigration station was opened on Ellis Island, New York, to process the hordes of applicants who arrived hoping to take up residency. In 1907 over 1.25 million people passed through the 'Island of Tears'.

The growth of passenger freight between Britain and America was not restricted to people seeking a new home. The globalisation of trade, culture and politics and the close relationship between the two countries saw increasing numbers of wealthy passengers crossing the Atlantic on a regular basis. They desired not only speedy transportation but also comfort and luxury, and were prepared to pay for the privilege. Consequently, shipbuilders focused on providing new ways of transporting passengers from all walks of life as quickly, yet as profitably, as possible, and the ocean-going liner was developed, with different standards of accommodation priced according to status and the size of one's wallet.

First-class passengers could expect to enjoy the height of comfort on their journey – a floating top-rated hotel experience – with quality entertainment, spacious cabins and only the best food and drink, while second-class customers could reserve a small berth or cabin, and enjoy a reasonable standard of accommodation. However, for those heading overseas because of poverty or persecution, necessity meant the cramped conditions of steerage – rooms situated between the passenger decks and the cargo hold, holding as many bunks as possible, with only the basic requirements for survival, often without heating, light or even proper ventilation. Even on the most luxurious liners, deaths occurred among the poor souls crammed below decks, even though they usually made up the majority of people on board.

In addition to commercial requirements, another darker factor lay behind the development of large-scale vessels during the first decade of the twentieth century – the arms race. Britain's international pre-eminence was largely due to its dominance of the seas through the Royal Navy, which had gone largely unchallenged since Nelson's legendary victory over Bonaparte's fleet at Trafalgar in 1805. A century of ruling the waves, however, had not led to complacency, and the Admiralty was involved in extensive research and development to ensure its ships were at the cutting edge of naval technology. An important relationship had developed between the commercial sector, where shipping magnates had invested vast sums of money building up the merchant marine – as shown by the ever-growing annual publication of British-registered vessels in *Lloyds Shipping Lists* – and the British government.

A navy capable of spanning the globe was incredibly expensive, so the Admiralty needed to be able to command suitable merchant-class vessels to support, and on occasion take part in, its operations during times of war. On occasion, the government was prepared to subsidise the development and commissioning of mercantile vessels capable of adaptation for naval use. The benefits were considerable, for both sides – shipping companies involved were able to afford larger and faster vessels with the capability of armed defence, and the government could point to the tax revenue advantages of supporting a key economic sector, while growing its reserve of ships for use during times of national crisis. Cunard, the main rivals of the White Star Line (which built the *Titanic*), were to benefit from this strategy, as *The Times* reported on 26 February 1903:

THE NEW SUBSIDIZED STEAMERS FOR THE CUNARD LINE

It was announced last year that the Government was prepared to advance money on terms advantageous to the Cunard Company if they constructed two large vessels of exceptional speed for the Transatlantic service, and further to add a large annual subsidy, conditional on the designs and tests meeting with the approval of the Admiralty. It was conclusively proved during the Cuban war that fast mail steamers with light armament but of great coal capacity were desirable adjuncts to a fighting fleet; it is possible that further consideration might have caused the vessels that were hired to have been employed during that war on more useful service than cable cutting; but the enormous disparity on the scene of action between two contending fleets is not likely to be reproduced in any coming war between two great European Powers. . . The Germans now have several large and fast steamers whose capabilities meet the views of their owners and of their Government, and they are faster over an ocean journey than any owned in this country at the present time. They are vessels of 21,000 tons of displacement, and in moderate weather make Atlantic passages at nearly 23 knots speed with a coal consumption of some 24 tons per hour, burned in producing about 37,000 indicated horse-power; they vary from 663 to 678 feet in length with 67 to 72 feet beam, and the largest of them has 28 feet draught. These would form admirable ocean scouts in war, and if loaded to their utmost coal supply would have an extended range at reasonable speed.

Designs for the new Cunard ships are nearly complete and model experiments have reached finality, but the vessels are so much beyond precedent in size and contemplated speed that an element of uncertainty causes anxious consideration. They will be approximately 760 feet on the water line with 80 feet in beam . . . The engines of the new vessels are contemplated for over 60,000 horse power and are expected to drive the vessels at a sea-speed of some 25 knots on a coal consumption of 46 tons per hour. The vessels will be luxuriously fitted in every way and will carry a whole colony of crew and of passengers, and each vessel will cost about a million and a quarter pounds sterling. Few existing firms of shipbuilders have plant adequate for constructing vessels of such unprecedented dimensions.'

The Times, 26 February 1903, National Maritime Museum
TRNISM/6/1 (618) folder 5

Subsidising the construction of merchant vessels to supplement the fleet freed up money to develop a new category of ship that would change the world. The first decade of the twentieth century was a time of escalating tension between Germany and Britain, particularly regarding competing colonial interests in Africa. Germany had been fiercely critical of Britain's handling of the Boer War and to protect and expand its own influence on the continent needed a fleet to rival Britain's. This resulted in the first arms race of the twentieth century, fought in the offices of naval architects and realised in shipyards across the British Isles. In 1905 the Admiralty confidently announced that it would take only a year and a day to commission and construct a new super-ship, and – true to its word – HMS *Dreadnought* was ready to set sail at the end of 1906.

This was the first in a new class of battleships that transformed naval warfare and led directly to the escalation in weaponry that would prove so devastating when global conflict finally broke out in August 1914. Having studied the 1904–5 Russo-Japanese War, in particular the way long-range guns had decimated the Russian fleet, the British opted for an all-big-gun battleship with a top speed of 21 knots – faster than any other contemporary military ship of comparable size, with screw shafts driven by steam turbines as opposed to conventional screw propellers – and thick armour plating covering the entire external structure, providing protection against similar weaponry. This made every other large military vessel obsolete overnight. The race was on to construct a new generation of warships, and as a result the high seas had suddenly become more dangerous.

The History of the White Star Line

The White Star Line at once leaped to a foremost place in Atlantic enterprise, and other companies, in their own interest, promptly imitated them in regard to that luxurious and complete comfort which to-day marks the Atlantic liner.

Liverpool Daily Post, 1 December 1899

These were the main political, social and military circumstances in which the *Titanic* was conceived. It is easy to view the struggles taking place for control of world trade as essentially nation against nation, but this is an oversimplification given the fierce rivalry that existed between the three leading British shipping companies that had emerged in the nineteenth century. The most venerable of the trio was the Cunard Steamship Company, whose origins can be traced to the business founded when Samuel Cunard was awarded the first British contract to carry mail via steamship across the Atlantic in 1839 – the British and North American Royal Mail Steam-Packet Company. It held the Blue Riband for the fastest transatlantic voyage for the best part of 30 years, then fell behind its rivals, reformed as the Cunard Steamship Company Limited to raise capital funds, and embraced the emerging new technology to regain its position of prominence. Two lines in particular rivalled Cunard in terms of size and ambition. The Inman Line (which traded under a variety of names such as the Liverpool, Philadelphia and New York Steamship Company and latterly the Inman and International Steamship Company) operated from 1850. Inman outperformed Cunard in the 1860s with the construction of faster ships, and began to win mail contracts from its elder rival. By the 1870s, Inman ships were carrying more passengers to New York than Cunard, offering quicker journey times and winning the Blue Riband on several occasions.

However, the key player for the story of the *Titanic* was the White Star Line, a company which had originally been founded in Liverpool by John Pilkington and Henry Threlfall Wilson but went bankrupt in 1867. A certain Thomas Henry Ismay then entered the scene, and bought the name and flag of the failed company for £1,000 the following year, with the express intention of creating a fleet of ocean-going vessels to challenge the dominant position of Cunard and Inman. Thomas Ismay was born in Maryport, Cumberland on 7 January 1837 and came from a shipbuilding family – both his grandfather and father had constructed wooden vessels in their own shipyards – and Ismay joined the family profession, working an apprenticeship in Liverpool with a company of shipbrokers before spending time at sea. He went into partnership with a friend of his father, Philip Nelson, though this business did not last, and married Margaret Bruce on 7 April 1859, daughter of shipowner Luke Bruce. He established himself in Liverpool, where he contrived to make his own way in the world. The capture of the White Star Line showed his driving ambition to succeed was wedded to his belief that big was better and iron was best.

As the inspiration behind the revived company, Ismay coupled his experience as director of a shipping line with his long-standing relationship with the financiers and merchants of Liverpool. One of his main supporters was the German-born Gustav Christian Schwabe, a remarkable character whose interests extended beyond maritime trade into the construction of ships. Indeed, Schwabe was instrumental in facilitating the partnership between his nephew Gustav Wilhelm Wolff and one of Schwabe's protégés, Edward James Harland, who had gained employment on the recommendation of Schwabe in the firm of marine engineers Robert Stephenson and Company in Newcastle upon Tyne. In 1858 Schwabe helped Harland purchase Robert Hickson's shipyard at Queen's Island, Belfast, the cornerstone for the company Harland and Wolff, founded in 1861. In 1869, over a game of billiards, Schwabe persuaded Ismay to assign the construction contract for his proposed fleet of White Star Line ships to Harland and Wolff; in return Schwabe would provide the necessary funds to make Ismay's vision come true. Shortly afterwards, in 1870, Ismay invited an old friend from his days as an apprentice, William Imrie, to join the management of the company, and the main planks of the resurrected White Star Line were in place.

Ismay died on 30 November 1899, and his obituary in the *Liverpool Daily Post* the following day contains a brief history of the company he'd run for so many years. It clearly shows that the large-scale commercial shipping companies operated under the shadow of government intervention and the constant threat of war, but also demonstrates the influence Ismay wielded over the company, and how highly he was rated by his contemporaries.

DEATH OF MR. T. H. ISMAY
A Remarkable Career
Revolution in Atlantic Enterprise

The announcement which we have to make to-day with profound regret, that Mr. Thomas H. Ismay, the founder of the White Star Line, expired at twenty minutes to seven last evening, at his residence, Dawpool, Cheshire, will be received in Liverpool with unqualified sorrow. The immediate cause of Mr. Ismay's death was failure of the heart's action after operations for an internal trouble. By this untimely death commerce is deprived of a giant leader, whose enterprises have conferred upon Liverpool in particular, and the country at large, benefits which are at first view difficult to appreciate. Mr. Ismay was not only an extraordinary genius in mercantile affairs, but a genial and popular man, personally esteemed by all the world, whose character, both personally and commercially, stood, through a great and long career, high above reproach . . .

Mr. Thomas Henry Ismay was a son of Mr. Joseph Ismay, shipowner, of Maryport, Cumberland. He was born in 1837, the year of the Queen's Accession. In 1853, at the age of sixteen, he came to Liverpool, and served an apprenticeship with Messrs. Imrie and Tomlinson, shipowners and shipbrokers. He was the architect of his own fortune, for, although his father carried on with some success the business of a shipbuilder at Maryport, of which place he is a native, he came to Liverpool having little capital except his own natural and acquired qualities. These, however, soon won for him a place as a business man of acknowledged value . . . In 1867 he acquired the business of the White Star Line of Australian clippers.

The history of the White Star Line takes us back to the old style of small sailing vessels, in which there had been little appreciable change for centuries past, and includes the transition from these to the magnificent sailing clippers which carried Her Majesty's Australian mails, and further to the new order of leviathan steamships such as now fly the White Star flag. It is unnecessary to describe at length the revolution effected in the Australian trade by the clipper-ships, which in the course of seven years conveyed half-a-million adventurers to the goldfields, and were until quite recently almost the exclusive carriers of the steadily increasing commerce between the Colonies and the Mother Country.

In 1867 the managing owner of the White Star Line retired, and an important change took place in the destinies of the line. Mr. Thomas Henry Ismay took over the flag, and very shortly signalised the change of ownership by introducing iron ships instead of the wooden vessels formerly employed. But the great event in the history of the flag came two years later, in 1869, when Mr. Ismay, deeming the moment ripe for the introduction into the Liverpool and New York trade of a high-class passenger service, induced some friends to join him in the formation of the Oceanic Steam Navigation Company.

The new company was initiated with boldness and judgment, and the shares of £1,000 each, fully paid, were at once privately taken up by Mr. Ismay's firm and their friends, including some of the most substantial names in England. In the year following the foundation of the Oceanic Steam Navigation Company, Mr. Ismay was joined in the management by Mr. William Imrie, of the late firm Imrie, Tomlinson, and Co., in whose office he and

Mr. Imrie had been fellow-apprentices. The firm now became Ismay, Imrie, and Co . . .

In forming the new company, he had resolved, as already mentioned, to compete for a share of the passenger traffic between Liverpool and the United States. This lucrative business, including a huge and steady emigration, was then shared between the Cunard, Guion, and Inman Companies. The project of establishing a new company was, however, well planned. Mr. Ismay saw that finality in the Atlantic trade was far from having been reached in 1870. He perceived, indeed, not only that great changes were ahead, but that fortune waited upon initiative. With that policy he began, and in that policy he continued. Thoroughly acquainted with the construction and management of ships, and with a remarkable power of organisation and method, he introduced a new style of steamer, more economical than any yet in use, but swift and elegant. This vessel, the first *Oceanic*, was built by Messrs. Harland and Wolff, who have since built steamers for Messrs. Ismay, Imrie, and Co., at a cost of some seven million sterling.

The points of departure on the part of the new company may thus be summarised: First, by increasing the length of their vessels in proportion to breadth, they enlarged the cargo capacity without adding expenses; secondly, they increased the engine power to ensure greater steadiness; thirdly, they introduced the midship staterooms and saloon. Atlantic liners which preceded the first *Oceanic* had saloon and staterooms in the after-part where the noise of the screws and the motion of the ship were at a maximum. The change to midships was so universally appreciated that the White Star Line at once leaped to a foremost place in Atlantic enterprise, and other companies, in their own interest, promptly imitated them in regard to that luxurious and complete comfort which to-day marks the Atlantic liner. Mr. Ismay was, in truth, the inventor of luxurious ocean travel. The result has been a development of traffic which thirty years ago would have exceeded the most sanguine dreams, and a knitting together of England and America in bonds of mutual interest and knowledge which must profoundly affect the history and well-being of the world.

The first *Oceanic* was launched on the 27th August, 1870, and sailed for New York on her first voyage under the White Star flag on the 2nd March 1871. She was followed in quick succession by the *Baltic, Republic, Adriatic,* and *Celtic,* forming a complete service of steamships equalling in speed and surpassing in accommodation any ships then afloat. The White Star Line is now one of the great shipping enterprises of the world . . .

In 1877, Mr. Ismay offered to place the whole of the White Star fleet of steamships, then – as now – among the swiftest in existence, at the disposal of Her Majesty's Government for service as cruisers or transports in event of war, the outcome of his proposals being the arrangement since made with some of the great steamship lines for securing the services of their vessels in time of national emergency. In 1889 and 1890 were introduced the celebrated twin-screw mercantile armed cruisers *Teutonic* and *Majestic,* each 10,000 tons, which have since made for themselves so great a reputation in the New York mail and passenger service . . . At the end of 1891 Mr. Ismay retired from the partnership with Ismay, Imrie, and Co., leaving the business of the firm to be carried on by Mr. Bruce Ismay . . .

In politics Mr. Ismay was a Liberal Unionist, and a member of the Reform Club, but he steadily declined to seek Parliamentary honours. He nevertheless found time to serve the public in other ways, having been appointed on several Royal and Departmental Commissions, including. . . (the) Board of Trade Life-Saving Appliance Committee (of which he was a chairman in 1889), concerning which Sir M. Hicks Beach afterwards said, in a speech to the Associated Chambers of Commerce: 'It was presided over most ably by a man whose name is a household word among shipping men' . . .

The close and lucrative association between the White Star Line and the shipbuilding industry of Belfast was marked by the presentation to Mr. Ismay, on the 20th July last, of the honorary freedom of that town. The name of the Right Hon. W. J. Pirrie, head of Messrs. Harland and Wolff, the famous shipbuilding firm, who have constructed the entire White Star fleet, was the first to be inscribed on the roll of Belfast's honorary freemen. Mr. Ismay's name was the second to be written on that distinguished roll, because as chief of the White Star Company he had contributed substantially to the prosperity of Belfast. The orders carried out by the Queen's Island firm for Mr. Ismay represented 300,000 tons of shipping, and involved an aggregate payment of £7,000,000. The disbursement of this enormous sum was spread over a period of thirty-five years, or practically the lifetime of the White Star Line up to 1899. To Mr. Ismay, therefore, Belfast was much indebted, and the ceremony of enrolling him as an honorary citizen was made the occasion of general rejoicing. The working men of the borough felt a tribute was due from them, and with the sanction of the Lord Mayor their several thousand modest subscriptions purchased the beautiful golden casket in which the scroll of citizenship was presented to Mr. Ismay. Such spontaneity from these artisans touched Mr. Ismay deeply, and drew from him a heartfelt acknowledgement . . .

Mr. Ismay said that during the long connection, extending over thirty-five years, between Messrs. Harland and Wolff and his firm, many difficult problems had presented themselves, involving much anxious thought; but he did not know that there had ever been any monetary dispute between them, nor could he recall an unfriendly word in the course of a unique business relationship . . . These remarks were received with enthusiasm. And well they might be. Was there ever such a business connection before? Those who knew Mr. Ismay will say that such commercial relationship was natural with a man of his broad mind and generous instincts.

Liverpool Daily Post 1 December 1899,
from the National Maritime Museum

This article was written shortly after Ismay's final act in control of White Star – commissioning *Oceanic (II)* – which was to have profound consequences for the direction the company would take over the next decade, and would ultimately create the circumstances in which the *Titanic* was envisaged and commissioned. Since establishing White Star as a major player on the commercial shipping stage, Ismay had raised the stakes for the whole industry and his competitors, in particular the Cunard liners, with whom White Star vied for control of the lucrative North American market using the speed, size and luxury of their respective fleets. After the decision to commission the second *Oceanic* in 1899, White Star Line made a conscious effort to focus on the quality of experience its passengers would enjoy, rather than speed, which meant that subsequent ships had to be even bigger and more impressive to not only attract first- and second-class passengers, but also to retain the capacity to take large numbers of poorer third-class passengers heading for a new life in Canada or the USA. The sheer cost of constructing such fleets meant that it became harder to remain competitive, and during the late nineteenth and early twentieth centuries many of the smaller or less competitive shipping lines were bought up or amalgamated into larger companies, increasingly financed abroad. As profits fell in the face of growing competition, the Inman Line ran into financial difficulties and declared voluntary liquidation so that it could be bought out by its largest creditor, the International Navigation Company, in 1886. The new venture was eventually consolidated into the American Line, a subsidiary of the International Navigation Company, in 1893.

The obituary of Thomas Ismay showed the importance of relationships at boardroom level between White Star and Harland and Wolff; yet the 1890s saw a changing of the guard during this critical time for the industry. Thomas Ismay was succeeded as managing director by his son Joseph Bruce Ismay, who was to play a central role in the *Titanic* story. Equally, Harland and Wolff lost its main founder Sir Edward Harland in 1895, and William James Pirrie – later Lord Pirrie – assumed control of the venture as chairman. Nevertheless, despite the continuity within the two company boards it became increasingly difficult for family-founded shipping lines to remain afloat without international finance. The passing of Thomas Ismay forced the White Star Line to enter into negotiations behind the scenes with major international financiers to secure the future of the company in an increasingly uncertain climate.

The new money was to come from America, with the creation in 1902 of the International Mercantile Marine Company. This was a trust fund established by Clement Griscom, who controlled the American Line and Red Star Line under the International Navigation Company banner, John Ellerman of the Leyland Line and Bernard Baker of the Atlantic Transport Line. Also purchased at the same time was the British-based Dominion Line. Bankrolling the venture was the considerable fortune of financier John Pierpoint Morgan, whose business acumen was behind General Electric and the United States Steel Corporation, as well as the powerful J. P. Morgan and Company financial house. To the shock of the shipping world, the final player in the partnership was revealed to be the White Star Line and J. Bruce Ismay. Although Griscom initially assumed the presidency of the new company, Ismay was appointed to the position in 1904 after pressure from White Star Line shareholders. Although the White Star vessels continued to fly the British flag, the government was so concerned by the appearance of this essentially American shipping giant that it granted the subsidies to Cunard to create its two superliners, described earlier in *The Times* in 1903.

The reason for Cunard's concerns – and those of the government – soon became clear. With funding from J. P. Morgan, White Star had real hopes that it would be able to rebuild its dominance under the International Mercantile Marine Company banner, and between 1901 and 1907 sent out a clear demonstration of intent with the construction of the so-called Big Four ships, *Celtic*, *Cedric*, *Baltic* and *Adriatic*. These were truly giant vessels of 24,000 tons, with the ability to carry up to 2,000 passengers in third class as well as 400 or so in first and second class. While speed had been sacrificed to sheer size, the numbers the ships could ferry across the Atlantic continued to create a profit for White Star, even though other lines within the International Mercantile Marine Company group failed to prove as successful, leading to fears that the ambitious venture might fail within a few years of its conception.

British dominance of the Atlantic sea trade was a source of great national pride, and even three years after the creation of the new group, there were still doubts that the International Mercantile Marine

Company would benefit British interests. Concerns for the future of White Star were expressed in *Fairplay* magazine in May 1905:

> What most people do feel is the keenest regret that such a magnificent line as the White Star, not to mention the other great lines associated with it, aggregating nearly one million tons of our best shipping, should have passed from British to American ownership, and from British to American control. The Combine fleets are American to the backbone; Americans found the capital, and it is Americans who appoint and pay the managers on this side. It is nothing but a mere pretence to say that through the technical wording of the Company's Act they are in any sense British, though through this technicality they are allowed to fly the British flag, a fact which most people regard as nothing less than a public scandal.
>
> *Fairplay* 25 May 1905 National Maritime
> Museum TRNISM/6/1 folder 8

Concerns over control of a key British company were also shared by long-standing partners Harland and Wolff, whose contracts to build White Star Line vessels had depended on agreements made through personal connections forged in the 1850s and 1860s. Although Harland and Wolff had constructed the Big Four, J Bruce Ismay still felt the need to write to Lord Pirrie to reassure the shipbuilder that their special relationship was safe, outlining his own position as president of the new company in the process:

March 2nd, '04
(off Queenstown)

My dear Pirrie,
Your kind messages reading as follows:
'Our most sincere congratulations. We all look forward to many years pleasant work with you, and assure you of our hearty and full co-operation,' reached me on board of the 'Cedric' the day I left New York,

and it is hardly necessary for me to say how very much I appreciate the kind thought that prompted you to send same, and how grateful I was to receive the assurance of your hearty and full co-operation.

You will readily understand I did not accept the position of President of the I.M.M. Co. without giving the matter earnest and careful consideration, and had I purely considered my own feeling would, without hesitation, have declined same, but finding Mr. Morgan, Mr. Steele, Mr. Griscom and many other friends interested in the I.M.M. Co. with very strong views as to what I should do, eventually acceded to their request. I may say that in coming to this decision I was largely influenced by personal feelings and also by the fact that I felt I should receive the hearty, loyal and active co-operation of all connected with the I.M.M. Co., for without this it would be quite impossible to hope to achieve any measure of success.

We must all realise that the fortunes of the I.M.M. Co. are at an extremely low ebb, and it means a great deal of anxious and hard work to pull it through, and although I am not at all sanguine as to the future of the Company, believe if we all work together, and do all possible in the years to come we may possibly see some slight return for our efforts, but the immediate future is surrounded with serious difficulties.

The most pressing one, to my mind, is the question of finance, and it is in this respect that you can give us much assistance and relief. I know the Company is largely indebted to your Firm, and we must do all possible to reduce this liability; all I ask is that you should make it as easy as possible, and not press us unduly. I do not think there is the least ground for any uneasiness on your part, as no doubt in time the indebtedness will be wiped out, and no one is more alive to the present position than Messrs. Morgan and Steele, who are quite prepared to allow your claims on the I.M.M. Co. to be considered as a prior indebtedness to that of the Company to their Firm.

It was most pleasing to me to see the evident determination on the part of Mr. Morgan to make the I.M.M. Co. a success, if possible, and he is, I am sure, willing and anxious to do all in his power to attain this end . . .

In the meantime, things generally are as bad as they can be, and the outlook gloomy in the extreme. We are in a state of war in the Mediterranean trade, in the Atlantic trade both passengers and freight (the Provision rate being 3/- per ton), and much fear from my latest advices that we are in for a serious upheaval in Australia and New Zealand, but shall do everything possible to avert the latter . . .

Well, I have undertaken a big job, and look to you to help me all you can, and feel sure I can rely on your loyal and hearty help and support. Again thanking you for your kind cable, and trusting Mrs. Pirrie and you are well, and with my kindest remembrances to both,
Believe me,
Yours very sincerely,
(Ismay)
The Right Hon. W. J. Pirrie, LLD, D.Sc.,
Queen's Island,
Belfast

National Maritime Museum TRNISM/2/2

Clearly, the new venture needed to win over public hearts and minds, and coupled with their long rivalry with Cunard – especially given the British-government-backed plans to build the two super-liners – it is easy to understand the background to White Star's grand schemes to take on and beat its domestic and international rivals to a degree never seen before. By 1907 Ismay and his backers at the International Mercantile Marine Company were ready to raise the stakes once again.

2

Building the Titanic

Conception

Messrs. Harland and Wolff of the Belfast shipbuilding works, are prepared to lay down ocean-going 'leviathans' of much greater dimensions than any yet attempted'

Freemans Journal 13 July 1909

The venture to create a fleet of three super-ships – the *Olympic, Titanic* and *Britannic* (to be called the *Gigantic* prior to the loss of the *Titanic*) – owed much to the success of the rival Cunard liners *Lusitania* and *Mauretania*, which were launched in September 1907 to great critical acclaim. The *Lusitania* went on to win the Blue Riband for the fastest transatlantic crossing. This had last been held by a White Star vessel in 1900, when the *Lucania* took the record. By coincidence, the *Lucania* was making the same journey when the *Lusitania* set out on its maiden voyage. New turbine technology as used on the *Lusitania* to drive the propellers meant that the *Lucania* was passed during the first day's sailing despite a head start. It was uncomfortably obvious to the White Star directors that in the race for dominance of the seas they were being left behind. The extent of newspaper coverage of the *Lusitania's* triumph shows how much the public were interested in events and the pride felt that the speediest ship on the seas was British once more.

SURF

The blue ribbon of the turf is an object of ambition with all those whose hobby is horse-racing and whose wealth enables them to indulge in its pursuit. Interest at the present time has, however, vanished from the Racecourse and centred itself in a contest for the blue ribbon, not of the turf, but of the surf. The Atlantic is the racecourse and surf, the mammoth new Cunarder *Lusitania* is the challenger of the World Record held by the German liner *Deutschland*. In 1900 the latter vessel steamed from New York to Plymouth in 5 days 7 hours 38 minutes, wresting the honour from the *Lucania* of the Cunard Line, which in 1895 made the voyage to New York in 5 days 8 hours. To beat the record of the *Deutschland*, the *Lusitania* would have to keep up an average speed of 24 knots an hour, but she did more than that as she covered a measured mile at the rate of 26¾ knots. In this ocean race the *Lucania*, which started a couple of hours ahead of the *Lusitania*, was overhauled and passed on the first day's run. It should be explained that the *Lucania* runs with the usual engines, but that the *Lusitania* is equipped with turbines. The difference is roughly this: the usual reciprocating engine works by admitting steam to each end of a cylinder alternately, thus driving the piston up and down. One end of the piston rod is attached to a crank and the straight movement is by this means converted into a circular one, with the result that a shaft with screw attached can be rotated. Of course, in a large ship there are several cylinders. With a turbine, the force of the steam is applied to the revolving of the shaft without the intermediaries of piston and crank.

If the *Lusitania* in her maiden voyage can beat all records, the advantages of the turbine engine will be apparent, and in the building of future ships it is likely to be favoured. Already there is an announcement that Harland and Wolff are engaged on the plans of a mammoth liner for the White Star fleet to be equipped with both types of engine arranged so that the escaping steam from the reciprocating engines may work the turbine. Should this plan prove successful the blue ribbon may not long remain with *Lusitania* . . .

LUSITANIA WINS

We have just received a wire stating that the *Lusitania* arrived in New York at 9 o'clock this (Friday) morning, thus beating the record of the *Deutschland* by something over an hour and a half.

Southern Star 14 September 1907,
Irish Newspaper Archives, British Library Digital Collection

As the report indicates, even before the *Lusitania* had captured the Blue Riband, Ismay and Lord Pirrie had become sufficiently concerned about the potential impact the Cunard vessels might have on their own business interests to discuss the possibility of creating their own new high-tech fleet. Over dinner one evening at Downshire House, Lord Pirrie's residence in London, in July 1907, they had begun to sketch out the operational parameters and commercial intentions for the new fleet, as well as the scale of the ships. As with so many pivotal moments in history, there is no written record of the event, or of the discussions that took place, only anecdotal accounts repeated by historians and elaborated upon by writers. All we know for certain is that following the dinner Ismay began to assemble the team that would be required to turn plans into reality.

Influential in the design process was naval architect Thomas Andrews, nephew of Lord Pirrie, who during his career was managing director and head of the draughting department for Harland and Wolff. Andrews was to lose his life when the *Titanic* sank, paying the ultimate price for design faults that would be revealed decades later when the wreck was rediscovered in 1985. Another key player at this early stage was Alexander Carlisle, the shipyard's chief draughtsman and general manager, who took responsibility for designing the superstructure of the vessels and would also advise on how the lifeboats were fitted; he resigned from Harland and Wolff in 1910 when he became a shareholder in the company commissioned to construct the hoist mechanisms that the ships would carry. Following the initial dinner conversation and dialogue with the creative minds at Harland and Wolff, events moved speedily onwards, with the public announcement that new ships would be constructed on 11 September 1907, and the names revealed on 22 April the following year. However, behind the scenes, the draughting process from conception to blueprint continued with further negotiation between White Star and Harland and Wolff, the contract letter confirming the commission being signed on 31 July 1908.

A history of the construction of the *Titanic* is highly technical. The following passages and contemporary extracts serve as a timeline for the key dates during the building process, highlight the public reaction to them and feature some of the more controversial aspects of design that were to contribute both to the loss of the vessel and the large number of casualties once the ship had started to sink. In parallel to the actual construction process is the impact the building process had on workers, contractors and interested onlookers, as recorded and reported in their own words at the time and in reflections after the event. The new fleet would also have a global impact, for example in terms of the changes required around the world at the ports receiving the huge ships. It is also important to mention the history of the *Olympic*, as its construction started first, and lessons learned while it was being built were used to modify the *Titanic* so that it became the largest operating ship of its day.

Even before a single metal plate or rivet had been hammered home, it was clear that the grand designs that Ismay, Pirrie, Andrews and Carlisle had drawn up for the new ships were on such a massive scale that the dockyard at Harland and Wolff would have to be modified, as the *Irish Independent* proudly announced early in 1908:

THE WHITE STAR LEVIATHANS

The White Star liners to be built at Belfast are intended to be about 840 feet long, 78 feet broad, about the same depth as the *Adriatic*, and of 52,000 gross tonnage. The new steamers will thus be larger than the big Cunarders. They will be named the *Olympic* and *Titanic*. The keels, it is thought, will be laid in July. About twelve months must elapse before the two new slips at Messrs. Harland and Wolff's yard, now in progress of lengthening to 1,000 feet, will be in readiness.

> *Irish Independent*, 23 April 1908, Irish Newspaper Archives,
> British Library Digital Collection

In fact, the *Titanic* was to be even larger, and by the time the main infrastructure of the ship was eventually completed and sea-launched for final outfitting in 1911, its dimensions were a massive 882 feet 9 inches long and 92 feet in breadth, with its height clearing 175 feet from the keel to the top of the funnels and a gross tonnage of 46,328 when finally launched from Belfast. The ship would have 9 decks, lettered A through G with the boilers below them. Fully loaded, 3,547 passengers and crew could be accommodated, in 840 staterooms – 416 first class, 162 second class and 262 third class – with 40 open berthing areas.

Once the letter of intent had been signed formalising the contract between White Star and Harland and Wolff to build the ships, work could begin on construction. Initially, the draughtsmen created models of the ships and laid out their lines in the yard's mould loft so that the construction process could be replicated and tested at scale before the real work began in the yards on Queen's Island. This was an important stage, one often overlooked by the press of the time, yet careful planning was vital to ensure that all calculations were correct. Mathematical equations and the laws of physics – assessing the number of boilers required to power sufficient engines to turn the intended propulsion system, for example – would then be translated into an actual costing for the purchase of exactly the right number of steel girders, plates and rivets required. Designing a ship was a precise art.

The US Senate board of inquiry final report into the *Titanic*'s sinking in 1912 provides a succinct summary of the final dimensions of the ship, as well as its estimated construction costs.

GENERAL PARTICULARS OF STEAMSHIP TITANIC

The *Titanic* was built by Harland and Wolff, of Belfast, Ireland. No restriction as to limit of cost was placed upon the builders. She was launched May 31, 1911. She was a vessel of 46,328 tons register; her length was 882.6 feet, and her breadth was 92.6 feet. Her boat deck and bridge were 70 feet above the waterline. She was, according to the testimony of President Ismay, 'especially constructed to float with her two largest watertight compartments full of water.'

The vessel, fully equipped, cost £1,500,000 sterling, or about $7,500,000.

At the time of the accident the vessel carried insurance of £1,000,000 sterling or about $5,000,000, the remaining risk being carried by the company's insurance fund.

The *Titanic* was a duplicate of the *Olympic*, which is owned by the same company, with a single exception of her passenger accommodations, and was built to accommodate 2,599 passengers, with additional accommodations for officers and crew numbering 903 persons.

US Senate board of inquiry final report

In terms of the technology that would be used to power the *Titanic*, the designers were keen to learn from their rivals at Cunard, particularly the way in which they had maximised power from fuel that translated into raw speed. To generate the steam that drove all vessels of the time, the ships were designed with 24 double-ended (six-furnace) and 5 single-ended (three-furnace) Scotch marine boilers installed below decks, burning coal used to convert water to high-pressure steam that then powered two four-cylinder reciprocating triple-expansion steam engines. The output of the engines was, for the time, breathtaking, each one producing 15,000 horsepower used to drive an outboard wing screw propeller – the propulsion system that had dominated naval transportation since the mid-nineteenth century when sails were replaced by the new technology. There was also a third screw propeller, situated down the centre of the ship, powered by one low-pressure Parsons turbine that produced 16,000 horsepower. This was cutting-edge technology that combined to generate 46,000 horsepower. Nevertheless, the ships would not be as fast as the earlier Cunard liners, as the *Titanic's* intended speed was 21 knots – 24 miles per hour – which could rise to 23 knots (26 miles per hour) top speed.

It was clear that three giants would eventually arise from Queen's Island, but this was not the only place where public attention was focused during this time. This was generally a period of great activity in ship-yards across Britain, both commercial and those run by the Admiralty. As part of the continued drive to retain maritime naval supremacy, more *Dreadnought*-class battleships were being commissioned and built at exactly the same time as Harland and Wolff was preparing to start work on the new liners. Such activity was particularly welcome since other sectors of the economy were not looking so healthy:

TRIUMPHS OF SHIPBUILDING

This week the two most powerful battleships ever constructed were launched from English yards. They are both of the *Dreadnought* type, but larger, and designed to carry far heavier armament. It is said that these two battleships represent the last word in naval construction. If for last we substitute latest, the statement may be fairly correct . . . Meanwhile the shipyards of Belfast are not empty, a huge White Star liner for the new Canadian service is being launched on Thursday, from Harland and Wolff's and it is said that work has already begun in the same yard on the first of two new Atlantic liners designed to eclipse the *Lusitania* and *Mauretania*, of the Cunard Company. If this proves correct, it is at least a hopeful sign for Belfast, where there is just now such a dearth of employ-ment. For the time being, at any rate, rivalry, whether between navies or steamship companies, is likely to benefit the artisan.

Irish Independent, 12 September 1908, Irish Newspaper
Archives, British Library Digital Collection

Not everyone believed that more naval vessels were required, and at the top level of government dissenting voices could be heard speaking out against the need to pour yet more funds into the expansion programme. The newly appointed president of the Board of Trade, Winston Churchill, had supported the chancellor of the exchequer's opposition to the first lord of the Admiralty's plans to expend even greater funds on the construction of more *Dreadnought*-class vessels, focusing instead on a desire to cement Britain's position at the heart of world trade and industry – which naturally included commercial shipping.

MR. CHURCHILL AT MANCHESTER . . .

I think it is not untrue to say that in these years we are passing through a decisive period in the history of our country. The wonderful century, which followed the battle of Waterloo and the downfall of the Napoleonic domination, which secured to this small island so long and so resplendent a reign, has come to an end. We have arrived at a new time. Let us realize it. And with that new time strange methods, huge forces, larger combinations – a Titanic world – have sprung up around us. The foundations of our power are changing. To stand still would be to fall; to fall would be to perish. We must go forward. We will go forward (cheers). We will go forward into a way of life more earnestly viewed, more scientifically organized, more consciously national than any we have known. Thus alone shall we be able to sustain and to renew through the generations which are to come the fame and the power of the British race (loud cheers).

The Times, 24 May 1909, British Library Digital Collection

Churchill may have had a point. The economic importance of the White Star's ongoing business relationship with Harland and Wolff is shown clearly in a piece that revealed the amount of money that would be spent in the creation of the new fleet of ships – in particular those sums set aside in wages for local workers.

£2,000,000 WAGES FOR BELFAST

It is estimated that at least £2,000,000 will be spent in wages in Belfast in connection with the building of the two mammoth White Star liners, *Olympic* and *Titanic*. Twelve thousand men are employed at Harland and Wolff's yard, the wages bill reaching £18,000 a week. Apart from any other orders, the outlay on the two liners represents wages for two years. While all records will be beaten by the enormous tonnage of the new liners, Lord Pirrie believes there is no limit to the size of ship that can be built except that imposed by accommodation in shipbuilding yards and docks.

Irish Independent, 18 September 1908, Irish Newspaper
Archives, British Library Digital Collection

While it is always tricky to assign modern values to historical sums of money, a conservative estimate for the injection of £2 million in wages into the local economy would equate to about £800 million in 2009, based on a comparison of average earnings.

Pirrie's comments about the size of future ships that his yard might build may seem arrogant to the modern observer – certainly with the benefit of hindsight given the fate that befell the *Titanic* – but the sheer scale of the project to build the three vessels meant that the economic benefits were not restricted to the workforce who would undertake the construction process. Echoing Churchill's words, this was a brave new world, and the venture had consequences across the Atlantic.

THE EXODUS TO EUROPE increases each year so rapidly that the ships are, yearly, growing larger and larger. It is reported here that Messrs. Harland and Wolff of the Belfast shipbuilding works, are prepared to lay down ocean-going 'leviathans' of much greater dimensions than any yet attempted. However, the limit of New York Dock accommodation has been reached. The latest of the great ocean steamers extend to the fullest capacity of the very longest piers, and the port authorities will not allow these piers to be extended further out into the water of the tideway. The only way, therefore, to accommodate the larger ships now is by encroaching upon the land, and tearing down all the huge buildings in the way. This course has been adopted in one case over here recently, but obviously in other cases the cost would be so enormous as to make it prohibitive, except in a few very special cases. This means that in order to provide for the annual and inevitable growth of the shipping, as well as for the largely increased size of the great ocean-going vessels, it is absolutely certain that docks will have to be erected on Long Island.

Freemans Journal, 13 July 1909, Irish Newspaper Archives,
British Library Digital Collection

This clearly shows that there was real expectation that the transatlantic shipping trade was still very much an industry with a positive future, with the continued desire to move between America and Europe leading to dramatic implications for the built environment on land, which would have to bow to the power of the waves as ships continued to grow in size. Although the loss of the *Titanic* brought a reality check, alterations were nevertheless required to take account of the size of other vessels under construction – not just those commissioned by White Star and Cunard, but also the Royal Navy battleships that were being launched during this period. Changes had to be made at both dockyards and ports – all at additional cost.

SHIPBUILDING DEVELOPMENTS ANTICIPATED – £30,000 TO BE EXPENDED

The Belfast Harbour Board have decided in anticipation of the demand for greater water draught that will be made by the new mammoth White Star liners *Olympic* and *Titanic*, and the even greater vessels that are expected to follow them, to proceed forthwith in the carrying out of an important scheme for the deepening of Victoria Channel ... On the motion of Mr. Andrews, seconded by Mr. Pollock, it was recommended that the Board do proceed with the

dredging of Victoria Channel to a depth of 32 feet below the level
of high water of ordinary spring tides at an estimated cost of £30,000.

Freemans Journal, 3 March 1909, Irish Newspaper Archives,
British Library Digital Collection

Similar works were required at many of the larger ports that White
Star used as points of departure and arrival for their regular voyages.
Southampton, for example, faced the prospect of making considerable
changes to its docks to accommodate the new fleet of White Star ships.

THE SOUTH COAST
SOUTHAMPTON DOCKS, NOV. I

A work of reconstruction that is about to take place at Southampton
will place the port ahead of any other port in the kingdom, if not
in the world, in regard to graving dock accommodation. The
coming of the large White Star liners *Titanic* and *Olympic,* now
under construction at Belfast, has made the dry-dock problem a
pressing one, and it has been decided to reconstruct the existing
Trafalgar Dock so that it will accommodate these vessels with ease.
The dock will then have a length of 800 ft., with a width of 100
ft. at the entrance and a width at the bottom of 108 ft. The work
will occupy about a year. The depth of water over the sill at high
tide will be 34 ft. The present swing-gates are to be replaced by a
caisson as in the case of the Prince of Wales Graving Dock. The
dock is to be lengthened riverward, but the important work is the
widening, and this will be effected by the removal of three of the
alters on each side ... The new deep-water dock is making rapid
progress, and the Harbour Board have now under consideration
a proposal for further deepening the channel in Southampton
Water. All the work that has to be done will be completed before
the *Titanic* and *Olympic* come round from Belfast.

The Times, 3 November 1909,
British Library Digital Collection

The race was therefore on to keep pace with the construction of the giants of the seas.

Construction

> If you had seen or known the process of extra work that went into the ship, you'd say it was impossible to sink her.
>
> Jim Thompson, Harland & Wolff caulker

Once contracts had been signed for the construction of the three super-liners – on 29 July 1908 Ismay and the White Star Line officials approved the original Harland and Wolff design for the *Titanic* and her sister ships – work could start in earnest.

The construction of a ship such as the *Titanic* fell into a number of stages. First, the keel needed to be laid down and plated, with the main skeleton or frame of the ship rising from the dockyard; this too would then be plated to form the hull. The internal structure would then be built, with final fitting of the superstructure – decks, funnels and internal fixtures and fittings – undertaken after an initial sea launch. At this point trials for seaworthiness would ensue.

The eventual size of the *Titanic*'s decks and engine space are given in the British wreck commissioner's final report in the section dealing with the superstructure of the ship. Particular attention, given the fate of the *Titanic*, was paid to describing the arrangements to make the bulkheads watertight on each deck, a key factor when the causes for the loss of the ship were considered later on in the final report.

The *Titanic* was a three-screw vessel of 46,328 tons gross and 21,831 net register tons, built by Messrs. Harland and Wolff for the White Star Line service between Southampton and New York. She was registered as a British steamship at the port of Liverpool, her official number being 131,428. Her registered dimensions were:

Length	852·5 ft.
Breadth	92·5 ft.

Depth from top of keel to top of beam at lowest
point of sheer of C deck, the highest deck which
extends continuously from bow to stern .....   64 ft. 9 in.

Depth of hold	59·58 ft.
Height from B to C	9·0 ft.
Height from A to B deck	9·0 ft.
Height from Boat to A deck	9·5 ft.

Height from Boat deck to waterline amidships
   at time of accident ....   60·5 ft.

Displacement at 34 ft. 7 in ....   52,310 tons.

The propelling machinery consisted of two sets of four-cylinder reciprocating engines, each driving a wing propeller, and a turbine driving the centre propeller. The registered horsepower of the propelling machinery was 50,000. The power which would probably have been developed was at least 55,000.

Structural arrangements. The structural arrangements of the *Titanic* consisted primarily of:

- (1) An outer shell of steel plating, giving form to the ship up to the top decks.
- (2) Steel decks. These were enumerated as follows:

	Height to next deck above	Distance from 34 ft. 7 in. waterline amidships	
		Above.	Below.
	Ft. In.	Ft. In.	Ft. In.
Boat deck, length about 500 ft.	- -	58 0	- -
A deck, length 9 6 about 500 ft.	48 6	- -	

[35]

B deck, length about 550 ft. with 125 ft. forecastle and 105 ft. poop	9 0	39 6	- -
C deck, whole length of ship.	9 0	30 6	- -
D deck, whole length of ship.	10 6	20 0 (tapered down at ends)	- -
E deck, whole length of ship.	9 0	11 0	5 6
F deck, whole length of ship.	8 6	2 6	13 6
G deck, 190 ft. forward of boilers, 210 ft. aft of machinery	8 0	- -	- -
Orlop deck, 190 ft. forward of boilers, 210 ft. aft of machinery	8 0	- -	- -

C D, E and F were continuous from end to end of the ship. The decks above these were continuous for the greater part of the ship, extending from amidships both forward and aft. The Boat deck and A deck each had two expansion joints, which broke the strength continuity. The decks below were continuous outside the boiler and engine rooms and extended to the ends of the ship. Except in small patches none of these decks was watertight in the steel parts, except the Weather deck and the Orlop deck aft.

- (3) Transverse Vertical Bulkheads. There were 15 transverse watertight bulkheads, by which the ship was divided in the direction of her length into 16 separate compartments. These bulkheads are referred to as A to P, commencing forward.

The watertightness of the bulkheads extended up to one or other of the decks D or E; the bulkhead A extended to C, but was only watertight to D deck. The position of the D, E and F decks, which were the only ones to which the watertight bulkheads extended, was in relation to the waterline (34 ft. 7 in. draught) approximately as follows:

Height above waterline (34 ft. 7 in.)

	Lowest part amidships		At bow		At stern	
	Feet	Inches	Feet	Inches	Feet	Inches
D	20	0	33	0	25	0
E	11	0	24	0	16	0
F	2	6	25	6	7	6

These were the three of the four decks which, as already stated, were continuous all fore and aft. The other decks, G and Orlop, which extended only along a part of the ship, were spaced about 8 ft. apart. The G deck forward was about 7 ft. 6 in. above the waterline at the bow and about level with the waterline at bulkhead D, which was at the fore end of the boilers. The G deck aft and the Orlop deck at both ends of the vessel were below the waterline. The Orlop deck abaft of the turbine engine room and forward of the collision bulkhead was watertight. Elsewhere, except in very small patches, the decks were not watertight. All the decks had large openings or hatchways in them in each compartment, so that water could rise freely through them.

There was also a watertight inner bottom, or tank top, about 5 ft. above the top of the keel, which extended for the full breadth of the vessel from bulkhead A to 20 ft. before bulkhead P – i.e. for the whole length of the vessel except a small distance at each end. The transverse watertight divisions of this double bottom practically coincided with the watertight transverse bulkheads; there was an additional watertight division under the middle of the reciprocating engine room compartment (between bulkheads K and L). There were three longitudinal watertight divisions in the double bottom, one at the centre of the ship, extending for about 670 ft., and one on each side, extending for 447 ft.

All the transverse bulkheads were carried up watertight to at least the height of the E deck. Bulkheads A and B, and all bulkheads from K (90 ft. abaft amidships) to P, both inclusive, further extended watertight up to the underside of D deck. A bulkhead further extended to C deck, but it was watertight only to D deck.

Bulkheads A and B forward, and P aft, had no openings in them. All the other bulkheads had openings in them, which were fitted with watertight doors. Bulkheads D to O, both inclusive, had each a vertical sliding watertight door at the level of the floor of the engine and boiler rooms for the use of the engineers and firemen. On the Orlop deck there was one door, on bulkhead N, for access to the refrigerator rooms. On G deck there were no watertight doors in the bulkheads. On both the F and E decks nearly all the bulkheads had watertight doors, mainly for giving communication between the different blocks of passenger accommodation.

All the doors, except those in the engine rooms and boiler rooms, were horizontal sliding doors workable by hand both at the door and at the deck above.

There were twelve vertical sliding watertight doors which completed the watertightness of bulkheads D to O inclusive, in the boiler and engine rooms. These were capable of being simultaneously closed from the bridge. The operation of closing was intended to be preceded by the ringing from the bridge of a warning bell.

These doors were closed by the bringing into operation of an electric current and could not be opened until this current was cut off from the bridge. When this was done the doors could only be opened by a mechanical operation manually worked separately at each door. They could, however, be individually lowered again by operating a lever at the door. In addition they would be automatically closed, if open, should water enter the compartment. This operation was done in each case by means of a float actuated by the water which was in either of the compartments which happened to be in the process of being flooded.

There were no sluice valves or means of letting water from one compartment to another.

British wreck commissioner's final report

Once the construction process was under way, progress was rapid for the first stages – by 15 December 1908 the keel of the *Olympic* had been laid, with plates being screwed into place the very next day. The *Titanic* followed: the keel was not laid until 22 March 1909, with the first keel plate put into place on 31 March. Thereafter, the hull began to take shape in earnest. The process of construction attracted regular attention.

IRELAND

THE NEW WHITE STAR LINERS

BELFAST, NOV. 6

Notable progress has been made in the constructive work of the mammoth White Star liners *Olympic* and *Titanic* at the Queen's Island shipbuilding works of Messrs. Harland and Wolff. These vessels, which when launched will be the largest afloat, will be driven by a combination of turbines and reciprocating engines, and the speed is expected to average about 21 knots.

The *Olympic* is in a slightly more advanced state than the *Titanic*, the vessel being more than half framed, and the decks aft, up to the upper deck, being plated. Amidships and forward the lower deck beams are being placed in position. From the engine room aft the hold columns and deck girders were fitted in conjunction with the framing, to obviate the necessity of the usual wood shoring aft. In vessels of such great height and length as the *Olympic* and *Titanic* shoring and staging become a more difficult problem than usual, owing to the great height from the ground at the ends of the ship, and the builders have overcome the trouble by means of a number of light iron lattice-work trestles which they have constructed for staging purposes. The shell plating of the *Olympic* appears above the upper turn of the bilge, the whole so far having been riveted by hydraulic machinery from the keel up. The weight of the rivets in the ship's double bottom alone is 270 tons, and number about 500,000, the largest being 1¼ in. in diameter. The heaviest plate weighs 4½ tons and is 36 ft. long. The stern frame, which is already in position, weighs 70 tons, the rudder 100 tons, and the boss arms 3½ tons aft and 45 tons forward. The largest beam used weighs over four tons and measures 92 ft. The large double gantries, over 200 ft. high, erected to deal with the work of constructing the new vessels, involved a cost, with the new slips and their substantial foundations, of about a quarter of a million, £130,000 having been expended on the steel work alone.

The Times, 3 November 1909,
British Library Digital Collection

With this stage complete, the sheer scale of the project became clear to all, as breathless onlookers recalled.

For months and months, in that monstrous iron enclosure there was nothing that had the faintest likeness to a ship, only something that might have been the iron scaffolding for the naves of half a dozen cathedrals laid end to end. At last a skeleton within the scaffolding began to take shape, at the sight of which men held their breaths. It was a shape of a ship, a ship so monstrous and unthinkable that it towered over the buildings and dwarfed the very mountains by the water. A rudder as big as a giant elm tree. Bosses and bearings of propellers the size of windmills. Twenty tons of tallow were spread upon the ways, so that when the moment came, the water she was to conquer should trust her finally from the earth.

A Belfast observer, 1911, *Titanic:
Death of a Dream*, Part One

The government was also keeping a close eye on progress, and saw an opportunity to capitalise on the work already required to make Belfast Harbour navigable for the White Star ships.

MAY MEAN £60,000 FOR DREDGING

At a cost of £30,000, the Belfast Harbour Commissioners are deepening the Victoria Channel, which will facilitate the safe navigation of the two giant White Star liners, *Olympic* and *Titanic*, now on the stocks at Harland and Wolff's yard. It is understood that the Government is anxious that the channel should be deepened to 35 feet for the safe entry of heavy battle-ships, but they have not offered any subsidy. The cost, over and above that already entered into, would mean another £30,000.

Irish Independent, 18 February 1910, Irish Newspaper Archives, British Library Digital Collection

The British wreck commissioner's final report on the sinking contains a vast amount of detail on the materials used in the construction of the hull and basic frame of the vessel, drawn from cross-examinations of the commissioners of the ship at both White Star and Harland and Wolff, with particular focus on the thickness of the steel used and the watertight nature of the superstructure.

Structure

The vessel was built throughout of steel and had a cellular double bottom of the usual type, with a floor at every frame, its depth at the centre line being 63 in., except in way of the reciprocating machinery, where it was 78 in. For about half of the length of the vessel this double bottom extended up the ship's side to a height of 7 ft. above the keel. Forward and aft of the machinery space the protection of the inner bottom extended to a less height above the keel. It was so divided that there were four separate watertight compartments in the breadth of the vessel. Before and abaft the machinery space there was a watertight division at the centre line only, except in the foremost and aftermost tanks. Above the double bottom the vessel was constructed on the usual transverse frame system, reinforced by web frames which extended to the highest decks.

At the forward end the framing and plating was strengthened with a view to preventing panting, and damage when meeting thin harbour ice.

Beams were fitted on every frame at all decks, from the Boat deck downwards. An external bilge keel, about 300 ft. long and 25 in. deep, was fitted along the bilge amidships.

The heavy ship's plating was carried right up to the Boat deck, and between the C and B deck was doubled. The stringer or edge plate of the B deck was also doubled. This double plating was hydraulic riveted.

All decks were steel plated throughout.

The transverse strength of the ship was in part dependent on the 15 transverse watertight bulkheads, which were specially stiffened and strengthened to enable them to stand the necessary pressure in the event of accident, and they were connected by double angles to decks, inner bottom, and shell plating.

The two decks above the B deck were of comparatively light scantling, but strong enough to ensure their proving satisfactory in these positions in rough weather.

Watertight Subdivision. In the preparation of the design of this vessel it was arranged that the bulkheads and divisions should be so placed that the ship would remain afloat in the event of any two adjoining compartments being flooded, and that they should be so built and strengthened that the ship would remain afloat under this condition. The minimum freeboard that the vessel would have, in the event of any two compartments being flooded, was between 2 ft. 6 in. and 3 ft. from the deck adjoining the top of the watertight bulkheads. With this object in view 15 watertight bulkheads were arranged in the vessel. The lower part of C bulkhead was doubled, and was in the form of a cofferdam. So far as possible the bulkheads were carried up in one plane to their upper sides, but in cases where they had for any reason to be stepped forward or aft, the deck, in way of the step, was made into a watertight flat, thus completing the watertightness of the compartment. In addition to this, G deck in the after peak was made a watertight flat. The Orlop deck between bulkheads which formed the top of the tunnel was also watertight. The Orlop deck in the forepeak tank was also a watertight flat. The electric machinery compartment was further protected by a structure some distance in from the ship's side, forming six separate watertight compartments, which were used for the storage of fresh water.

Where openings were required for the working of the ship in these watertight bulkheads they were closed by watertight sliding doors which could be worked from a position above the top of the watertight bulkhead, and those doors immediately [next to] the inner bottom were of a special automatic closing pattern, as described below. By this subdivision there were in all 73 compartments, 29 of these being above the inner bottom.

Watertight doors. The doors (12 in number) immediately above the inner bottom were in the engine and boiler room spaces. They were of Messrs. Harland and Wolff's latest type, working vertically. The doorplate was of cast iron of heavy section, strongly ribbed. It closed by gravity, and was held in the open position by a clutch which could be released by means of a powerful electro-magnet controlled from the captain's bridge. In the event of accident, or at any time when it might be considered desirable, the captain or officer on duty could, by simply moving an electric switch, immediately close all these doors. The time required for the doors to close was between 25 and 30 seconds. Each door could also be closed from below by operating a hand lever fitted alongside the door. As a further precaution floats were provided beneath the floor level, which, in the event of water accidentally entering any of the compartments, automatically lifted and thus released the clutches, thereby permitting the doors in that particular compartment to close if they had not already been dropped by any other means. These doors were fitted with cataracts which controlled the speed of closing. Due notice of closing from the bridge was given by a warning bell.

A ladder or escape was provided in each boiler room, engine room, and similar watertight compartment, in order that the closing of the doors at any time should not imprison the men working therein.

Ship's Side Doors. Large side doors were provided through the side plating, giving access to passengers' or crew's accommodation as follows:

On the saloon (D) deck on the starboard side in the forward third class open space one baggage door.

In way of the forward first class entrance, two doors close together on each side.

On the upper (E) deck, one door each side at the forward end of the working passage.

On the port side abreast the engine room, one door leading into the working passage. One door each side on the port and starboard sides aft into the forward second class entrance.

All the doors on the upper deck were secured by lever handles, and were made watertight by means of rubber strips. Those on the saloon deck were closed by lever handles but had no rubber.

Accommodation Ladder. One teak accommodation ladder was provided, and could be worked on either side of the ship in the gangway way door opposite the second class entrance on the upper deck (E). It had a folding platform and portable stanchions, hand rope, etc. The ladder extended to within 3 ft. 6 in. of the vessel's light draft, and was stowed overhead in the entrance abreast the forward second class main staircase. Its lower end was arranged so as to be raised and lowered from a davit immediately above.

Masts and Rigging. The vessel was rigged with two masts, and fore and aft sails. The two pole masts were constructed of steel, and stiffened with angle irons. The poles at the top of the mast were made of teak.

A look-out cage, constructed of steel, was fitted on the foremast at a height of about 95 ft. above the waterline. Access to the cage was obtained by an iron vertical ladder inside of the foremast, with an opening at C deck and one at the lookout cage. An iron ladder was fitted on the foremast from the hounds to the masthead light.

British wreck commissioner's final report

Men who worked on the construction had very fond memories of the experience. Jim Thompson worked at Harland and Wolff, and recalled his time in the shipyard with pride. His words contain no trace of irony, spoken over sixty years after the *Titanic* had sunk.

I was on the *Titanic* from [when] they laid the keel 'til she left Belfast . . . Well, I loved it, I loved it, and I loved my work and I loved the men, and I got on well with all . . . Oh, well, it was a great advantage, if you'd call it that, yet and the privilege of working on it . . . [as a] caulker; that is, making the ship watertight. Wouldn't you say that was a very important job? . . .If you had seen or known the process of extra work that went into the ship, you'd say it was impossible to sink her . . . Yes, it was a marvellous bit of work, yes, a marvellous bit of work . . . Well, I remember all the first-class compartments, the special rooms, which was a privilege to see. They were so nice that you couldn't just describe them. You couldn't, I bet you wouldn't think it was a ship when you were inside. Of course everything was so highly decorated.

Jim Thompson, Harland & Wolff caulker in a 1976 interview with Radio Ulster, BBC *Titanic* Archive

Yet there were more critical voices about the design of the *Titanic* higher up within Harland and Wolff. A fascinating account of life at the company and what it was like to work on the construction of vessels such as the *Titanic* was written retrospectively in 1946 by an engineer named David Watson. He raises several points about safety features on the *Titanic*, in particular the thickness of the bilge. He also comments on the role played during construction by Alexander Thomas Andrews, who died when the vessel sank.

D. Watson. Born 15th March 1875, started work as (a boy in the Queens Rd. shipyard of Messrs Harland & Wolff . . .) as a catch boy on 2nd week of April 1889 . . . I started to serve my time to the riveting about 1893, finished 1899, but during my apprenticeship I was not a good timekeeper, especially, sleeping in three or four mornings in a week, 5 AM being then the starting time, for three offences I got sent home for a month or 6 weeks 3 or 4 times during my apprenticeship. I also lost many days through carelessness, but in my last years I hardly lost one hour, as things were not going too well with me at home. . . I was offered the job as leading hand & counter at the latter end of 1902. I accepted the job, I was put in charge of 22 old truck drilling machines scattered all over the different ships where there was work suitable for this class of drill. As their weight was 4 hundred it was necessary to have a riggers squad to shift one each time. It was not an easy job for me as most of the men employed on operating these drills left. . . as they had been used to more freedom in making up their wages, which was not very high. £1 or £2 a week was reckoned a good pay at that time and it was seldom when strictly counted that they could earn even this amount. Therefore most of them threw up the job having me in a difficulty to have them replaced. There was a time that I even went to the coal quay and asked two men if they would take the job. They at once dropped their shovels and came along. One of them stayed. The other left after two days. The one who stayed on was my own father-in-law. Drilling was not a recognised trade at that time, therefore I got men from anywhere and everywhere I could. There was no such thing as twist drills, we were obliged to use plain drills & spoon reamed, so when I started any stranger I could only depend on a few of the old hands to teach them to dress these class of tools, but I myself learned to do them thro time.

So when a new man started I stood by him until he learned to do in his own tools, but my greatest, worst, & most difficult experience was the drilling at shurstrakes of very large ships such as the *Celtic, Cedric, Baltic, Adriatic, Titanic* and *Olympic* where all plates on these heavy shells & shurstrakes had to be drilled solid with the exception of the shell frames which were reamed but a size larger and with the crude tools then in use. The large & heavy electric drills used in the doing of this work then were hung over the side of the ships, suspended from the jib of a Bogie, placed on rails running with tons of pig iron & were shifted by a large hatchet. These machines were comprised of two magnets and a big motor. The drills or reamer were opperated (*sic*) between the powerful magnets & was controlled by two men, one on each side of the machine, which weighed over half a ton and were pulled up or down by chain blocks, three of these were rigged up on each side of the ship, & when these were ready for working my next trouble was to find 24 extra men to opperate (*sic*) them as it was night & day work until the shell & shurstrake was finished. Also it was a great worry keeping ahead of the Hya Riveting machines, for if they were kept back at all there was sure to be trouble, as the late Mr. Thomas Andrews, who went down with the *Titanic*, the nephew of the late Lord Pirrie, hardly ever left this job until it was finished, in fact he would even come down in the middle of the night to see if there was any hold backs or any stuff going on. He was a very earnest & determined man, but at the same time most fair and considerate where any difficulty or hitch occurred, so long as one told the truth, but God help any one he caught telling lies, a stickler for economy, and to quote one incident, on his coming up on the deck where one day there was a very big drilling job, he took exception to four old men employed on the truck drills. This was about the years 1908 or 09. The oldest of these was about 60. Their names were as follow[s], John McMillan from Consber, William Henderson (my father-in-law), Isaac Stuart who was the father of Stuart Brothers, Shipping Agents, Waring St., & lastly an old chap called Bullneck. I don't remember his real name. He had a grey whisker & beard all round his face making him look older than he actually was. I told Mr. Andrews that these four were my most conscientious workers as they were doing more work than the younger men on the job, now especially pointing out one old man named John McMillan whom I knew wrought as a general jobber in Andrews' Mills. I am sure Mr. Andrews knew him alright. I gave this man a great recommendation so there was no further excuse required from paying off.

I may add that at this time, although I was only a leading hand and Counter I had full authority for starting or stopping my own men the same as any Head Foreman. Also at one time I had 6/- per week higher wages than the other leading hands. . . I got this in two rises of 3/- a time. Eventually in the early part of 1918 I was put on the staff with 48/- per week advance in my wages. This was alright until a slump came in 1922 when there were a number of us Assistant Foremen reduced to leading hands again, but unfortunately I did not get the 6/- extra per week back, all this economy stunt started at that time until about 1927 when things became a little better until about 1931 and in 1932 the yard closed altogether. Previous to this a leading hand was paid for sickness & holidays also, but these privileges were taken away in about 1931 and all lost time meant lost pay. Before these days a leading hand was much better off during his absence than when he was working as there was sickness & mutual aid benefits, also friendly societies added to his weekly wage's full pay. We in our department had one man not now in the yard who took full advantage of these privilages (*sic*) by taking a month off quite frequently. This was one of the things which the firm caught on to. There was no longer any leading hands after 1932. The title was changed & we were only on the books as Charge Hands. Therefore one was just like a ganger or squad leader, but as the years from 1921 to 1934 were a time of comparative slackness we were very lucky to be working at all.

Time came about 1924 when it was necessary to close up the main yard entirely as there were no orders on hand to fill up the slips. This was in the nineteen twenties. I myself for the first time was transferred to what was then called the East Yard (now the Musgrave Yard), taking charge of a big Castle Liner, but luckily enough a number of oil tanker[s] came in for repair of course. I got charge of these ships & which proved to be a very good job for me as I was paid time and a quarter & time and a half during the time I was employed on them.

Mr. Davidson was the manager and no doubt at that time he was hot stuff to deal with, mostly using shipyard language when giving any orders. This was before he began to act the fool but after all he was very fair, his bark being worse than his bite. At the same time he was, in my opinion, a most capable man for the job as it was most difficult making a good job on these type of ships because of the cylindrical tanks as these were old cargo ships converted into oil tankers to make up for the shortage of our oil tanker loss during the 1914–1918 war . . . After the war there was no more of this type built. Lord Pirrie getting badly nipped in buying us all the steel left over when this type of ship was no longer wanted, he must have lost nearly a million in the deal. I believe this had a lot to do with his sudden death, which took place when passing through the Panama Canal, accompanied by the late Lady Pirrie and Dr. Morrow. I shall never forget that funeral, the coffin was brought over on a ship which berthed at the end of the Thompson Wharf, where a great number of Gentlemen were gathered dressed in their best mourning clothes with Caster hats & umbrellas. The cortege had reached about halfway up Grosvenor Rd when the motors began to quicken their pace. It was most amusing to watch these gentry trying to keep up behind the hearse. Some of them were actually trotting, their tail coats flying in the air, until they reached the Falls Rd where the motors increased their speed, leaving them standing, looking at each other, without even saying goodbye.

With regard to Thomas Andrews there is no doubt that Lord Pirrie meant that he would eventually become the head Director of Harland & Wolff, which certainly would have happened had he lived. According to a little book on the life of Mr. Andrews, a Gentleman fellow traveller on the *Titanic* states that while in conversation with him during the trip he asked him how he was feeling, his reply was that the only thing that worried him a little was the fact of going farther and farther away from home. Little did he think of how far he would be going as it was understood that this ship, the *Titanic*, was unsinkable. It was given out at the time the very passengers crying this out during the time she was going down underneath them . . . One thing I remarked was the difference in the design of bilge on these very large type of ships in comparison to the *Cedric, Baltic* & *Adriatic* etc., as the bilges of these ships were double heavy plated and strapped, being from over 2in. to 3in. thick, wherein *Titanic's* bilge was single plated, being only a good one inch in thickness and I am of the opinion that if the *Titanic* had been similarly bilged she would have kept afloat for a much longer period and probably would not have sunk at all . . . on the other White Star liners mentioned surely there would have been a greater resistance when striking the iceberg.

David Watson's engineer's notebook 1946,
National Maritime Museum, ref. LMQ/1/14/1

The actual construction of the ships was not without danger, with a total of five fatalities among the workforce whilst the *Olympic* and *Titanic* were being built. Shipbuilding had long been a risky business, with disfigurement and loss of limbs common during the welding and riveting of the the massive plates together to form the skin of the vessel. Other dangers came from faulty or overloaded hoisting gear. A terrible accident occurred at the shipyard in February 1910: two men died after a crane collapsed on a gantry above the *Olympic* whilst hoisting five iron plates that were to be bolted onto the bulkhead of the ship.

AT QUEEN'S ISLAND YARD

CRANE ACCIDENT ON NEW LINER

TWO KILLED – ONE INJURED

Belfast, Tuesday

A terrible accident, resulting in the death of two men and serious injury to a third, took place late this evening at the North Yard of Messrs. Harland and Wolff's Shipbuilding Works, Belfast, where the giant White Star Liners (*Olympic* and *Titanic*) are in the course of construction. The accident occurred on the *Olympic*, which is in a fairly advanced stage, and caused havoc in a squad which was working amidships on the huge liner, underneath the giant Gantry, which is a conspicuous object at Queen's Island. A few minutes after five o'clock the squad was busily at work, under the supervision of a plater, with an apprentice, a holder-on, and two helpers. A ten-ton crane on the Gantry was hoisting five plates for the bulkhead of the ship, when, without the slightest warning, several of the plates slipped from the sling, and fell right on to the gang of men below. One of the helpers named Robert Kilpatrick was struck on the back of the skull by a plate which fell sideways, and literally clove his head in two. The second helper, whose name was Lynas, was also struck by the plates, and HURLED TO THE GROUND, THIRTY FEET BELOW, being killed on the spot. The holder-on, named Arthur McQuoid, was also involved in the smash, and knocked on to a staging underneath, as was also the unfortunate man Kilpatrick. By what seemed a miracle the plater and the apprentice got clear, and escaped uninjured. The plates were what are known as 'twenties', and the combined weight of the load in the sling amounted to five or six tons. They are by no means the largest size of plates, hence the fact that so many were being lifted at once by the crane, which is one of several of various lifting powers on the huge Gantry . . . The accident is the most serious which has happened at the Queen's Island since the disaster on the new Hamburg-American liner *Arcadia*, two years ago. On that occasion a staging broke, and five men fell on to the tank top of the vessel, four of them being killed, and the other seriously injured.

Freemans Journal, 9 February 1910,
Irish Newspaper Archives, British Library Digital Collection

By April 1910, framing on the *Titanic* was under way, though during this phase the ship claimed its first casualty – a fifteen-year-old riveter catch-boy. Samuel Joseph Scott, employed to catch any rivets dropped by the men bolting the girders and external structures into place, plunged to his death from the hull. The rivet he had been chasing would have cost only a few pence. Sufficient progress had been made on the super-structure for plating to begin in earnest by October. However, by this date work on the *Olympic* had reached the momentous stage when it could be launched for the next stage of work, and the world looked on in awe as the first of the White Star liners took to the water.

Launch and final preparations

The picture of the monstrous mass gliding gently to the waters of the Lagan and taking its first dip at the opening of a valve will be historic to Belfast and memorable in the annals of the shipbuilder's ancient craft.

Sunday Independent (Irish), 23 October 1910

On 20 October 1910 vast crowds of press and reporters were joined by dignitaries from the shipping world and thousands of interested bystanders to watch the launch of the *Olympic*. Given the huge media interest, special arrangements were made to highlight the ship, such as painting it white so that it would show up more clearly in press photographs, even though it was then repainted black for service. In the build-up to the event, newspapers devoted a large number of column inches to paint a picture of the unfolding scene at the shipyard, and included vivid descriptions of working conditions during this phase of construction.

MAMMOTH WHITE STAR LINERS

PREPARATIONS TO LAUNCH SS. OLYMPIC

Rapid progress is apparent in the preparations for the launch of the gigantic White Star liner, *Olympic*, next month. Though little can be seen of her and the *Titanic* owing to the forest of scaffolding and the enormous gantries with which they are encircled, the hull of the former painted white is distinctly visible at both bow and stern. The rudder is not yet fitted, and owing partly to the impossibility of obtaining a view of the vessels, the realisation at the glance of their enormous length is hardly apparent at close quarters, and it is not until the spectator is half a mile away and comparison can be made with even large steamers on the stocks of Messrs. Harland and Wolff, that their huge mass appears to dominate Belfast. Even from the dock of the Liverpool and Belfast steamer *Graphic*, approaching the city, when off the Copeland nearly 20 miles away, the great shipbuilding yard looms up before it is to be seen itself in any detail.

What it means for Harland and Wolff to be working overtime can be more vividly understood when the horn known as the Buzzer sounds at 3.30 pm. Drawn up for workmen only along the broad road, a mile or so long, are 40 to 50 electric cars, and in less than 5 minutes the whole road is black with men who pour out of different gates of the works like a swarm of bees to the number probably of 18,000 to 20,000. One of the sights of Belfast is the view of Harland and Wolff's yard at the present time with the night shift in full swing. The rows of powerful electric lights and the glow of the furnace across the dark water might easily suggest the scene of a great conflagration were it not accompanied by the incessant clatter of a thousand hammers on the plates of the leviathans which forcibly convey the impression that not an hour is being lost to have the *Olympic* ready at the appointed time . . .

SOME INTERESTING FACTS

The White Star line has issued an artistically illustrated leaflet giving some interesting figures concerning their new leviathans *Olympic* and *Titanic*. The former vessel is to be launched at Belfast on the 20th prox. Some idea of the enormous dimensions of these two vessels will be grasped when it is stated that the rudder weighs alone 100 tons and the weight of the castings comprising the stern frame and brackets amounts to 280 tons more than those of any other steamer. They were manufactured at Darlington and special railway arrangements had been made for their conveyance to Hartlepool, whence they were shipped to Belfast. The largest beam used weighs over 4 tons, and measures 92 feet, and there are 2,500,000 rivets in the ship – Each engine crank shaft weighs 118 tons, bedplate 195 tons, and the heaviest cylinder with liner, 50 tons, wing propeller, 38 tons. The weight for the casting for the turbine cylinder is 163 tons, and of the propeller, which is of solid bronze, 22 tons; the anchors are over 19 feet in length, and over 15 tons in weight.

Southern Star, 8 October 1910,
Irish Newspaper Archives, British Library Digital Collection

Pride in the Irish shipbuilding industry was clearly felt and loudly expressed, as was the assumption that the two new vessels would put the Cunard liners firmly in their place once all work on them had been concluded successfully during the next phase of construction:

OLYMPIC LAUNCHED

THE BIGGEST SHIP AFLOAT

IRISH FIRM'S TRIUMPH

In the presence of an enormous gathering, representative of the trade and commerce of the three Kingdoms, the largest ship in the world, the triple screw steamer *Olympic*, built by Messrs. Harland and Wolff for the White Star Line, Ltd., was launched on Thursday at Queen's Island, Belfast.

The monster vessel left the slips precisely at the appointed hour (11a.m.), and with grace and ease floated into the Lagan, amidst the cheers of the thousands that had assembled. Lord Pirrie was heartily congratulated by the representatives of the owner and the numerous guests present on the success of the achievement.

The giant Cunarders, *Mauretania* and *Lusitania*, temporarily robbed Belfast of the distinction of having built the largest vessel in the world, which was gained twelve years ago on the building of the *Oceanic*, and retained with the *Cedric*, *Celtic*, *Baltic*, and *Adriatic* for eight years after. Now, however, the *Olympic* and her sister ship, the *Titanic*, still in the slips, place the Irish shipyard ahead once more.

Sunday Independent (Irish), 23 October 1910,
Irish Newspaper Archives, British Library Digital Collection

Similar feelings of wonder at mankind's ability to construct such an amazing vessel were echoed in other papers:

IRELAND'S SHIPBUILDING RECORD

The building of the largest vessel afloat on the waters of the world is no small thing for one of the smallest and sparest of countries to have to its credit. This is a solid achievement . . . The *Olympic* is a marvel of the time; there has never been in all history anything so vast on the seas. All the ages of the world, till our age, would have refused to believe such a monstrous creation possible. Could the men dead only fifty years ago be brought to life to see it looming up before them, they could scarcely conceive what it was intended for, and they could have no idea at all how so vast a weight could be kept on the surface of the water and be guided and controlled by the hands of men. The *Olympic* needs a great many men. Her crew is a regiment of 500, a villageful in itself . . . The whole vessel, as the official account tells, is divided into thirty steel compartments, separated by heavy bulkheads. An automatic device on the bridge controls all these great doors at will, so that one man's hand can close all simultaneously, and an electric light register on the bridge tells, by the showing of a light, when each door is closed. The man on the bridge knows in a glance whether all is working well. Fire, the terrible danger of the sea, is guarded against by similarly effective and simple safeguards, and an affected area can be immediately cut off from all communication with the rest until all the peril is over . . .

The mere details of the launching bring vividly before the mind the great power of the vessel and the triumph of engineering which it represents. The picture of the monstrous mass gliding gently to the waters of the Lagan and taking its first dip at the opening of a valve will be historic to Belfast and memorable in the annals of the shipbuilder's ancient craft. It appears that there was some anxiety at least in the minds of the great inexpert public; probably the chiefs had no thought of the kind: they had made the most elaborate preparations for the most stupendous task of its kind that has ever been attempted in the world, and they carried out their plans without a hitch, so easily that it might seem nothing strange was being attempted. Yet this launching cost no less than £50,000 to the Belfast Harbour Commissioners for the special works that had to be taken in hand if the work was to be performed. The channel, for one thing, had to be deepened to meet the unforeseen case. And the catching and steadying of the great vessel as she took to the water was in itself a great undertaking, as it is easy to realise when it is considered that it had to be held by an apparatus of cables, drags, and anchors weighing something like 200 tons. From the moment of the first beginning of the glide from the stocks it took less than two minutes to bring the *Olympic* to a standstill in the water, so that the heaviest weight ever set afloat took to the water with less turmoil than accompanies the setting off of a curach [coracle].

Even with the extensive works taken in hand for this exceptional feat of launching, the *Olympic* is too vast to be finished on the stocks. It will still require some eight months' work to make all ready for the trial trip. Before the great new vessel carries its first passengers over the Atlantic, its sister ship, the *Titanic*, will be in about the state of the *Olympic* to-day. This represents a mighty business in Ireland, one which many a country must envy us. Here we hold an absolute record, and we can show something done in Ireland better than anything of its kind in England, Germany or America. Belfast, of course, has the first credit, but the whole country has its share in the work done in the second city of Ireland.

(*Freemans Journal*, 21 October 1910, Irish Newspaper Archives, British Library Digital Collection)

Yet it wasn't just the ships themselves that grabbed the attention of the world. Even changes to Harland and Wolff's shipyard made the news, such the opening of the new graving dock on 1 April 1911 in preparation for dry-docking the *Olympic* for her final fitting-out.

THE LARGEST IN THE WORLD

The Opening Ceremony of the Huge Graving Dock in Belfast was carried out yesterday. The great White Star Liner Olympic *was after-wards towed into the New Dock*

The largest graving dock in the world was opened in Belfast yesterday for the dry-docking of the largest steamer in the universe, the 45,000-ton White Star liner *Olympic*, recently launched from Messrs. Harland and Wolff's shipbuilding yard. The dock was begun in 1903, but owing to subsidences in the Alexandra Dock, which lies close by, the contract was delayed for some years, and instead of being completed in three years and four months, as originally arranged, it has taken almost eight years to complete the task. That the undertaking was of A STUPENDOUS NATURE may be judged by the cost, as the scheme involved an expenditure of £350,000.

The normal length of the dock is 850 feet, but by a contrivance of a caisson gate, which closes the entrance, it can at any time be placed against the outer quoin facing the entrance sill, so as to give an additional length of 886 feet 6 inches. The entrance to the dock is in clear width 96 feet, and the width of the dock at flood level is 100 feet, while that between the lines of coping is 128 feet. The depth of the dock floor at its centre below the level of high water at ordinary spring tides is 37 feet 3 inches, and at high water level of ordinary spring tides 33 feet 9 inches. THE BOTTOM OF THE DOCK FLOOR at the sides of the dock below the coping level is 43 ft. 6 in., and the thickness of the floor of the dock is 17 ft. 6 in., while at the side walls it is 18 ft. 9 in. The pumping of the dock engines and pumps, three sets in all, are nearly 3,000 horsepower, and are capable of emptying the dock of 23,000,000 of gallons inside 119 minutes.

The contractors of the dock were Messrs. Walter Scott and Middleton, Westminster, and Messrs. McLoughlin and Harvey Ltd. built the pumping station. It is interesting to note that when the Belfast Alexandra Dock was completed in 1885 it measured 800 ft. long and 50 ft. broad, and it was then the largest dock in the world.

There was a large and fashionable attendance of specially invited guests at THE OPENING CEREMONY, which included Lord and Lady Pirrie . . . The leviathan vessel Olympic was towed from her temporary berth at 10.30, and crossed the line of the dock at 10.50, being safely docked at 11.30. The most elaborate care was taken to avoid any hitch, a number of divers in diving dress occupying a prominent position during the docking operations.

At luncheon following the opening of the new graving dock at Belfast yesterday Lord Pirrie said he really did feel that the dock was not only not too large, but that before long the requirements of shipbuilding would necessitate even greater provision. The Harbour Board of Belfast should feel very proud of the fact that they had anticipated the necessities and requirements of the port in building a dock which many people at the time the scheme was being discussed, thought was far ahead of the requirements of the port.

Sunday Independent, 2 April 1911, Irish Newspaper Archives, British Library Digital Collection

Just under two months later it was the turn of the *Titanic* to slip into the water and begin the next stage of construction. At 12.05 p.m. on 31 May 1911 two rockets were fired, with a third set off five minutes later; and at 12.13 p.m., the *Titanic* started to move down the ramp. This was one of the events of the year, with thousands flocking to the dockyard expecting to send her on her way to fame and glory as the fastest and most luxurious ship in the world. The process took only 62 seconds and the correspondent from the *Sunday Independent* was suitably impressed by the whole occasion:

TITANIC AFLOAT

BELFAST'S SHIPBUILDING FEAT

HAPPY COINCIDENCE

An interesting coincidence connected with the launch this week of the new White Star liner, *Titanic*, from the Queen's Island ship-building yard, Belfast, which left the ways for the water just a few days after her huge sister, the *Olympic*, from the same yard, departed for her trial trip, was that Wednesday, also, both Lord Pirrie, the famous master builder, and Lady Pirrie celebrated their dual birthday. It is by many accepted as a happy augury for the career of both the great ships that the successful launching of the one and the first extended trial trip of the other synchronised with the natal day of both the head of the building firm and of his amiable wife.

LORD PIRRIE'S TRIUMPH

Lord Pirrie designed both the ships, and has personally taken responsibility for their construction from start to finish, so that within the space of a few days he has witnessed the triumph of two gigantic feats in the most advanced phase of modern marine designing and engineering.

The *Titanic* is slightly larger than the *Olympic*, yet 62 seconds sufficed to unloose her from the terra firma on which her massive frame was constructed and to see her securely afloat.

The scene at her launching was one never to be forgotten. A sun of almost tropical heat shone down on many thousands gathered on the stands and along the quays. Fog signals were exploded; the sirens in the Lough shrieked and a great cheer went up as the leviathan glided gracefully into the waters of the Lagan.

A BRILLIANT SCENE

Prior to the launch crowded vehicles of various descriptions were conveying passengers to the Queen's Island. There were motor cars, outside cars, taxi-cabs, and tram cars, and all of them were crowded. Several stands were erected on 'the Island', and the beauty and fashion of Belfast were well represented.

Upwards of 100 journalists, representing papers in Ireland, England, Scotland, and Wales were afforded special accommodation. A prominent figure at the launch was Mr. F. T. Ballen, the well-known journalist and novelist of the sea, who afterwards delivered a speech at a luncheon held at the Grand Central Hotel.

Mr. J. Pierpont Morgan, the United States shipping and financial magnate, was one of the distinguished gathering. He followed the proceedings at the launch with the greatest interest.

Lord Pirrie was early at the Island, and, before the launch, inspected the various portions of the ship with the greatest care. As soon as the 'triggers' were released by a signal from Lord Pirrie, there was a momentary lull; then there was a cry of 'There she goes!' and the cheers were loud and long. The spectacle was indeed a thrilling one.

BRAVO BELFAST!

It was a remarkable achievement that the *Titanic* should have been launched within about seven months of her sister, the *Olympic*. Between them they represent well over 100,000 tons displacement. This latest White Star monster's dimensions are:

Length overall . . . 882 feet
Gross tonnage . . . 45,000 tons
Displacement . . . . 60,000 tons
Speed . . . . 21 knots

The *Titanic* has 10 decks. The bridge deck extends 550 feet amidships; the forecastle and poop decks, on the same level, being, respectively, 128 feet and 106 feet long. The promenades and boat deck are over 500 feet long. For first-class passengers there are 30 suite rooms on the bridge deck and 30 on the shelter deck. In all there are nearly 350 first-class rooms, 100 of these being single berth rooms. There is accommodation for over 750 first-class passengers. For second-class passengers the rooms are arranged as two- or four-berth rooms, the total number of second-class passengers being over 550. For third-class passengers, there is a large number of enclosed berths, there being 84 two-berth rooms. The total number of third-class passengers provided for is over 1,100.

The arrangement of the machinery secures for the passengers the utmost comfort by the smooth working of the ship. It is also the most satisfactory from an engineering point of view.

Sunday Independent, 4 June 1911, Irish Newspaper Archives, British Library Digital Collection

It was not just company top brass that were impressed with the launch. The workers who had helped to construct the vessel took enormous pride in the occasion, as one of them later remembered: 'I was there and not only that but I had my eldest daughter there . . . Well, what you remember about it, the parts of people that was there. All the highest nobility and they were there and it was a sight to see the dresses of male and female, and you would see what the comparison was between the rich and the poor' (Jim Thompson, BBC *Titanic* Archive).

It is unusual to find such eyewitness accounts today, mainly because of the passing of time and lack of written testimony, but also because of the public's fascination with the stories of the survivors rather than the workforce that constructed the vessel. Consequently, it is primarily from newspaper accounts that we obtain a sense of the wonderment that the onlooking crowds must have felt. The journalist from the *Cork Informer*, for example, was also impressed by the scene, highlighting the trouble-free nature of the launch and conveying the pride and excitement of all those who were there to witness the event in his report of 1 June 1911.

The vessel launched yesterday from the yard of Harland and Wolff deserves well her name *Titanic*, for none other would more aptly apply. The day was observed as a holiday by all who could leave work, some of these people joining the many of the leisured class who travelled long distances in order to witness the launch . . . On the river were many craft from small to large, and these were full to over-flowing with sightseers. Five minutes before the appointed time there boomed out a double rocket, that being the signal that all was clear. Once more the whistle rang out, then the signal rockets boomed, the mountain of metal commenced to move, and there burst forth from the throats of the thousands of men, women and children that were assembled at the yard, from those that filled the boats on the river, and from the great human belt that fringed the opposite shore, a cheer that seemed like tumult – it was a wild roar.

> Quoted in Senan Molony, *The Titanic: Lost Words*,
> Tunbridge Wells; Ticktock Media Ltd, 2005

It did not go unnoticed that this was also the day that the *Olympic* made her maiden voyage – a true statement of intent about White Star's ability to compete with Cunard once again. However, it was also reported that the *Titanic* claimed another life shortly afterwards. Riveter Robert James Murphy fell 50 feet from one of the upper decks while working on the structure, and died from his injuries. He was 49.

Of course, there was still much work to do even after the *Titanic* was successfully launched. The *Leitrim Observer* carried a progress report four months after the triumphal scenes described in May. It is clear that, for the first time, the lofty ambitions for the ship, sketched out during the planning process, were starting to take shape in reality.

THE WHITE STAR LINER TITANIC

Rapid progress has been made at Belfast in the construction of the White Star triple-screw steamer *Titanic*, sister to the *Olympic*,

45,000 tons, the largest vessel in the world. The *Titanic*, which was launched on May 31st has now the steel structure of her hull practically completed; the electric turbine and auxiliary machinery, refrigerating plant, steering gear, and all the boilers are on board; the funnel uptakes complete; and one of the funnels is erected in position, as also are the masts.

As regards the state of things on some of the principal decks, it may be mentioned that the 2nd and 3rd class accommodation aft, on the lower deck is well advanced; whilst on the middle deck the stateroom bulkheads are finished throughout, and work is proceeding in the Engineers' accommodation. The stateroom bulkheads on the upper deck are also practically complete and well under way on the saloon deck, where the 1st and 2nd class dining saloon and 1st class reception room joinery grounds are all up and ready for proceeding with the framing, panelling, and ceiling.

On the shelter deck the 3rd class smoking room and general room joinery grounds are finished and the framing has been commenced. The framing of all the 1st class staterooms on this deck is well in hand. As further indicating the progress that has been made, it may be added that the main staircase is in position; also the electric elevators, the work in connection with which is advancing speedily.

The *Titanic* is scheduled to sail from Southampton and Cherbourg for New York in the White Star Line's Mail and Passenger Service on April 10th, 1912.

Leitrim Observer, 28 October 1911, Irish Newspaper Archives, British Library Digital Collection

This shows that by this stage the builders were so confident with the progress they were making that they were able to schedule and announce the date of the *Titanic's* maiden voyage. As interest in the ship continued to grow as work progressed, the paper followed up its story two weeks later, noting that after a minor collision the *Olympic* was undergoing repairs.

PROSPEROUS BELFAST

Belfast shipyards offer just now the unique spectacle of the two biggest ships afloat lying in dock. The *Titanic* is not yet finished, and some two thousand men are still at work on her, while as many more are in Harland and Wolff's workshops preparing the material for the equipment of this leviathan. Her sister ship, the *Olympic*, is meanwhile being repaired after the injuries she received in her recent collision with a British cruiser off the Isle of Wight. There must be fully five thousand men at work on these two vessels alone; but the other yards and docks are not idle, so that it is no wonder Belfast is comparatively prosperous with its thriving shipbuilding and other industries.

Leitrim Observer, 11 November 1911, Irish Newspaper Archives, British Library Digital Collection

The British wreck commissioner's final report describes in considerable detail the amount of work required to construct the superstructure during the period from launch to final sea trials before being put into service, and what the finished structure looked like.

DETAILED DESCRIPTION – DECKS AND ACCOMMODATION

The Boat deck was an uncovered deck, on which the boats were placed. At its lowest point it was about 92 ft. 6 in. above the keel. The overall length of this deck was about 500 ft. The forward end of it was fitted to serve as the navigating bridge of the vessel and was 190 ft. from the bow. On the after end of the bridge was a wheel house, containing the steering wheel and a steering compass. The chart room was immediately abaft this. On the starboard side of the wheel house and funnel casing were the navigating room, the captain's quarters, and some officers' quarters. On the port side were the remainder of the officers' quarters. At the middle line abaft the forward funnel casing were the wireless telegraphy rooms and the operators' quarters. The top of the officers' house formed a short deck. The connections from the Marconi aerials were made on this deck, and two of the collapsible boats were placed on it. Aft of the officers' house were the first-class passengers' entrance and stairways, and other adjuncts to the passengers' accommodation below. These stairways had a minimum effective width of 8 ft. They had assembling landings at the level of each deck, and three elevators communicating from E to A decks, but not to the Boat deck, immediately on the fore side of the stairway.

All the boats except two Englehardt life rafts were carried on this deck. There were seven lifeboats on each side, 30 ft. long, 9 ft. wide. There was an emergency cutter, 25 ft. long, on each side at the fore end of the deck. Abreast of each cutter was an Englehardt life raft. One similar raft was carried on the top of the officers' house on each side. In all there were 14 lifeboats, 2 cutters, and 4 Englehardt life rafts.

The forward group of four boats and one Englehardt raft were placed on each side of the deck alongside the officers' quarters and the first-class entrance. Further aft at the middle line on this deck was the special platform for the standard compass. At the after end of this deck was an entrance house for second-class passengers, with a stairway and elevator leading directly down to F deck. There were two vertical iron ladders at the after-end of this deck, leading to A deck, for the use of the crew. Alongside and immediately forward of the second-class entrance was the after group of lifeboats, four on each side of the ship.

In addition to the main stairways mentioned, there was a ladder on each side amidships, giving access from A deck below. At the forward end of the Boat deck there was on each side a ladder leading up from A deck, with a landing there, from which, by a ladder, access to B deck could be obtained direct. Between the reciprocating engine casing and the third funnel casing there was a stewards' stairway, which communicated with all the decks below as far as E deck. Outside the deck houses was promenading space for first-class passengers.

- *A Deck.* The next deck below the Boat deck was A deck. It extended over a length of about 500 feet. On this deck was a long house, extending nearly the whole length of the deck. It was of irregular shape, varying in width from 24 ft. to 72 ft. At the forward end it contained 34 staterooms, and abaft these a number of public rooms, etc., for first-class passengers, including two first-class entrances and stairway, reading room, lounge and the smoke room. Outside the deck house was a promenade for first-class passengers. The forward end of it on both sides of the ship, below the forward group of boats and for a short distance further aft, was protected against the weather by a steel screen, 192 ft. long, with large windows in it. In addition to the stairway described on the Boat deck, there was near the after-end of the A deck, and immediately forward of the first-class smoke room, another first-class entrance, giving access as far down as C deck. The second class stairway at the after-end of this deck (already described under the Boat deck) had no exit on to the A deck. The stewards' staircase opened on to this deck.
- *B Deck.* The next lowest deck was B deck, which constituted the top deck of the strong structure of the vessel, the decks above and the side plating between them being light plating. This deck extended continuously for 550 ft. There were breaks or wells both forward and aft of it, each about 50 ft. long. It was terminated by a poop and forecastle. On this deck were placed the principal staterooms of the vessel, 97 in number, having berths for 198 passengers, and aft of these was the first-class stairway and reception room, as well as the restaurant for first-class passengers and its pantry and galley. Immediately aft of this restaurant were the second-class stairway and smoke room. At the forward end of the deck outside the house was an assembling area, giving access by the ladders, previously

mentioned, leading directly to the Boat deck. From this same space a ladderway led to the forward third-class promenade on C deck. At the after-end of it were two ladders giving access to the after third-class promenade on C deck. At the after-end of this deck, at the middle line, was placed another second-class stairway, which gave access to C, D, E, F and G decks.

At the forward end of the vessel, on the level of B deck, was situated the forecastle deck, which was 125 ft. long. On it were placed the gear for working the anchors and cables and for warping (or moving) the ship in dock. At the after-end, on the same level, was the poop deck, about 105 ft. long, which carried the after-warping appliances and was a third-class promenading space. Arranged above the poop was a light docking bridge, with telephone, telegraphs, etc., communicating to the main navigating bridge forward.

- **C Deck.** The next lowest deck was C deck. This was the highest deck which extended continuously from bow to stern. At the forward end of it, under the forecastle, was placed the machinery required for working the anchors and cables and for the warping of the ship referred to on B deck above: there were also the crew's galley and the seamen's and firemen's mess room accommodation, where their meals were taken. At the after-end of the forecastle, at each side of the ship, were the entrances to the third-class spaces below. On the port side, at the extreme after-end and opening on to the deck, was the lamp room. The break in B deck between the forecastle and the first class passenger quarters formed a well about 50 ft. in length, which enabled the space under it on C deck to be used as a third-class promenade. This space contained two hatchways, the No. 2 hatch and the bunker hatch. The latter of these hatchways gave access to the space allotted to the first- and second-class baggage hold, the mails, specie and parcel room, and to the lower hold, which was used for cargo or coals. Abaft of this well there was a house

450 ft. long and extending for the full breadth of the ship. It contained 148 staterooms for first class, besides service rooms of various kinds. On this deck, at the forward first-class entrance, were the purser's office and the enquiry office, where passengers' telegrams were received for sending by the Marconi apparatus. Exit doors through the ship's side were fitted abreast of this entrance. Abaft the after-end of this long house was a promenade at the ship's side for second-class passengers, sheltered by bulwarks and bulkheads. In the middle of the promenade stood the second-class library. The two second-class stairways were at the ends of the library, so that from the promenade access was obtained at each end to a second-class main stairway. There was also access by a door from this space into each of the alleyways in the first-class accommodation on each side of the ship, and by two doors at the after-end into the after-well. This after-well was about 50 ft. in length and contained two hatchways called No. 5 and No. 6 hatches. Abaft this well, under the poop, was the main third-class entrance for the after-end of the vessel, leading directly down to G deck, with landings and access at each deck. The effective width of this stairway was 16 ft. to E deck. From E to F it was 8 ft. wide. Aft of this entrance on B deck were the third-class smoke room and the general room. Between these rooms and the stern was the steam steering gear and the machinery for working the after capstan gear, which was used for warping the after-end of the vessel. The steam steering gear had three cylinders. The engines were in duplicate, to provide for the possibility of breakdown of one set.

- *D Deck.* The general height from D deck to C deck was 10 ft. 6 in., this being reduced to 9 ft. at the forward end, and 9 ft. 6 in. at the after-end, the taper being obtained gradually by increasing the sheer of the D deck. The forward end of this deck provided accommodation for 108 firemen, who were in two separate watches. There was the necessary lavatory accommodation, abaft the firemen's quarters at the sides of the ship.

On each side of the middle line immediately abaft the firemen's quarters there was a vertical spiral staircase leading to the forward end of a tunnel, immediately above the tank top, which extended from the foot of the staircase to the forward stokehole, so that the firemen could pass direct to their work without going through any passenger accommodation or over any passenger decks. On D deck abaft of this staircase was the third-class promenade space which was covered in by C deck. From this promenade space there were four separate ladderways with two ladders, 4 ft. wide to each. One ladderway on each side forward led to C deck, and one, the starboard, led to E deck and continued to F deck as a double ladder and to G deck as a single ladder. The two ladderways at the after end led to E deck on both sides and to F deck on the port side. Abaft this prom-enade space came a block of 50 first-class staterooms. This surrounded the forward funnel. The main first-class reception room and dining saloon were aft of these rooms and surrounded the No. 2 funnel. The reception room and staircase occupied 83 ft. of the length of the ship. The dining saloon occupied 112 ft., and was between the second and third funnels. Abaft this came the first-class pantry, which occupied 56 ft. of the length of the ship. The reciprocating engine hatch came up through this pantry. Aft of the first-class pantry, the galley, which provides for both first- and second-class passengers, occupied 45 ft. of the length of the ship. Aft of this were the turbine engine hatch and the emergency dynamos. Abaft of and on the port side of this hatch were the second-class pantry and other spaces used for the saloon service of the passengers. On the starboard side abreast of these there was a series of rooms used for hospitals and their attendants. These spaces occupied about 54 ft. of the length. Aft of these was the second-class saloon occupying 70 ft. of the length. In the next 88 ft. of length there were 38 second-class rooms and the necessary baths and lavatories. From here to the stern was accommodation for third class passengers and the main third-class lavatories for the passengers in the after-end of the ship. The watertight bulkheads come up to this deck throughout the length from the stern as far forward as the bulkhead dividing the after boiler room from the reciprocating engine room. The watertight bulkhead of the two compartments abaft the stern was carried up to this deck.

• *E Deck.* The watertight bulkheads, other than those mentioned as extending to D deck, all stopped at this deck. At the forward end was provided accommodation for three watches of trimmers, in three separate compartments, each holding 24 trimmers. Abaft this, on the port side, was accommodation for 44 seamen. Aft of this, and also on the starboard side of it, were the lavatories for crew and third-class passengers; further aft again came the forward third-class lavatories. Immediately aft of this was a passageway right across the ship communicating directly with the ladderways leading to the decks above and below and gangway doors in the ship's side. This passage was 9 ft. wide at the sides and 15 ft. at the centre of the ship.

From the after end of this cross passage main alleyways on each side of the ship ran right through to the after end of the vessel. That on the port side was about 8 ½ ft. wide. It was the general communication passage for the crew and third-class passengers and was known as the 'working passage'. In this passage at the centre line in the middle of the length of the ship direct access was obtained to the third-class dining rooms on the deck below by means of a ladderway 20 ft. wide. Between the working passage and the ship's side was the accommodation for the petty officers, most of the stewards, and the engineers' mess room. This accommodation extended for 475 ft. From this passage access was obtained to both engine rooms and the engineers' accommodation, some third-class lavatories and also some third-class accommodation at the after end. There was another cross passage at the end of this accommodation about 9 ft. wide, terminating in gangway doors on each side of the ship. The port side of it was for third-class passengers and the starboard for second class. A door divided the parts, but it could be opened for any useful purpose, or for an emergency. The second-class stairway leading to the Boat deck was in the cross passageway. The passage on the starboard side ran through the first- and then the second-class accommodation, and the forward main first-class stairway and elevators extended to this deck, whilst both the second-class main stairways were also in communication with this starboard passage. There were four first-class, eight first or second alternatively, and 19 second-class rooms leading off this starboard passage.

The remainder of the deck was appropriated to third-class accommodation. This contained the bulk of the third-class accommodation. At the forward end of it was the accommodation for 53 firemen constituting the third watch. Aft of this in three watertight compartments there was third-class accommodation extending to 147 ft. In the next watertight compartment were the swimming bath and linen rooms. In the next watertight compartments were stewards' accommodation on the port side, and the Turkish baths on the starboard side. The next two watertight compartments each contained a third-class dining room.

The third-class stewards' accommodation, together with the third-class galley and pantries, filled the watertight compartment. The engineers' accommodation was in the next compartment directly alongside the casing of the reciprocating engine room. The next three compartments were allotted to 64 second-class staterooms. These communicated direct with the second-class main stairways. The after compartments contained third-class accommodation. All spaces on this deck had direct ladderway communication with the deck above, so that if it became necessary to close the watertight doors in the bulkheads an escape was available in all cases. On this deck in way of the boiler rooms were placed the electrically driven fans which provided ventilation to the stokeholds.

• **G Deck.** The forward end of this deck had accommodation for 15 leading firemen and 30 greasers. The next watertight compartment contained third-class accommodation in 26 rooms for 106 people. The next watertight compartment contained the first-class baggage room, the post office accommodation, a racquet court, and seven third-class rooms for 34 passengers. From this point to the after-end of the boiler room the space was used for the 'tween deck bunkers. Alongside the reciprocating engine room were the engineers' stores and workshop. Abreast of the turbine engine room were some of the ship's stores. In the next watertight compartment abaft the turbine room were the main body of the stores. The next two compartments were appropriated to 186 third-class passengers in 60 rooms; this deck was the lowest on which any passengers or crew were carried.

- ***Below G Deck.*** were two partial decks, the Orlop and Lower Orlop decks, the latter extending only through the forepeak and No. 1 hold; on the former deck, abaft the turbine engine room, were some store rooms containing stores for ship's use.

  Below these decks again came the inner bottom, extending fore and aft through about nine-tenths of the vessel's length, and on this were placed the boilers, main and auxiliary machinery and the electric light machines. In the remaining spaces below G deck were cargo holds or 'tween decks, seven in all, six forward and one aft. The firemen's passage, giving direct access from their accommodation to the forward boiler room by stairs at the forward end, contained the various pipes and valves connected with the pumping arrangements at the forward end of the ship, and also the steam pipes conveying steam to the windlass gear forward and exhaust steam pipes leading from winches and other deck machinery. It was made thoroughly watertight throughout its length, and at its after-end was closed by a watertight vertical sliding door of the same character as other doors on the inner bottom. Special arrangements were made for pumping this space out, if necessary. The pipes were placed in this tunnel to protect them from possible damage by coal or cargo, and also to facilitate access to them.

On the decks was provided generally, in the manner above described, accommodation for a maximum number of 1,034 first-class passengers, and at the same time 510 second-class passengers and 1,022 third-class passengers. Some of the accommodation was of an alternative character, and could be used for either of two classes of passengers. In the statement of figures the higher alternative class has been reckoned. This makes a total accommodation for 2,566 passengers.

Accommodation was provided for the crew as follows; about 75 of the deck department, including officers and doctors, 326 of the engine room department, including engineers, and 544 of the victualling department, including pursers and leading stewards.

Access of passengers to the Boat deck. The following routes led directly from the various parts of the first-class passenger accommodation to the Boat deck: From the forward ends of A, B, C, D, and E decks by the staircase in the forward first-class entrance direct to the Boat deck. The elevators led from the same decks as far as A deck, where further access was obtained by going up the top flight of the main staircase.

The same route was available for first-class passengers forward of midships on B, C, and E decks.

First-class passengers abaft amidships on B and C decks could use the staircase in the after main entrance to A deck, and then could pass out on to the deck, and by the midships stairs besides the house ascend to the Boat deck. They could also use the stewards' staircase between the reciprocating engine casing and Nos. 1 and 2 boiler casing, which led direct to the Boat deck. This last route was also available for passengers on E deck in the same divisions who could use the forward first-class main stairway and elevators.

Second-class passengers on D deck could use their own after-stairway to B deck, and could then pass up their forward stairway to the Boat deck, or else could cross their saloon and use the same stairway throughout.

Of the second-class passengers on E deck, those abreast of the reciprocating engine casing, unless the watertight door immediately abaft them was closed, went aft and joined the other second-class passengers. If, however, the watertight door at the end of their compartment was closed, they passed through an emergency door into the engine room, and directly up to the Boat deck, by the ladders and gratings in the engine room casing.

The second-class passengers on E deck in the compartment abreast the turbine casing on the starboard side, and also those on F deck on both sides below could pass through M watertight bulkhead to the forward second-class main stairway. If this door were closed, they could pass by the stairway up to the serving space at the forward end of the second-class saloon, and go into the saloon and thence up the forward second-class stairway.

Passengers between M and N bulkheads on both E and F decks could pass directly up to the forward second-class stairway to the Boat deck.

Passengers between N and O bulkheads on D, E, F and G decks could pass by the after second-class stairway to B deck, and then cross to the forward second-class stairway and go up to the Boat deck.

Third-class passengers at the fore end of the vessel could pass by the staircases to C deck in the forward well and by ladders on the port and starboard sides at the forward end of the deck houses, thence direct to the Boat deck outside the officers' accommodation. They might also pass along the working passage on E deck and through the emergency door to the forward first-class main stairway, or through the door on the same deck at the forward end of the first-class alleyway and up the first-class stairway direct to the Boat deck.

The third-class passengers at the after-end of the ship passed up their stairway to E deck, and into the working passage, and through the emergency doors to the two second-class stairways, and so to the Boat deck, like second-class passengers. Or, alternatively, they could continue up their own stairs and entrance to C deck, thence by the two ladders at the after-end of the bridge on to the B deck, and thence by the forward second-class stairway direct to the Boat deck.

Crew. From each boiler room an escape or emergency ladder was provided direct to the Boat deck by the fidleys, in the boiler casings, and also into the working passage on E deck, and thence by the stair immediately forward of the reciprocating engine casing, direct to the Boat deck.

From both the engine rooms ladders and gratings gave direct access to the Boat deck.

From the electric engine room, the after tunnels, and the forward pipe tunnels, escapes were provided direct to the working passage on E deck, and thence by one of the several routes already detailed from that space.

From the crew's quarters they could go forward by their own staircases into the forward well, and thence, like the third-class passengers, to the Boat deck.

The stewards' accommodation being all connected to the working passage or the forward main first-class stairway, they could use one of the routes from thence.

The engineers' accommodation also communicated with the working passage, but, as it was possible for them to be shut between two watertight bulkheads, they had also a direct route by the gratings in the engine room casing to the Boat deck.

On all the principal accommodation decks the alleyways and stairways provided a ready means of access to the Boat deck, and there were clear deck spaces in way of all first-, second- and third-class main entrances and stairways on Boat deck and all decks below.

British wreck commissioner's final report

Outfitting was not restricted to decks and crew accommodation; the intention of the venture was to make the ships as luxurious as possible. Consequently, the *Titanic* was fitted with a swimming pool, gymnasium, Turkish bath, libraries, squash court and even a restaurant – the

Café Parisienne – for first-class passengers, whose common rooms were often finished with the highest-quality wood panelling, bespoke furniture, electric lights, exclusive crockery and china, works of art and similar luxury trappings. It was Ismay's desire to create not only the largest but also the most impressive liner in the world. But to enjoy the ultimate experience would not be cheap: the most expensive one-way transatlantic ticket would cost £870 or $4,350.

Yet one element continued to be controversial even during construction – the lifeboats. A succinct summary contained in the final report of the US inquiry indicates the quantity and arrangement of lifeboats on board.

BOAT DAVITS AND LIFEBOATS OF
THE STEAMSHIP TITANIC.

The *Titanic* was fitted with 16 sets of double-acting boat davits of modern type, capable of handling 2 or 3 boats per set of davits. The davits were thus capable of handling 48 boats, whereas the ship carried but 16 lifeboats and 4 collapsibles, fulfilling all the requirements of the British Board of Trade. The *Titanic* was provided with 14 lifeboats, of capacity for 65 persons each, or 910 persons; 2 emergency sea boats, of capacity for 35 persons each, or 70 persons; 4 collapsible boats, of capacity for 49 persons each, or 196 persons. Total lifeboat capacity, 1,176. There was ample lifebelt equipment for all.

US Senate board of inquiry final report

The *Belfast Evening News* stressed the modernity of the equipment chosen to operate the lifeboats in case there was need to lower them into the water: 'The *Titanic* will be fitted with patent davits which will enable the lifeboats to be lowered expeditiously. The lifeboats will be arranged on the double-banked principle, and will be operated by the new Wellin gear, which combines a maximum of efficiency and a minimum of complexity and space . . . The *Olympic's* lifeboats have been fitted with a similar appliance.' (*Belfast Evening News*, 31 May 1911, National Maritime Museum LMQ/7/3/B)

These details were of particular importance given the role of Alexander Carlisle, who had responsibility for selecting the system used in both the *Olympic* and *Titanic* and left Harland and Wolff in 1910 when he became a shareholder in the Wellin Davit and Engineering Company. Fitting sixteen davits theoretically enabled four lifeboats to be suspended from each davit, making a total number of 64 for the entire ship and a capacity of 4,160 people – more than the maximum number of passengers and crew the *Titanic* was designed to carry. Carlisle, though, recommended that only three boats be attached to each davit, making a total of 48 and a capacity of 3,120 – only slightly less than the ship could hold. However, the decision was taken to load only one boat per davit to enable greater deck space, with an additional four collapsible boats on top of the officers' quarters, making a total of only 20 lifeboats with a capacity far beneath the numbers a standard voyage could expect to contain – yet still in excess of Board of Trade regulations insisted upon as a minimum requirement to receive a safety certificate. Carlisle himself spoke at the subsequent inquiry:

> When I pointed out that I expected the Board of Trade and the Government would require much larger boat accommodation on these large ships, I was authorised then to go ahead and get out full plans and designs, so that if the Board of Trade did call upon us to fit anything more we would have no extra trouble or extra expense ... I came over from Belfast in October, 1909, with these plans that were worked out, and also the decorations, and Mr. Ismay and Mr. Sanderson and Lord Pirrie and myself spent about four hours together... The lifeboat part I suppose took five or ten minutes... It was said they thought it would be desirable to fit them [the Wellin davits] in the ship... I showed them the advantage, and that it would put them to no expense or trouble in case the Board of Trade called upon them to do something at the last minute... One [interview] took place in October, 1909, and the other in January, 1910 ... Mr. Ismay was the only one who spoke or said anything about it... Mr. Sanderson, I think, never spoke...

The White Star and other friends give us a great deal of liberty,
but at the same time we cannot build a ship any bigger than they
order, or put anything in her more than they are prepared to pay
for. We have a very free hand, and always have had; but I do not
think that we could possibly have supplied any more boats to the
ship without getting the sanction and the order of the White Star
Line. . . Personally I consider there were not enough [lifeboats on
board]. . . I have said so over and over again. . . I said it at the
merchant Shipping Advisory committee on the 19th and 26th of
May [1911]. . . before either of the ships went to sea. . . I said it to
the entire meeting, whoever was present heard me say it. . . I showed
them the plans of my proposals; I could not do any more. . . If they
[the White Star Line] go and make certain changes in these [new]
ships, naturally they would have to make them in the *Adriatic* and
other boats. . . The [Life-Saving Appliances] Committee was practically at the end when I was asked to join it [in 1911]. I was only
at the last two meetings, and the majority of the points had been
well considered, and it was understood that if any Act of Parliament
was brought in by the Board of Trade it would not only affect a
ship like the *Titanic*, but that it would go back on all the old ships
afloat, and it would therefore be unfair to go in for putting too
many boats when they possibly could not get room on the older
ships.

Board of Trade Inquiry, 1912, Day 20

On 3 February 1912, the *Titanic* was dry-docked in the Belfast Harbour
Commission's new graving dock, the Thompson Dock, where her
propellers were fitted and a final coat of paint applied. 'Under the super-
intendence of Lord Pirrie, who seemed to be quite as energetic as any
of his workmen, the White Star liner *Titanic* (sister ship to the *Olympic*)
was successfully dry-docked at Belfast on Saturday morning. Here she
will be completed and made ready for sea' (*Irish Independent*, 5 February
1912, Irish Newspaper Archives, British Library Digital Collection). All
was complete within a matter of weeks, and the final stages of fitting
out began. 'The White Star liner *Titanic* left the new graving dock at

Belfast yesterday and moored to the fitting-out jetty, where she will be completed. The operation, which was most successful, occupied less than an hour. The gigantic vessel will leave Belfast in about six weeks' time, and sail from Southampton for New York on her maiden voyage on the 10th April' (*Sunday Independent,* 18 February 1912, Irish Newspaper Archives, British Library Digital Collection).

The British wreck commissioner's report describes the results of the final fitting-out process:

The vessel was constructed under survey of the British Board of Trade for a passenger certificate, and also to comply with the American Immigration Laws.

Steam was supplied from six entirely independent groups of boilers in six separate watertight compartments. The after boiler room, No. 1, contained five single-ended boilers. Four other boiler rooms, Nos. 2, 3, 4 and 5, each contained five double-ended boilers. The forward boiler room, No. 6, contained four double-ended boilers. The reciprocating engines and most of the auxiliary machinery were in a seventh separate watertight compartment aft of the boilers; the low-pressure turbine, the main condensers and the thrust blocks of the reciprocating engine were in an eighth separate watertight compartment. The main electrical machinery was in a ninth separate watertight compartment immediately abaft the turbine engine room. Two emergency steam-driven dynamos were placed on the D deck, 21 ft. above the level of the load waterline. These dynamos were arranged to take their supply of steam from any of the three of the boiler rooms Nos. 2, 3 and 5, and were intended to be available in the event of the main dynamo room being flooded.

The ship was equipped with the following:

(1) Wireless telegraphy.
(2) Submarine signalling.
(3) Electric lights and power systems.
(4) Telephones for communication between the different working

positions in the vessel. In addition to the telephones, the means of communication included engine and docking telegraphs, and duplicate or emergency engine room telegraph, to be used in the event of any accident to the ordinary telegraph.

(5) Three electric elevators for taking passengers in the first class up to A deck, immediately below the Boat deck, and one in the second class for taking passengers up to the Boat deck.

(6) Four electrically driven boat winches on the Boat deck for hauling up the boats.

(7) Life-saving appliances to the requirements of the Board of Trade, including boats and lifebelts.

(8) Steam whistles on the two foremost funnels, worked on the Willett-Bruce system of automatic control.

(9) Navigation appliances, including Kelvin's patent sounding machines for finding the depth of water under the ship without stopping; Walker's taffrail log for determining the speed of the ship; and flash signal lamps fitted above the shelters at each end of the navigating bridge for Morse signalling with other ships.

MACHINERY

Description. The propelling machinery was of the combination type, having two sets of reciprocating engines driving the wing propellers, and a low-pressure turbine working the centre propeller. Steam was supplied by 24 double-ended boilers, and 5 single-ended boilers, arranged for a working pressure of 215 lbs. per square inch. The turbine was placed in a separate compartment aft of the reciprocating engine room and divided from it by a watertight bulkhead. The main condensers, with their circulating pumps and air pumps, were placed in the turbine room. The boilers were arranged in six watertight compartments, the single-ended boilers being placed in the one nearest the main engines, the whole being built under Board of Trade survey for passenger certificate.

Reciprocating Engines. The reciprocating engines were of the four-crank triple expansion type. Each set had four inverted, direct-acting cylinders, the high-pressure having a diameter of 54 in., the intermediate-pressure of 84 in., and each of the two low-pressure cylinders of 97 in., all with a stroke of 6 ft. 3 in. The valves of the high-pressure and intermediate cylinders were of the piston type, and the low-pressure cylinder had double-ported slide valves, fitted with Stephenson link motion. Each engine was reversed by a Brown's type of direct-acting steam and hydraulic engine. There was also a separate steam-driven high-pressure pump fitted for operating either or both of the reversing engines. This alternative arrangement was a stand-by in case of breakdown of the steam pipes to these engines.

Turbine. The low-pressure turbine was of the Parson's reaction type, direct coupled to the centre line of shafting and arranged for driving in the ahead direction only. It exhausted to the two condensers, placed one on each side of it. A shut-off valve was fitted in each of the eduction pipes leading to the condensers. An emergency governor was fitted and arranged to shut off steam to the turbine and simultaneously change over the exhaust from the reciprocating engines to the condensers, should the speed of the turbine become excessive through the breaking of a shaft or other accident.

Boilers. All the boilers were 15 ft. 9 in. in diameter, the 24 double-ended boilers being 20 ft. long, and the single-ended 11 ft. 9 in. long. Each double-ended boiler had six, and each single-ended boiler three furnaces, with a total heating surface of 144,142 sq. ft. and a grate surface of 3,466 sq. ft. The boilers were constructed in accordance with the rules of the Board of Trade for a working pressure of 215 lbs. per square inch. They were arranged for working under natural draught, assisted by fans, which blew air into the open stokehold.

Auxiliary Steam Pipes. The five single-ended boilers and those in boiler rooms Nos. 2 and 4 had separate steam connections to the pipe supplying steam for working the auxiliary machinery, and the five single-ended boilers and the two port boilers in boiler room No. 2 had separate steam connections to the pipe supplying steam for working the electric light engines. A cross connection was also made between the main and auxiliary pipes in the recip- rocating engine room, so that the auxiliaries could be worked from any boiler in the ship. Steam pipes also were led separately from three of the boiler rooms (Nos. 2, 3, 5) above the watertight bulk- heads and along the working passage to the emergency electric light engines placed above the loadline in the turbine room. Pipes were also led from this steam supply to the pumps in the engine room, which were connected to the bilges throughout the ship.

Main Steam Pipes. There were two main lines of steam pipes led to the engine room, with shut-off valves at three of the bulk- heads. Besides the shut-off valves at the engine room bulkhead, a quick-acting emergency valve was fitted on each main steam pipe, so that the steam could at once be shut off in case of rupture of the main pipe.

Condensing Plant and Pumps. There were two main condensers, having a combined cooling surface of 50,550 square feet, designed to work under a vacuum of 28 ins. with cooling water at 60 deg. Fahr. The condensers were pear-shaped in section, and built of mild steel plates.

Four gunmetal centrifugal pumps were fitted for circulating water through the condensers. Each pump had suction and discharge pipes of 29 in. bore, and was driven by a compound engine. Besides the main sea suctions, two of the pumps had direct bilge suctions from the turbine room and the other two from the reciprocating engine room. The bilge suctions were 18 in. diameter. Four of Weir's 'Dual' air pumps were fitted, two to each condenser, and discharged to two feed-tanks placed in the turbine engine room.

Bilge and Ballast Pumps. The ship was also fitted with the following pumps: Five ballast and bilge pumps, each capable of discharging 250 tons of water per hour; three bilge pumps, each of 150 tons per hour capacity.

One ash ejector was placed in each of the large boiler compartments to work the ash ejectors [sic], and to circulate or feed the boilers as required. This pump was also connected to the bilges, except in the case of three of the boiler rooms, where three of the ballast and bilge pumps were placed. The pumps in each case had direct bilge suctions as well as a connection to the main bilge pipe, so that each boiler room might be independent. The remainder of the auxiliary pumps were placed in the reciprocating and turbine engine rooms. Two ballast pumps were placed in the reciprocating engine room, with large suctions from the bilges direct and from the bilge main. Two bilge pumps were also arranged to draw from bilges. One bilge pump was placed in the turbine room and one of the hot salt-water pumps had a connection from the bilge main pipe for use in emergency. A 10 in. main ballast pipe was carried fore and aft through the ship with separate connections to each tank, and with filling pipes from the sea connected at intervals for trimming purposes. The five ballast pumps were arranged to draw from this pipe. A double line of bilge main pipe was fitted forward of No. 5 boiler room and aft of No. 1.

British wreck commissioner's final report

All that remained was to hire the crew – recruits were signed up from 25 March in various places and then sent to Belfast – and head for Southampton under the temporary command of Captain Herbert Haddock, who would then hand over control of the vessel to the man appointed to oversee the maiden voyage, Captain Edward John Smith. The time had finally come for the *Titanic* to leave Belfast. From Southampton, she would head via Cherbourg and Queenstown for New York having first conducted several important sea trials to test seaworthiness and safety, as well as practise emergency drills such as lowering the lifeboats. The intended departure date was 1 April 1912, but not everything went to plan. 'The White Star liner *Titanic*, which has just been completed by Messrs. Harland and Wolff, at Belfast, was to have left for her trial trip yesterday, but owing to the strong wind her departure was postponed until to-day' (*Irish Independent*, 2 April 1912, Irish Newspaper Archives, British Library Digital Collection).

The US inquiry report described the trials in its final report. Significantly, it noted flaws in the testing procedures of the lifeboats.

TRIAL TESTS STEAMSHIP TITANIC

The committee finds from the evidence that between six and seven hours was spent in making trial tests of this vessel at Belfast Lough on Monday, the 1st of April last. A few turning circles were made, compasses adjusted, and she steamed a short time under approximately a full head of steam, but the ship was not driven at her full speed. One general officer of the steamship company was on board during the trial tests, while the builders were represented by Mr. Thomas Andrews, who had superintended the building of the vessel. Mr. Andrews conducted certain tests at Southampton and represented the builders both at Southampton and on the first voyage.

With a partial crew, the ship sailed from Belfast, immediately after the trial, for Southampton, where she arrived on Wednesday, April 3, about midnight. She made fast with her port side to the wharf, where she remained until April 10, about 12 o'clock noon, when she sailed for Cherbourg, Queenstown, and New York.

ONLY TWO LIFEBOATS LOWERED

Many of the crew did not join the ship until a few hours before sailing, and the only drill while the vessel lay at Southampton or on the voyage consisted in lowering two lifeboats on the starboard side into the water, which boats were again hoisted to the boat deck within a half hour. No boat list designating the stations of members of the crew was posted until several days after sailing from Southampton, boatmen being left in ignorance of their proper stations until the following Friday morning.

US Senate board of inquiry final report

Despite the postponement, vast crowds once again turned out to see the departure from Belfast, including Francis John Parkinson junior, whose father Francss John Parkinson senior had worked on the *Titanic*. He later recalled:

'It was very, very . . . very, very wonderful indeed. There were thousands waving goodbye to the ship. It was emotional, and there was a tinge of sadness about it all too. These men had spent all those years, something like four years, getting it ready, and making it a first class job, and then just something they'd loved and were going to miss seeing. It was very, very much just part of themselves.'

Titanic: Death of a Dream, Part One

This time everything went to plan, and the *Titanic* finally left the shipyard en route to her date with destiny. The newspapers were full of praise for the vessel, and flagged up the fact that the construction process had incorporated modifications learned throughout the building of the *Olympic*.

The White Star liner *Titanic*, 46,323 tons, the largest vessel in the world, left Belfast on Tuesday, and is due to arrive at Southampton this morning, and will sail on her first voyage on April 10th. The production of two such notable vessels as the *Olympic* and *Titanic*, and the completion of the second so shortly after the first, is worthy of special comment. The *Olympic* and *Titanic* are essentially similar in design and construction, and yet, so rapidly are we moving in these days of progress, that already the experience gained with the *Olympic* is being taken advantage of in the *Titanic*. Consequently there are several changes carried out in the second ship with a view to meeting even more completely than before the requirements of the service, and the large number of passengers with whom this type of ship is proving so popular.

Irish Independent, 4 April 1912,
Irish Newspaper Archives, British Library Digital Collection

On Wednesday 3 April, the *Titanic* arrived in Southampton, before being moored up in anticipation of imminent departure for Cherbourg. One final step was required – acquiring an official certificate from the Board of Trade, as the US inquiry report notes: 'On Wednesday morning, the day the ship sailed from Southampton, Capt. Clark, a representative of the British Board of Trade, came aboard and, after spending a brief time, issued the necessary certificate to permit sailing' (US Senate board of inquiry final report). Only one small mishap occurred: a fire broke out in one of No. 6 boiler room's bunkers that continued throughout the ship's stay in Southampton. While it was contained, it was not fully extinguished until after the *Titanic* had already set sail on its maiden voyage.

Part Two

The Maiden Voyage and Loss of the *Titanic*

3

Introduction

This collection of testimonies will transport you back in time to the night in question, and vividly reveal what it was like to be on board the *Titanic* as it struck the iceberg and then made its final descent to the ocean floor.

The events of 14 and 15 April 1912 have long since passed into legend, horrifying and fascinating both historians and the general public in equal measure ever since. Many books have been written about the tragedy, as noted earlier, in an attempt to provide an explanation of why the *Titanic* sank. However, the passages and extracts that follow provide a very different style of account. They are filled with the confusion and uncertainty that you would naturally expect during an unfolding disaster, with conflicting accounts and disagreements over what actually happened. They are drawn from a variety of sources – crew, passengers and those first on the scene to help with the rescue – and as a result what follows is a highly emotive and personal version of events, witnessed and recalled by people caught up in the unfolding momentum of the sinking ship. To help make sense of the passing of time, a narrative chronology has been provided, counting down the days, hours and minutes between setting sail from Southampton and the fatal iceberg strike.

In some instances memories were recorded mere days and weeks after the event, the pain and terror still fresh; others tell their stories in an official capacity at the various inquiries that were held into the accident; further attempts by the historian Walter Lord to recapture what it was like to be involved on that fatal night via a process of retrospective interview have also been included. All are subjective, and many of the later accounts of the tragedy are naturally coloured by the passing of time. Nevertheless, this collection of testimonies will transport you back in time to the night in question, and vividly reveal what it was like to be on board the *Titanic* as it struck the iceberg and began its final descent to the ocean floor.

The personal testimonies have been deliberately allowed to stand by themselves, with as little commentary as possible so as not to detract from the power of the recollections. To help understand who each person was, where applicable a brief biography is provided, outlining their role on board the ship if a member of the crew, and the fate that befell them. In addition, at the start of each section there is a brief timeline with an overview of how events unfolded.

Although powerful in their own right, individual accounts make it difficult to get a sense of the scale of the tragedy, and the statistics compiled by the various inquiries provide some indication of the sheer number of people involved, the figures on the page acting as a stark backdrop to the testimonies, each total representing individuals with hopes, dreams and aspirations of an exciting trip, a reunion with friends and family or the promise of a better life overseas.

PASSENGER LIST AND SURVIVORS OF
STEAMSHIP TITANIC

The *Titanic* arrived at Cherbourg late the same afternoon. The *Titanic* left Cherbourg and proceeded to Queenstown, Ireland, arriving there on Thursday about midday, departing for New York immediately after embarking the mails and passengers. Her passenger list was made up as follows:

First-class passengers who sailed on the *Titanic*:

Women and Children	156
Men	173
Total	**329**

First-class passengers, survivors:
Women and Children	145
Men	54
Total	**199**

First-class passengers, lost:
Women and Children	11
Men	119
Total	**130**

Second-class passengers who sailed on the *Titanic*:
Women and Children	128
Men	157
Total	**285**

Second-class passengers, survivors:
Women and Children	104
Men	15
Total	**119**

Second-class passengers, lost:
Women and Children	24
Men	142
Total	**166**

Third-class passengers who sailed on the *Titanic*:
Women and Children	224
Men	486
Total	**710**

Third-class passengers, survivors:
Women and Children	105
Men	69
Total	**174**

Third-class passengers, lost:

Women and Children	119
Men	417
Total	**536**

US Senate board of inquiry final report

The report stated that the number of crew totalled 899. The British wreck commissioner's final report contains some discrepancies to the US report in the compilation of the accompanying passenger lists. What follows is the official list of statistics, focusing firstly on the crew who sailed on the vessel:

Crew and Passengers

When the *Titanic* left Queenstown on 11th April the total number of persons employed on board in any capacity was 885.
The respective ratings of these persons were as follows:

Deck Department	66
Engine Department	325
Victualling Department	494
Total	885

Eight bandsmen were included in the second-class passenger list. In the Deck Department the Master, Edward Charles [John] Smith, held an Extra Master's Certificate. Chief Officer H. F. [T.] Wilde held an Ordinary Master's Certificate. [actually Extra Master's].

1st Officer W. M. Murdoch held an Ordinary Master's Certificate. [actually Extra Master's].

2nd Officer C. H. Lightoller held an Extra Master's Certificate.
3rd Officer H. J. Pitman held an Ordinary Master's Certificate.
4th Officer J. G. Boxhall held an Extra Master's Certificate.
5th Officer H. G. Lowe held an Ordinary Master's Certificate.
6th Officer J. P. Moody held an Ordinary Master's Certificate.

In the Engine Department were included the Chief Engineer and 7 senior and 17 assistant engineers.

In the Victualling Department there were 23 women employed. The total number of passengers on board was 1,316.

Of these	Male	Female	Total
1st class	180	145	325
2nd class	179	106	285
3rd class	510	196	706
			1,316

Of the above   6 children were in the 1st class.

24 children were in the 2nd class.

79 children were in the 3rd class.

_____

or 109 in all.

About 410 of the 3rd class passengers were foreigners, and these, with the foreigners in the 1st and 2nd class and in the Victualling Department would make a total of nearly 500 persons on board who were presumably not English-speaking, so far as it is possible to ascertain. The disposition of the different classes of passengers and of the crew in the ship has already been described. In all 2,201 persons were on board.

British wreck commissioner's final report

For those interested in particular individuals, a full list of everyone on board can be found in a variety of sources, such as the online passenger lists described in the preface.

4

Setting Out (10–13 April)

The ship is like a palace. There is an uninterrupted deck run of 165 yards for exercise and a ripping swimming bath, gymnasium and squash racket court & huge lounge & surrounding verandahs. My cabin is ripping, hot and cold water and a very comfy looking bed & plenty of room.

A summary of the key events that occurred during the first few days of the *Titanic*'s maiden voyage from Southampton, England to Cherbourg, France then Queenstown, Ireland and finally towards its final destination New York, USA.

Wednesday 10 April

RMS Titanic set sail from Southampton for New York. Six powerful tugs pulled her into the River Test where she was able to engage her engines. Disaster was narrowly avoided when the *Titanic* sailed past the *New York*, built in 1888 and one of the finest liners of her day, yet nothing in comparison to the *Titanic*. All six of the *New York*'s moorings snapped under the pressure of the waves created by the *Titanic*. The *New York* floated free, and Captain Gale of the tug *Vulcan* tried unsuccessfully to throw the ship a line. When she was just four feet from *Titanic* a second line from the *Vulcan* brought her under control.

08.00 First of the boat trains leaves Waterloo for Southampton.
09.30 Bruce Ismay, MD of the White Star Line, inspects the ship

with his wife and young children. He remains aboard alone for the crossing. He is accompanied by the naval architect from Harland and Wolff, Thomas Andrews.

12.15 *Titanic* whistle blown three times to signal departure.

12.20 Near-collision with the drifting *New York*.

17.30 *Titanic* anchors between the breakwaters at Cherbourg.

Thursday 11 April

Titanic arrives at Queenstown, Ireland, shortly before noon, and then sets out for New York.

06.45 *Titanic* passes Land's End bound for Ireland.

09.00 Hours before *Titanic* is due to arrive, people assemble near Queenstown harbour to catch a glimpse of her.

12.15 *Titanic* drops her anchor off the lighthouse at Roche's Point.

13.55 Anchor weighed as *Titanic* leaves Queenstown.

14.15 British army officer John Morrogh takes the last photograph of the *Titanic*.

Friday 12 April

09.00 Crew lifeboat assignment lists posted. Most do not read them.

10.00 Captain leads his officers in a thorough inspection of the ship.

12.00 *Titanic* has made 386 miles since leaving Queenstown.

19.00 *Titanic* receives warning from *La Touraine* about two thick ice fields ahead.

23.00 *Titanic's* wireless apparatus breaks down.

Saturday 13 April

05.00 *Titanic's* wireless back in working order.
10.30 Captain Smith informed that the bunker fire in boiler room 6 has finally been extinguished.
12.00 Notices posted show that a distance of 519 miles has been covered since Friday.

Approaching noon on Friday 12 April 1912, the appointed time for the *Titanic* to set sail on its maiden commercial voyage had arrived. All passengers shared a sense of wonderment and excitement, from those about to enjoy the luxuries of first class to the hopeful men, women and children who had booked passage in third class looking to start a new life on the other side of the ocean. The hustle and bustle of the quayside, packed with onlookers and well-wishers, is described by a second-class passenger, Charlotte Collyer, writing a few weeks after the *Titanic* had sunk. She had been heading to America with her husband Harvey and young daughter Marjorie to start a new life as a fruit farmer in Payette, Idaho. Friends of the family had emigrated some time before, and had written to the Collyers to encourage them to follow their lead. This was partly for economic reasons, but also designed to improve Charlotte's health as she suffered from tuberculosis.

The day before we were due to sail [our neighbours] made much of us, it seemed as if there must have been hundreds who called to bid us goodbye and in the afternoon members of the church arranged a surprise for my husband. They led him to a seat under the old tree in the churchyard and then some of them went up into the belfry and, in his honour, they rang all the chimes that they knew. It took more than an hour and he was very pleased. Somehow it made me a little sad. They rang the solemn old chimes as well as the gay ones and to me it was too much of a farewell ceremony . . . The next morning we went to Southampton and then my husband drew from the bank all his money, including the sum he had received for our store. The clerk asked him if he

HSR12/3012

Heathville
—   March 16th 1912.

My dear Father
        I returned from
my "good-bye" visits last
evening, & although they
have been a wee bit
trying, yet it has
been comforting to
feel that I shall be
missed a little when
I sail. I should have
written this earlier

Letter from Marion Wright to her father written 16 March 1912 describing her preparations for the voyage to New York as a second-class passenger on *Titanic*.

did not want a draft, but he shook his head and put the notes in a wallet which he kept to the end in the inside breast pocket of his coat. It came to several thousand dollars in American money. We had already sent forward the few personal treasures that we had kept from our old home so that when we went on board the *Titanic* our every earthly possession was with us. We were travelling second cabin and from our deck which was situated well forward, we saw the great send off that was given to the boat. I do not think that there had ever been so large a crowd in Southampton and I am not surprised that it should have come together . . . The *Titanic* was wonderful, far more splendid and huge than I had dreamed of. The other crafts in the harbour were like cockle shells beside her, and they, mind you, were the boats of the American and other lines that a few years ago were thought enormous. I remember a friend said to me, 'Aren't you afraid to venture on the sea?' but now it was I who was confident. 'What, on this boat!' I answered. 'Even the worst storm could not harm her.'

American Semi-Monthly Magazine, May 1912

Many of the other passengers were also looking for a new life. Miss Marion Wright wrote to her father in the months before departure, describing how she was looking forward to a new life as a fruit farmer in the Willamette Valley near Cotton Grove, Oregon with her intended husband.

Heathville, The Park, Yeovil
December 31st 1911

Dear Father,

Just a line to wish you a very happy New Year. I hope your neuritis hasn't been troubling you this last week, I'm afraid it would have been if you had been with me these last few days, for I have had the windows open all day long, it has been so mild & to hear the birds singing makes one think it is spring time. I narrowly escaped a nasty accident yesterday. I was coming along the Park Rd just by the Christchurch buildings, when Mrs. Bob Brutton's retriever dog came off the pavement straight into my cycle. I jammed the brakes on to stop myself, & luckily escaped any damage. I didn't even fall, although the impact sent me clean off the cycle, I managed to keep my balance by running several yds leaving my cycle one side of the Rd . . . I'm thankful I came off with only a nasty shaking. I went into Miss Brutton's to apologize for any harm I might have done to the dog & she tells me he is deaf . . .

National Maritime Museum, ref. HSR/Z/30/1-17

Regardless of class of accommodation, everyone was amazed by the opulence of their surroundings. A first-class passenger, Mrs Ida Straus, wrote about her first impressions, whilst presciently hinting that the sheer enormity of the vessel did not guarantee security.

On Board R.M.S. Titanic
Wednesday

Dear Mrs. Burbidge
    You cannot imagine how pleased I was to find your exquisite basket of flowers in our sitting-room on the steamer. The roses and carnations are all so beautiful in color and as fresh as though they had just been cut. Thank you so much for your sweet attention which we both appreciate very much.
    But what a ship! So huge and so magnificently appointed. Our rooms are furnished in the best of taste and most luxuriously and they are really rooms not cabins. But size seems to bring its troubles – Mr. Straus, who was on deck when the start was made, said that at one time it stroked painfully near to the repetition of the Olympic's *experience on her first trip out of the harbor, but the danger was soon averted and we are now well on to our course across the channel to Cherbourg.*
    Again thanking you and Mr. Burbidge for your lovely attention and good wishes and in the pleasant anticipation of seeing you with

[99]

us next Sunday (?). I am with cordial greetings in which Mr. Straus
heartily joins,
   Very sincerely yours,
   Ida R. Straus

                  National Maritime Museum LMQ/7/2/30

It seems that the second-class accommodation was almost as grand.
Charlotte Collyer's husband, Harvey, wrote to his parents on 11 April
in slightly more earthy language about the first day of the voyage from
Southampton to Queenstown.

Titanic April 11th

My dear Mum and Dad
   *It don't seem possible we are out on the briny writing to you. Well
dears so far we are having a delightful trip the weather is beautiful
and the ship magnificent. We can't describe the tables it's like a floating
town. I can tell you we do swank we shall miss it on the trains as
we go third on them. You would not imagine you were on a ship.
There is hardly any motion she is so large we have not felt sick yet
we expect to get to Queenstown today so thought I would drop this
with the mails. We had a fine send off from Southampton and Mrs
S and the boys with others saw us off. We will post again at New
York then when we get to Payette.*
   *Lots of love, don't worry about us. Ever your loving children
Harvey, Lot & Madge*

   Donald Hyslop, Alastair Forsyth, and Sheila Jemima, *Titanic
Voices: Memories from the Fateful Voyage* (Southampton: Sutton
Publishing Ltd, 1997)

The incident at Southampton involving the *New York* clearly made an
impression on one passenger, Lawrence Beesley, who wrote to his son
Kit while on board the *Titanic* on 10 April. Beesley was travelling to
Toronto to visit his brother, and was one of the lucky male survivors
from the wreck.

On Board R.M.S. Titanic
10 April 1912

My dear Kit,

We had an exciting experience just as we were passing the last wharf in Southampton water. The New York was lying alongside the Oceanic . . .

The suction of this monster ship as she approached, drew the New York outward and one by one her hawsers broke . . . Only one in the bow held. Out came her stern toward our port side. Just in the nick of time a tug came up & they made fast a steel rope . . . checked the outward swing. The Titanic, meanwhile, went hard astern, & the New York's stern just cleared our bows.

Meanwhile, two more tugs got hold of the New York, one from her bows & another from the starboard of her stern . . . and brought her clean around the corner of the wharf. We then went ahead safe and clear but twice it was a near thing, first of a collision between her stern and our side, when the first tug came on the scene, & afterwards when we just cleared her stern when we went astern ourselves. She had only enough steam up to work her stern winches, not enough for her main engines.

Anyhow it was exciting when the hawsers began popping one after the other, & the men ran in bunches to escape the flying ends of rope. Now we are running past the Isle of Wight. I hope not to have any more accidents. The ship is like a palace. There is an uninterrupted deck run of 165 yards for exercise and a ripping swimming bath, gymnasium and squash racket court & huge lounge & surrounding verandahs. My cabin is ripping, hot and cold water and a very comfy looking bed & plenty of room.

Write and tell me how you are getting on. One letter a week ought not to overtire you.

Your loving Dad

National Maritime Museum, ref. LMQ/7/3/B

Marion Wright was more frustrated by the delay than frightened by the possibility of a collision.

On board R.M.S. Titanic
April 1912

Dearest Dad,

Just a few lines to post to you from Queenstown. I find Mr. Collett very pleasant, & this evening I have been talking to a girl who is on the same errand as myself, i.e. to be married to a fruit rancher. She is going to California by herself & so far seems very pleasant, so if all's well I shall be happy with them I hope. We are very late so far, about 3 hours behind. We had a very near *collision with the American line boat* New York *which delayed us over an hour, & instead of arriving at Cherbourg at 5 o'c we did not get there till 7 o'c & after, & consequently shall be late all through. I am told we shall probably get into New York, provided all goes well, late Tuesday night which means we shall land early Wednesday morning. It is lovely on the water, & except for the smell of new paint, everything is very comfortable on board. The food is splendid, & so far I have had 3 meals. I hope you & mother got to Charlton in fairly decent time & that the colds will soon be better. So far the vessel doesn't seem a bit crowded, & there are dozens of tables empty in the dining saloon. I don't know if there are a lot coming from Queenstown, the passengers from Cherbourg were brought on a small steamer & conveyed from thence to this boat. It is now 9.30, I am soon going to retire & hope to have a good night's rest. Good night & goodbye. God be with you all & bring me safe home in a few years' time to see you all once again. Much love & many thanks for all you have given me,*

Ever your loving child,
Marion

National Maritime Museum, ref. HSR/Z/30/1-17

A second-class passenger, Robertha Josephine Watt, described the departure to Walter Lord in 1963. Born in Scotland in 1899, Bertha had been only twelve when the *Titanic* set sail, and travelling with her mother Bessie Watt to Portland, Oregon, where they were to be reunited

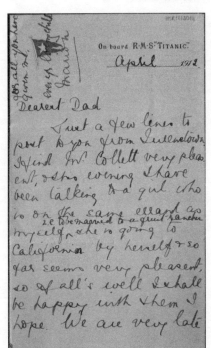

On board R·M·S "Titanic"

april 1912

Dearest Dad

Just a few lines to post to you from Queenstown. I find Mr. Collett very pleasant, & this evening I have been talking to a girl who is on the same errand as myself, i.e. to be married to a gentleman she is going to California by herself & so far seems very pleasant, so if all's well I shall be happy with them I hope. We are very late

Letter from Marion Wright to her father written onboard *Titanic* and posted at Queenstown. Continued on page 104.

...vided all goes well late Tuesday night which means we shall land early Wednesday morning. It is lovely on the water except for the smell of new paint. everything is very comfortable on board. the food is splendid, so far I have had 3 meals. I hope you shall be brother get to Charlton in fairly decent time. That the colds will soon be better. so far

so far, about 3 hours behind, we had a very near collision with the American Line boat New York which delayed us over an hour, instead of sailing at Cherbourg on board, at 5 oc. we did not get here till 7 oc & after, & consequently, shall be late all through, I am told we shall probably get into New York, pro-

the vessel doesn't seem
a bit crowded, & there are
dozens of tables empty
in the dining-saloon. I don't
know if there are a lot
coming on from Queenstown,
the passengers from Cherbourg
were brought on a small
steamer & conveyed from
thence to the this boat. It
is now 9.30, I am soon going
to retire & hope to have a
good night's rest. Good-
night & good-bye re. God be
with you all & bring me
safe home in a few years
time. to see you all once
again. Much love & many than

with Bertha's father. By a quirk of fate the pair were originally booked
to travel on the *New York,* but transferred to the *Titanic.*

> We were coming to join my Dad who was an architect in Portland,
> Oregon. I well remember arriving at Southampton and boarding
> the *Titanic.* Like all young ones I guess I covered every corner of
> it before too long. It was truly a lovely ship and at that time we
> felt very lucky to have been able to book passage on her. We had
> been booked on the *New York* and due to some strike, she was
> taken off the run and so at the very last we decided on the *Titanic.*
> A queer little incident happened that afternoon. I remember
> mother and some ladies having tea and as sometimes happened
> in those days one of them read the tea cups. Can't remember this
> lady's name but in one cup she said, 'I can't see anything, it's like
> there was just a blank wall and nothing beyond,' quite a good
> prediction for so many. Leaving the dock we had a spot of trouble
> also, another ship seemed to break a mooring and swung toward
> us, but somehow an actual collision was averted.

National Maritime Museum LMQ/7/2/37

Charlotte Collyer also recalled the incident, and instead of her being
worried by the near collision, it only served to reinforce the idea that
the *Titanic* was invincible. 'Before we left the harbour I saw the accident to the *New York,* the liner that was dragged from her moorings
and swept against us in the Channel. It did not frighten anyone, as it
only seemed to prove how powerful the *Titanic* was' (*American Semi-
Monthly Magazine,* May 1912).

During the course of the journey, Bertha Watt and Charlotte's daughter
Marjorie Collyer became friends and spent time together playing; while
the Collyers were berthed with Marion Wright.

However, it was not just passengers that left behind their memories
of the *Titanic's* first few days at sea. An account survives of the first
stages of the journey from crewman George Arthur Beedum, who

enlisted as a bedroom steward on 4 April having previously served on board the *Olympic*. Aged 34, Beedum wrote to his mother and young family from the ship before its final departure from Queenstown.

On board R.M.S. Titanic
Don't Forget

Dear Mother,

I have done two days. Got back Thursday morning. You can hardly tell the difference between the two boats. I have been 'standing by' the ship to-day to see she doesn't run away. Nobody has been working on her, being Good Friday. I have a days pay to come. Mr. B keeps me in work. I have not seen him [since I] went to the office last Saturday but his head man told me I was to go on the Titanic *on Thursday so I cleared off home straight away. Had a nice little time but all too short. Lill has not been very well. I shall be glad when we are all down in Southampton. I expect she will come down when I come home again to have a look around. Am glad to hear Uncle J. is better, hope he continues. I am signing on in Rooms. Last trip was not above the average. Nobody was travelling because of the coal strike. We came back practically empty but I think we are full up out & back this trip. I found a stowaway last trip but I told you all about it. I did not get your letter, that's on its way to America. I expect I have not got a stamp so shall not be able to post this till tomorrow. I should like to know how Uncle J is if you drop a line. Don't forget* Titanic *not* Olympic. *I am quite well so goodbye with fondest love,*
    George

Mr. B. will come with us this trip I expect.

Titanic
Friday Evening

My Dearest Lill,
    Good Friday & I have been at work all day. I got on board yesterday about 9 o/c. The crowd have not started yet, they come tomorrow. There

is very little difference between the two ships. I have been 'standing by' today simply seeing the ship does not run away. The others are not working. I signed on for rooms. It's been a lovely day today. Now how is your neck? Stick to that stuff my girl whatever you do. I cannot find any note paper only this sheet in my bag so I must have another look. I have found a few sheets. When I signed on I found I had left my discharge book home on the dresser. Please send it on to the Titanic. Now my girl I don't know what else to write about. I cannot get a stamp until tomorrow morning. I am going to take the pipe for a stroll somewhere or the other. I do like being here by myself, so goodbye my little dears. Hope Charlie sleeps alright now, so tata with love & kisses,
  Da Da

On board R.M.S. Titanic
Tuesday

My dear Lill & Charlie
  This is the last night & thank goodness we are off tomorrow. I should never do another week alone like I have this one. On Sunday I went all over the place house hunting. You had better let me know for certain at Plymouth what you are going to do in the way of coming down next time home. I don't suppose we shall leave the ship till 5 o/c on the Saturday night. I hope your neck is better. Let me know all about it for certain at Plymouth. My cold has been rotten & I shall be glad to get away to have a good square meal. As usual I expect you will say I am wrong in my money. I have not been paid for Good Friday, there were only 10 of us working & none have been paid through some fool leaving us off the list. I am sending 10/-, that's 4/- short, so I've managed to exist on about 6/- counting 2/- I had from you, so it's a happy life. I have no news to tell you, only the last 3 days I've felt rotten & what with no dusters or anything to work with I wish the bally ship at the bottom of the sea. I heard from mother today. Uncle John is a little better but cannot get up. Hope Charlie is having a nice holiday, so goodbye with love to both of you,
  George

I have been thinking if it were possible to go right in for our own house. Just think it over & see if anything could be done,
   Dad

On board R.M.S. Titanic
Thursday Morning

My dear little treasures
   Just for a bit of luck I am on watch from 12 to 4. I received your letter & am very glad you are going to the hospital, the lump is bound to hurt with the codeine, perhaps it might be drawing it gradually to a head, let's hope so. We have a more decent crowd on board this time although not so many. There is a lot to come on at Queenstown I think, the more the merrier. If you are not well enough don't come down this time but be sure & let me know at Plymouth. As we left to-day the American boat New York *broke her moorings & drifted right across our bows, missed the* Oceanic *by about a foot. We had to reverse engines sharp & one of our tugs went & got her under control before any damage was done, anyhow it was a narrow squeak for all of us. We have a lot of new faces this time everywhere on the boat. I have just had a shave etc. & shall be glad when 4 o/c comes, then I turn in till about 7.30. Now I don't know what else to write about. Only my chest is not so sore today. I did not go to mother's, though I should have liked to. Now I'll finish, don't forget don't come down if you don't feel well enough, it would only be a waste of time & would not do you any good whatever. Now tata, glad you liked the pictures & I suppose those chocolate eggs have all disappeared down that great big hole. With fondest love to both of you,*
   Da Da
              National Maritime Museum, ref. LMQ/7/3/B

We do not know whether Beedum wrote again to his loved ones; these are his last known thoughts – a cheerful account of the near-miss with the *New York* and fond memories of family life back home, even finding time to make plans for a house of their own. These dreams and aspirations were never realised; Beedum was one of the 1,517 souls who died that night, sucked to a watery grave as the ship went down. His body, to date, has not been found.

5

The Final Day and the Iceberg (14–15 April)

We remained then, about 1500 persons, with no way to escape. It was sure death for all of us. I cannot say enough about the wonderful calm with which each one contemplated it. We said good-bye to all our friends and each one prepared himself to die decently.

What follows is an account of the principal moments that occurred during the final 24 hours of the *Titanic,* in particular the reports of floating ice that were received during the hours leading up to the iceberg strike, and the unfolding drama as the ship slowly sank. It is drawn from the official US and British inquiry reports into the sinking, incorporating known communications between the *Titanic* and other vessels in the vicinity, as well as reported actions taken by the crew members once the iceberg had been struck at 11.45 p.m. on Sunday 14 April.

Sunday 14 April

09.00 *Titanic* receives a warning from the *Caronia* of bergs, growlers and field ice in her track. This warning was passed on to Bruce Ismay by the captain and was not returned until the evening.
11.30 Scheduled boat drill is cancelled.

11.40 *Noormadic* sends another ice warning about the same location.

12.00 *Titanic* has run 546 miles in the last 24 hours.

13.00 Captain Smith shows Second Officer Charles Lightoller an ice warning from the *Caronia* and it is posted in the chartroom.

13.30 Second-class Purser Reginald Barker tells passenger Lawrence Beesley that the ship's speed is a disappointment.

13.40 *Baltic* message received: 'Capt. Smith, *Titanic*. Have had moderate variable winds and clear fine weather since leaving. Greek steamer *Athenai* reports passing icebergs and large quantity of field ice today in latitude 41.51 north, longitude 49.52 west. Last night we spoke [with] German oil tanker *Deutschland,* Stettin to Philadelphia, not under control; short of coal; latitude 40.42 north, longitude 55.11. Wishes to be reported to *New York* and other steamers. Wish you and *Titanic* all success.' The message is given to Capt. Smith, who puts it in his pocket and heads for A deck, where he encounters Bruce Ismay talking to the Wideners on the promenade. Smith hands Ismay the message, which Ismay puts in his pocket.

17.00 *Titanic* reaches 'the corner', a location 42 degrees north latitude and 47 degrees west longitude, where in spring steamships normally headed due west on course for the Nantucket Lightship and took a more southerly route to avoid the ice found near the Grand Banks. However, the Captain orders a delay in changing course until 5.45 p.m., causing the ship to travel an additional sixteen miles south-west.

17.45 *Titanic* changes course but is approximately ten miles south of the normal shipping route for that time of year. Smith's decision is possibly due to the number of ice warnings received so far.

18.00 Second Officer Charles Lightoller comes on duty for a four-hour watch. Lightoller asks Sixth Officer James Moody to calculate when they will reach ice from the messages received from other ships. Moody calculates that they will reach the ice at about 11 p.m.

18.10 Bruce Ismay encounters Mrs Ryerson and Mrs Thayer on

A deck and shows them the message the captain has given to him, commenting that they are in among the icebergs but are not travelling very fast at 20 or 21 knots. However, they are planning on starting up the boilers that evening.

19.10 Captain Smith approaches Bruce Ismay in the smoking room and asks for the telegram back so that he can post it in the officers' chartroom.

19.15 First Officer William Murdoch is temporarily acting as officer of the watch while Second Officer Lightoller has dinner in the officers' messroom. Murdoch asks Lamp Trimmer Samuel Hemming, who has arrived on the bridge to report that all the ship's navigational lights have been lit, to close the forward scuttle hatch as there is a glow coming from it that might hinder their chances of spotting ice.

19.30 Junior Marconi Operator Harold Bride intercepts a message sent from the *Californian* to the *Antillian*: '6.30 p.m., apparent time, ship; latitude 42.3 north, longitude 49.9 west. Three large bergs five miles to southward of us.' Bride acknowledges the warning and sends it to the bridge.

19.35 Second Officer Lightoller returns to the bridge from dinner and comments on how much the temperature had dropped in his absence. First Officer Murdoch mentions that it has dropped four degrees in half an hour to 39 degrees Fahrenheit.

20.30 The temperature reaches freezing and Second Officer Lightoller orders Quartermaster Robert Hichens to take his compliments to the ship's carpenter and warn him to take precautions against the ship's fresh-water supply freezing.

20.55 Captain Smith arrives on the bridge and remarks to Second Officer Lightoller about the cold and the calmness of the sea. Lightoller replies that the temperature is just one degree above freezing. Lightoller remarks to the captain that it is a pity there is no breeze while they are going through the ice region, as this will make it more difficult to spot ice. Smith says that if the weather becomes in the slightest bit hazy they will have to slow down.

Upper part of *Titanic*'s stern frame in position in the Harland and Wolff shipyard in Belfast.

QUEENS ISLAND SHIPYARD BELFAST   WAG 3191

Sister ships *Titanic* and *Olympic* next to each other in the Harland and Wolff shipyard. *Titanic* was having the last of her shell plating completed the day before *Olympic* was launched on 20 October 1910. *Olympic*, being the first of the White Star Line's three super-ships to be launched, was initially painted light grey so the photographers could get better pictures of her in the water.

A port main engine in the engine works erecting shops at Harland and Wolff.

Harland and Wolff workers fitting the starboard tail shaft prior to launching the ship.

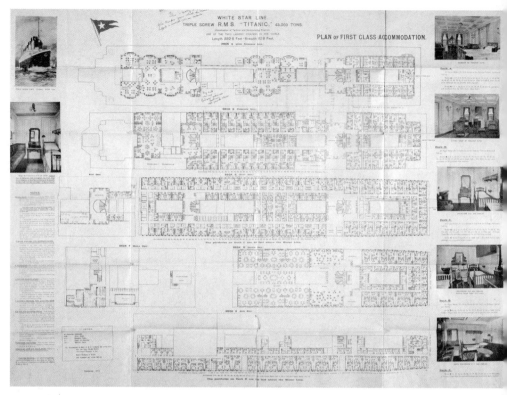

A plan of the layout of the *Titanic* given to passengers.

Harland and Wolff workmen leaving the Queen's Island dockyard in Belfast with *Titanic* in the background.

Some of the Harland and Wolff employees
who built *Titanic* pose for a press photograph
in front of their masterpiece.

This photo was taken from the tender *America*,
which pulled alongside *Titanic*'s open gangway
door. Captain Smith can be seen at the very top
peering down from the starboard bridge.

Second-class passengers promenading on the boat
deck where the lifeboats were stored. It was decided
not to 'clutter' the deck with more lifeboats than
were required by Board of Trade regulations so that
passengers could enjoy a stroll more easily.

American short-story writer Jacques Fotrell standing on the deck outside the gymnasium, taken by first-class passenger Father Browne. Fotrell was another victim of the *Titanic* disaster. Father Browne travelled from Southampton to Queenstown and took most of the last surviving photos of *Titanic*'s maiden voyage.

FACING PAGE

(*Above*) Second-class passengers looking down on to 'A' deck, taken by Father Browne.

(*Below*) The bridge of the *Olympic*, identical to that of the *Titanic*.

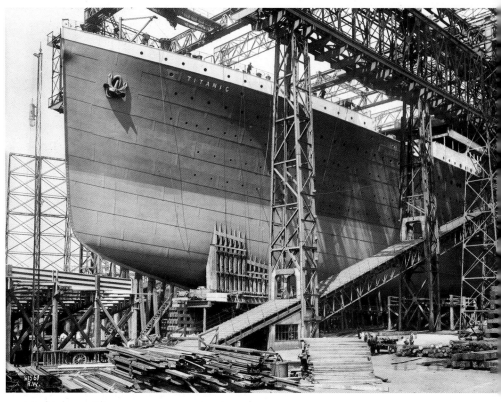

Port bow view of the *Titanic* prior to her launch.

Titanic entering the water for the first time on launch day in Belfast.

21.20 Captain Smith leaves the bridge, with the instruction to Lightoller, 'If in the slightest degree doubtful, let me know.' The captain leaves the bridge for a dinner party in the knowledge that this is the most crucial part of the voyage.

21.30 Lightoller instructs Sixth Officer Moody to telephone the crow's nest and tell the lookouts to keep a sharp watch for small ice and growlers, and to pass the word to subsequent watches. Moody speaks to Lookout George Symons.

21.35 Senior Marconi Operator Phillips is interrupted while sending passenger messages to Cape Race by a message from the steamer *Mesaba* addressed to the *Titanic* and all eastbound ships, which reads 'Ice report. In latitude 42 north to 41.25 north, longitude 49 west to longitude 50.3 west. Saw much heavy pack ice and great number large icebergs, also field ice. Weather good, clear.' Phillips acknowledges the message but does not deliver it to the bridge. Phillips has had a long day and a large number of passenger messages to get through. In light of the number of ice warnings he has already delivered, he does not think the message important enough to take to the bridge.

22.00 Change of the watch for officers and crew. First Officer William Murdoch takes over from Second Officer Lightoller. The lights are put out in the third-class public rooms to encourage the passengers to go to bed.

23.00 Senior Marconi Operator Phillips is interrupted while sending private messages to Cape Race by a nearby Leyland steamer, whose proximity makes the message very loud. The *Californian*, just 35 miles to the north-west, sends: 'Say, old man, we are stopped and surrounded by ice.' Phillips is startled by the loudness of the message and replies, 'Shut up! Shut up! I am busy. I am working Cape Race.'

23.30 Lookout Fred Fleet comments to his colleague Lee that the horizon has developed a slight haze.

23.35 The *Californian*'s only wireless operator Cyril Evans, who has listened in to Phillips busily working Cape Race for a while, shuts down his wireless set and goes to bed.

23.40 Lookout Fred Fleet spots a dark object immediately ahead, rings the crow's-nest bell and telephones the bridge with the warning 'Ice right ahead.' Sixth Officer Moody passes the message to First Officer Murdoch, who has just seen the berg and telegraphed the engine room the signal 'Full speed astern' whilst instructing Quartermaster Hichens to turn the wheel 'Hard a starboard.' *Titanic*, travelling at 22 knots, grazes the iceberg on her starboard side. Once the bow begins to swing Murdoch orders 'Hard a port,' hoping to swing the ship clear of the berg, but it is too late. Murdoch closes all the ship's watertight doors.

23.45 Captain Smith appears on the bridge and asks what they have struck.

Monday 15 April

00.10 Captain Smith steps into the Marconi room for the second time and tells Bride to send the call for assistance.

00.15 *Titanic* sends its first distress message, giving an estimated position of latitude 41.46 north, longitude 50.24 west.

00.25 Ship's position corrected to 41.46 north, 50.14 west. CQD radio distress call from *Titanic* received by *Carpathia* says, 'Come at once. We have struck a berg.'

00.26 Fires drawn from the boilers to cool them before contact with water. Steam noisily blown out of the funnels.

00.30 *Titanic* to *Frankfurt*: 'Tell your Captain to come to our help. We are on the ice.'

00.35 An approaching ship's lights are seen. The order is given for rockets to be fired.

00.45 First lifeboat, number 7 launched on the starboard side with only 28 of 65 places filled.

00.55 Lifeboats 6 and 5 launched on opposite sides of the *Titanic*.

01.00 Lifeboat 3 launched. Crewmen still 'all standing about', according to Fireman Alfred Shiers, who left in 3. 'They did not think it was serious.'

01.10 Lifeboat 8 told to row for the light on the port side. Lifeboat 1 departs from the starboard side with only 12 occupants.

01.20 The engineers called off their work at the pumps and ordered up top.

01.25 *Olympic* asks her sister ship, 'Are you steering southerly to meet us?' *Titanic* replies, 'We are putting the women off in boats.'

01.45 Last signal from *Titanic* heard by the *Carpathia*, rushing to the rescue: 'Engine room full up to boilers.'

01.50 Lifeboats 2, 9, 10, 11, 12, 13, 14, 15 and 16 have all left. Only five boats remain.

01.55 Lifeboat 4 is launched. Captain Smith tells wireless officers that they have done their full duty.

02.00 Bruce Ismay leaves in collapsible boat C.

02.05 Collapsible boat D leaves. Other passengers attempt to free boats A and B from the roof of the officer's quarters

02.20 Boat A is swept off, waterlogged. Boat B is capsized by waves. *Titanic* finally sinks.

The British wreck commissioner's inquiry report into the accident covered all aspects of the disaster from initial warnings of ice in the vicinity to the actual collision itself. The salient points of the report are given here, starting with the hours leading up to the collision when ice was first reported from other vessels.

MESSAGES RECEIVED

The *Titanic* followed the Outward Southern Track until Sunday, the 14th April, in the usual way. At 11.40 p.m. on that day she struck an iceberg and at 2.20 a.m. on the next day she foundered.

At 9 a.m. (*Titanic* time) on that day a wireless message from the S.S. *Caronia* was received by Captain Smith. It was as follows: 'Captain, *Titanic*. – Westbound steamers report bergs, growlers and field ice in 42° N. from 49° to 51° W., 12th April. Compliments. Barr.'

It will be noticed that this message referred to bergs, growlers and field ice sighted on the 12th April – at least 48 hours before the time of the collision. At the time this message was received the *Titanic's* position was about lat. 43° 35' N. and long. 43° 50' W. Captain Smith acknowledged the receipt of this message.

At 1.42 p.m. a wireless message from the S.S. *Baltic* was received by Captain Smith. It was as follows: 'Captain Smith, *Titanic*. – Have had moderate, variable winds and clear, fine weather since leaving. Greek steamer *Athenai* reports passing icebergs and large quantities of field ice to-day in lat. 41° 51' N., long. 49° 52' W. Last night we spoke German oiltank steamer *Deutschland*, Stettin to Philadelphia, not under control, short of coal, lat. 40° 42' N., long. 55° 11' W. Wishes to be reported to *New York* and other steamers. Wish you and *Titanic* all success. Commander.'

At the time this message was received the *Titanic* position was about 42° 35' N., 45° 50' W. Captain Smith acknowledged the receipt of this message also.

Mr. Ismay, the Managing Director of the White Star Line, was on board the *Titanic*, and it appears that the Master handed the *Baltic's* message to Mr. Ismay almost immediately after it was received. This no doubt was in order that Mr. Ismay might know that ice was to be expected. Mr. Ismay states that he understood from the message that they would get up to the ice 'that night'. Mr. Ismay showed this message to two ladies, and it is therefore probable that many persons on board became aware of its contents. This message ought in my opinion to have been put on the board in the chart-room as soon as it was received. It remained, however, in Mr. Ismay's possession until 7.15 p.m., when the Master asked Mr. Ismay to return it. It was then that it was first posted in the chartroom.

This was considerably before the time at which the vessel reached the position recorded in the message. Nevertheless, I think it was irregular for the Master to part with the document, and improper for Mr. Ismay to retain it, but the incident had, in my opinion, no connection with or influence upon the manner in which the vessel was navigated by the Master.

This is a highly contentious issue, and one that has formed the basis for charges of negligence against both Captain Smith and Ismay, made in reports that circulated at the time of the sinking and inquiry and by historians thereafter. It is clear that reports of ice were being passed to the *Titanic* from other vessels, and that its senior officers were aware that they were approaching a section of the ocean where the risk of meeting floating ice was significant. Ismay's action in taking and retaining the message has also been seen by some as linked to a desire to get to New York as quickly as possible, which Ismay denied.

It appears that about 1.45 p.m. (*Titanic* time) on the 14th a message was sent from the German steamer *Amerika* to the Hydrographic Office in Washington, which was in the following terms: '*Amerika* passed two large icebergs in 41° 27' N., 50° 8' W., on the 14th April.'

This was a position south of the point of the *Titanic's* disaster. The message does not mention at what hour the bergs had been observed. It was a private message for the Hydrographer at Washington, but it passed to the *Titanic* because she was nearest to Cape Race, to which station it had to be sent in order to reach Washington. Being a message affecting navigation, it should in the ordinary course have been taken to the bridge. So far as can be ascertained, it was never heard of by anyone on board the *Titanic* outside the Marconi room. There were two Marconi operators in the Marconi room, namely, Phillips, who perished, and Bride, who survived and gave evidence. Bride did not receive the *Amerika* message nor did Phillips mention it to him, though the two had much conversation together after it had been received. I am of the opinion that when this message reached the Marconi room it was put aside by Phillips to wait until the *Titanic* would be within call of Cape Race (at about 8 or 8.30 p.m.), and that it was never handed to any officer of the *Titanic*.

At 5.50 p.m. the *Titanic's* course (which had been S. 62° W.) was changed to bring her on a westerly course for New York. In ordinary circumstances this change in her course should have been made about half an hour earlier, but she seems on this occasion to have continued for about ten miles longer on her southwesterly course before turning, with the result that she found herself, after altering course at 5.50 p.m. about four or five miles south of the customary route on a course S. 86° W. true. Her course, as thus set, would bring her at the time of the collision to a point about two miles to the southward of the customary route and four miles south and considerably to the westward of the indicated position of the *Baltic*'s ice. Her position at the time of the collision would also be well to the southward of the indicated position of the ice mentioned in the *Caronia* message. This change of course was so insignificant that in my opinion it cannot have been made in consequence of information as to ice.

The official verdict seems to play down the effect of the crew's actions in changing course, and to conclude that no significant action was taken in response to the messages received by the *Titanic* to divert away from the threat of ice – although it is acknowledged that the information received by the crew implied that the ship was out of the danger zone:

In this state of things, at 7.30 p.m. a fourth message was received, and is said by the Marconi operator Bride to have been delivered to the bridge. This message was from the S.S. *Californian* to the S.S. *Antillian*, but was picked up by the *Titanic*. It was as follows: 'To Captain, *Antillian*, 6.30 p.m. apparent ship's time; lat. 42° 3' N., long. 49° 9' W. Three large bergs five miles to southward of us. Regards. Lord.'

Bride does not remember to what officer he delivered this message.

By the time the *Titanic* reached the position of the collision (11.40 p.m.) she had gone about 50 miles to the westward of the indicated position of the ice mentioned in this fourth message. Thus it would appear that before the collision she had gone clear of the indicated positions of ice contained in the messages from the *Baltic* and *Californian*. As to the ice advised by the *Caronia* message, so far as it consisted of small bergs and field ice, it had before the time of the collision possibly drifted with the Gulf Stream to the eastward; and so far as it consisted of large bergs (which would be deep enough in the water to reach the Labrador current) it had probably gone to the southward. It was urged by Sir Robert Finlay, who appeared for the owners, that this is strong evidence that the *Titanic* had been carefully and successfully navigated so as to avoid the ice of which she had received warning. Mr. Ismay, however, stated that he understood from the *Baltic* message that 'we would get up to the ice that night.'

There was a fifth message received in the Marconi room of the *Titanic* at 9.40 p.m. This was from a steamer called the *Mesaba*. It was in the following terms: 'From *Mesaba* to *Titanic* and all east-bound ships. Ice report in lat. 42° N. to 41° 25' N., long. 49° to long. 50° 30' W. Saw much heavy pack ice and great number large icebergs. Also field ice. Weather good, clear.'

This message clearly indicated the presence of ice in the immediate vicinity of the *Titanic*, and if it had reached the bridge would perhaps have affected the navigation of the vessel. Unfortunately, it does not appear to have been delivered to the Master or to any of the officers. The Marconi operator was very busy from 8 o'clock onward transmitting messages via Cape Race for passengers on board the *Titanic*, and the probability is that he failed to grasp the significance and importance of the message, and put it aside until he should be less busy. It was never acknowledged by Captain Smith, and I am satisfied that it was not received by him. But, assuming Sir Robert Finlay's contentions to be well founded that the *Titanic* had been navigated so as to avoid the *Baltic* and the *Californian* ice, and that the *Caronia* ice had drifted to the eastward and to the southward, still there can be no doubt, if the evidence of Mr. Lightoller, the second officer, is to be believed, that both he and the Master knew that the danger of meeting ice still existed.

Two issues here make uncomfortable reading: the fact that messages were not being satisfactorily relayed to the bridge from the radio room, and that the radio operators were kept busy transmitting messages for passengers. It is easy with hindsight to attribute blame given what happened, but it should be borne in mind that this was an experienced crew and a well-navigated course, which may explain some of the complacency.

Mr. Lightoller says that the Master showed him the *Caronia* message about 12.45 p.m. on the 14th April when he was on the bridge. He was about to go off watch, and he says he made a rough calculation in his head which satisfied him that the *Titanic* would not reach the position mentioned in the message until he came on watch again at 6 p.m. At 6 p.m. Mr. Lightoller came on the bridge again to take over the ship from Mr. Wilde, the chief officer, (dead). He does not remember being told anything about the *Baltic* message, which had been received at 1.42 p.m. Mr. Lightoller then requested Mr. Moody, the sixth officer (dead), to let him know 'at what time we should reach the vicinity of ice', and says that he thinks Mr. Moody reported 'about 11 o'clock'. Mr. Lightoller says that 11 o'clock did not agree with a mental calculation he himself had made and which showed 9.30 as the time. This mental calculation he at first said he had made before Mr. Moody gave him 11 o'clock as the time, but later on he corrected this, and said his mental calculation was made between 7 and 8 o'clock, and after Mr. Moody had mentioned 11. He did not point out the difference to him, and thought that perhaps Mr. Moody had made his calculations on the basis of some 'other' message. Mr. Lightoller excuses himself for not pointing out the difference by saying that Mr. Moody was busy at the time, probably with stellar observations. It is, however, an odd circumstance that Mr. Lightoller, who believed that the vicinity of ice would be reached before his watch ended at 10 p.m., should not have mentioned the fact to Mr. Moody, and it is also odd that if he thought that Mr. Moody was working on the basis of some 'other' message, he did not ask what the other message was or where it came from. The point, however, of Mr. Lightoller's evidence is that they both thought that the vicinity of ice would be reached before midnight. When he was examined as to whether he did not fear that on entering the indicated ice region he might run foul of a growler (a low-lying berg) he answers: 'No, I judged I should see it with sufficient distinctness' and at a distance of a 'mile and a half, more probably two miles'. He then adds: 'In the event of meeting ice there are many things we look for. In the first place, a slight breeze. Of course, the stronger the breeze the more visible will the ice be, or, rather, the breakers on the ice.'

He is then asked whether there was any breeze on this night, and he answers: 'When I left the deck at 10 o'clock there was a slight breeze. Oh, pardon me, no; I take that back. No, it was calm, perfectly calm.' And almost immediately afterwards he describes the sea as 'absolutely flat'. It appeared, according to this witness, that about 9 o'clock the Master came on the bridge and that Mr. Lightoller had a conversation with him which lasted half an hour. This conversation, so far as it is material, is described by Mr. Lightoller in the following words: 'We commenced to speak about the weather. He said, 'There is not much wind.' I said, 'No, it is a flat calm,' as a matter of fact. He repeated it, he said, 'A flat calm.' I said, 'Quite flat; there is no wind.' I said something about it was rather a pity the breeze had not kept up whilst we were going through the ice region. Of course, my reason was obvious, he knew I meant the water ripples breaking on the base of the berg. We then discussed the indications of ice. I remember saying, 'In any case, there will be a certain amount of reflected light from the bergs.' He said, 'Oh, yes, there will be a certain amount of reflected light.' I said or he said – blue was said between us – that even though the blue side of the berg was towards us, probably the outline, the white outline, would give us sufficient warning, that we should be able to see it at a good distance, and as far as we could see, we should be able to see it. Of course, it was just with regard to that possibility of the blue side being towards us, and that if it did happen to be turned with the purely blue side towards us, there would still be the white outline.

Further on Mr. Lightoller says that he told the Master nothing about his own calculation as to coming up with the ice at 9.30 or about Mr. Moody's calculation as to coming up with it at 11.

The conversation with the Master ended with the Master saying, 'If it becomes at all doubtful let me know at once; I will be just inside.' This remark Mr. Lightoller says undoubtedly referred to ice.

At 9.30 the Master went to his room, and the first thing that Mr. Lightoller did afterwards was to send a message to the crow's nest 'to keep a sharp look-out for ice, particularly small ice and growlers', until daylight. There seems to be no doubt that this message was in fact sent, and that it was passed on to the next look-outs when they came on watch. Hichens, the quartermaster, says he heard Mr. Lightoller give the message to Mr. Moody, and both the men in the crow's nest at the time (Jewell and Symons) speak to having received it. From 9.30 to 10 o'clock, when his watch ended, Mr. Lightoller remained on the bridge 'looking out for ice'. He also said that the night order book for the 14th had a footnote about keeping a sharp look-out for ice, and that this note was 'initialled by every officer'. At 10 o'clock Mr. Lightoller handed over the watch to Mr. Murdoch, the first officer (dead), telling him that 'we might be up around the ice any time now'. That Mr. Murdoch knew of the danger of meeting ice appears from the evidence of Hemming, a lamp trimmer, who says that about 7.15 p.m. Mr. Murdoch told him to go forward and see the forescuttle hatch closed, 'as we are in the vicinity of ice and there is a glow coming from that, and I want everything dark before the bridge'.

This section of evidence reveals that key members of the crew on the next watch were alerted to the possibility that ice was in the vicinity, and that instructions were sent to the lookouts on the basis of the previous messages passed to the *Titanic* from other ships. Furthermore, Captain Smith was aware that there was some difference of opinion as to when ice might start to appear in the path of the ship, and instructed his officers to alert him if – or when – it was sighted, but was sufficiently confident that there was no immediate danger that he was prepared to leave the bridge at 9.30pm.

The foregoing evidence establishes quite clearly that Captain Smith, the Master, Mr. Murdoch, the first officer, Mr. Lightoller, the second officer, and Mr. Moody, the sixth officer, all knew on the Sunday evening that the vessel was entering a region where ice might be expected, and this being so, it seems to me to be of little importance to consider whether the Master had by design or otherwise succeeded in avoiding the particular ice indicated in the three messages received by him.

Speed of the Ship

The entire passage had been made at high speed, though not at the ship's maximum, and this speed was never reduced until the collision was unavoidable. At 10 p.m. the ship was registering 45 knots every two hours by the Cherub log.

The quartermaster on watch aft, when the *Titanic* struck, states that the log, reset at noon, then registered 260 knots, and the fourth officer, when working up the position from 7.30 p.m. to the time of the collision, states he estimated the *Titanic*'s speed as 22 knots, and this is also borne out by evidence that the engines were running continuously at 75 revolutions.

The theory that the ship was running flat out to reach New York as quickly as possible, under instruction from Ismay and with the compliance of Captain Smith, is discounted in the short passage above in the official inquiry, using evidence from the log, officers and technical information from the engines.

Weather Conditions

From 6 p.m. onwards to the time of the collision the weather was perfectly clear and fine. There was no moon, the stars were out, and there was not a cloud in the sky. There was, however, a drop in temperature of 10 deg. in slightly less than two hours, and by about 7.30 p.m. the temperature was 33 deg. F., and it eventually fell to 32 deg. F. That this was not necessarily an indication of ice is borne out by the Sailing Directions. The Nova Scotia (S.E. Coast) and Bay of Fundy Pilot (6th edition, 1911, page 16) says: 'No reliance can be placed on any warning being conveyed to a mariner by a fall of temperature either of the air or sea, on approaching ice. Some decrease in temperature has occasionally been recorded, but more often none has been observed.'

Sir Ernest Shackleton was, however, of the opinion that 'if there was no wind and the temperature fell abnormally for the time of the year, I would consider that I was approaching an area which might have ice in it'.

Clearly, professional opinion about clues offered by the weather was divided, though it is interesting to read the views of the polar explorer Sir Ernest Shackleton expressed as part of the inquiry, given that he was to fall foul of ice during the ill-fated expedition on board the *Endurance* only two years later.

The Collision

Mr. Lightoller turned over the ship to Mr. Murdoch, the first officer, at 10 o'clock, telling him that the ship was within the region where ice had been reported. He also told him of the message he had sent to the crow's nest, and of his conversation with the Master, and of the latter's orders.

The ship appears to have run on, on the same course, until, at a little before 11.40, one of the look-outs in the crow's nest struck three blows on the gong, which was the accepted warning for something ahead, following this immediately afterwards by a telephone message to the bridge 'Iceberg right ahead.' Almost simultaneously with the three gong signal Mr. Murdoch, the officer of the watch, gave the order 'Hard-a-starboard,' and immediately telegraphed down to the engine room 'Stop. Full speed astern.' The helm was already 'hard over', and the ship's head had fallen off about two points to port, when she collided with an iceberg well forward on her starboard side.

Mr. Murdoch at the same time pulled the lever over which closed the watertight doors in the engine and boiler rooms.

The Master 'rushed out' on to the bridge and asked Mr. Murdoch what the ship had struck.

Mr. Murdoch replied: 'An iceberg, Sir. I hard-a-starboarded and reversed the engines, and I was going to hard-a-port round it but she was too close. I could not do any more. I have closed the watertight doors.'

From the evidence given it appears that the *Titanic* had turned about two points to port before the collision occurred. From various experiments subsequently made with the S.S. *Olympic*, a sister ship to the *Titanic*, it was found that travelling at the same rate as the *Titanic*, about 37 seconds would be required for the ship to change her course to this extent after the helm had been put hard-a-starboard. In this time the ship would travel about 466 yards, and allowing for the few seconds that would be necessary for the order to be given, it may be assumed that 500 yards was about the distance at which the iceberg was sighted either from the bridge or crow's-nest.

That it was quite possible on this night, even with a sharp look-out at the stemhead, crow's nest and on the bridge, not to see an iceberg at this distance is shown by the evidence of Captain Rostron, of the *Carpathia*.

The injuries to the ship, which are described in the next section, were of such a kind that she foundered in two hours and forty minutes.

It is clear from this extract that events happened at great speed – only seconds passed between sighting the iceberg and the attempt to avoid it – and that once the strike had taken place, safety precautions such as closing the watertight bulkheads were implemented at once. However, the subsequent tests with the *Olympic* demonstrate the narrow margins that the crew faced between sighting and collision based on the speed the ship was travelling. This is one of the reasons for contemporary criticism of the ship's speed in an area where icebergs were known to be.

From the evidence gathered from survivors and recounted to the inquiry, it was possible to estimate the damage caused by the strike, and the effect it had on the internal structure of the ship.

Description of the Damage to the Ship and its Gradual Final Effect

Extent of the Damage

The collision with the iceberg, which took place at 11.40 p.m., caused damage to the bottom of the starboard side of the vessel at about 10 feet above the level of the keel, but there was no damage above this height. There was damage in: The forepeak, No. 1 hold, No. 2 hold, No. 3 hold, No. 6 boiler room, No. 5 boiler room.

The damage extended over a length of about 300 ft.

Time in which the damage was done

As the ship was moving at over 20 knots, she would have passed through 300 ft. in less than 10 seconds, so that the damage was done in about this time

Flooding in the First Ten Minutes

At first it is desirable to consider what happened in the first 10 minutes.

The forepeak was not flooded above the Orlop deck – i.e., the peak tank top, from the hole in the bottom of the peak tank.

In No. 1 hold there was 7 ft. of water.

In No. 2 hold five minutes after the collision water was seen rushing in at the bottom of the firemen's passage on the starboard side, so that the ship's side was damaged abaft of bulkhead B sufficiently to open the side of the firemen's passage, which was 3½ ft. from the outer skin of the ship, thereby flooding both the hold and the passage.

In No. 3 hold the mail room was filled soon after the collision. The floor of the mail room is 24 ft. above the keel.

In No. 6 boiler room, when the collision took place, water at once poured in at about 2 feet above the stokehold plates, on the starboard side, at the after end of the boiler room. Some of the firemen immediately went through the watertight door opening to No. 5 boiler room because the water was flooding the place. The watertight doors in the engine rooms were shut from the bridge almost immediately after the collision. Ten minutes later it was found that there was water to the height of 8 feet above the double bottom in No. 6 boiler room.

No. 5 boiler room was damaged at the ship's side in the starboard forward bunker at a distance of 2 feet above the stokehold plates, at 2 feet from the watertight bulkhead between Nos. 5 and 6 boiler rooms. Water poured in at that place as it would from an ordinary fire hose. At the time of the collision this bunker had no coal in it. The bunker door was closed when water was seen to be entering the ship.

In No. 4 boiler room there was no indication of any damage at the early stages of the sinking.

The matter-of-fact tone of the report somehow heightens the sense of the calamity that was unfolding. It is clear that terrible damage had been inflicted on the infrastructure of the ship, and that water had breached large sections very quickly. Those closest to the ruptures to the hull, and witnessing the water pouring in, would have realised that this was no minor incident.

Gradual Effect of the Damage

It will thus be seen that all the six compartments forward of No. 4 boiler room were open to the sea by damage which existed at about 10 feet above the keel. At 10 minutes after the collision the water seems to have risen to about 14 feet above the keel in all these compartments except No. 5 boiler room. After the first ten minutes, the water rose steadily in all these six compartments.

The forepeak above the peak tank was not filled until an hour after the collision when the vessel's bow was submerged to above C deck. The water then flowed in from the top through the deck scuttle forward of the collision bulkhead. It was by this scuttle that access was obtained to all the decks below C down to the peak tank top on the Orlop deck.

At 12 o'clock water was coming up in No. 1 hatch. It was getting into the firemen's quarters and driving the firemen out. It was rushing round No. 1 hatch on G deck and coming mostly from the starboard side, so that in 20 minutes the water had risen above G deck in No. 1 hold.

In No. 2 hold about 40 minutes after the collision the water was coming in to the seamen's quarters on E deck through a burst fore and aft wooden bulkhead of a third-class cabin opposite the seamen's wash place. Thus, the water had risen in No. 2 hold to about 3 ft. above E deck in 40 minutes.

In No. 3 hold the mail room was afloat about 20 minutes after the collision. The bottom of the mail room which is on the Orlop deck, is 24 feet above the keel.

The description of how the water surged through the ship, room by room, deck by deck, testifies to the failure of the watertight bulkheads to contain the initial flood caused by the strike. Despite the best efforts of the crew, they were driven back – at first slowly, and then with increasing speed as the battle to contain and pump out the damaged sections was lost.

The watertight doors on F deck at the fore and after ends of No. 3 compartment were not closed then.

The mail room was filling and water was within 2 ft. of G deck, rising fast, when the order was given to clear the boats.

There was then no water on F deck.

There is a stairway on the port side on G deck which leads down to the first-class baggage room on the Orlop deck immediately below. There was water in this baggage room 25 minutes after the collision. Half an hour after the collision water was up to G deck in the mail room.

Thus the water had risen in this compartment to within 2 ft. of G deck in 20 minutes, and above G deck in 25 to 30 minutes.

No. 6 boiler room was abandoned by the men almost immediately after the collision. Ten minutes later the water had risen to 8 ft. above the top of the double bottom, and probably reached the top of the bulkhead at the after end of the compartment, at the level of E deck, in about one hour after the collision.

In No. 5 boiler room there was no water above the stokehold plates, until a rush of water came through the pass between the boilers from the forward end, and drove the leading stoker out.

It has already been shown in the description of what happened in the first ten minutes, that water was coming into No. 5 boiler room in the forward starboard bunker at 2 ft. above the plates in a stream about the size of a deck hose. The door in this bunker had been dropped probably when water was first discovered, which was a few minutes after the collision. This would cause the water to be retained in the bunker until it rose high enough to burst the door which was weaker than the bunker bulkhead. This happened about an hour after the collision.

No. 4 boiler room. One hour and 40 minutes after collision water was coming in forward, in No. 4 boiler room, from underneath the floor in the forward part, in small quantities. The men remained in that stokehold till ordered on deck.

Nos. 3, 2 and 1 boiler rooms. When the men left No. 4 some of them went through Nos. 3, 2 and 1 boiler rooms into the reciprocating engine room, and from there on deck. There was no water in the boiler rooms abaft No. 4 one hour 40 minutes after the collision (1.20 a.m.), and there was then none in the reciprocating and turbine engine rooms.

Electrical engine room and tunnels. There was no damage to these compartments.

From the foregoing it follows that there was no damage abaft No. 4 boiler room.

All the watertight doors aft of the main engine room were opened after the collision.

Half an hour after the collision the watertight doors from the engine room to the stokehold were opened as far forward as they could be to No. 4 boiler room.

Final Effect of the Damage

The later stages of the sinking cannot be stated with any precision, owing to a confusion of the times which was natural under the circumstances.

The forecastle deck was not under water at 1.35 a.m. Distress signals were fired until two hours after the collision (1.45 a.m.). At this time the fore deck was under water. The forecastle head was not then submerged though it was getting close down to the water, about half an hour before she disappeared (1.50 a.m.).

When the last boat, lowered from davits (D), left the ship, A deck was under water, and water came up the stairway under the Boat deck almost immediately afterwards. After this the other port collapsible (B), which had been stowed on the officers' house, was uncovered, the lashings cut adrift, and she was swung round over the edge of the coamings of the deckhouse on to the Boat deck.

Very shortly afterwards the vessel, according to Mr. Lightoller's account, seemed to take a dive, and he just walked into the water. When he came to the surface all the funnels were above the water.

Her stern was gradually rising out of the water, and the propellers were clear of the water. The ship did not break in two; and she did eventually attain the perpendicular, when the second funnel from aft about reached the water. There were no lights burning then, though they kept alight practically until the last.

The subsequent rediscovery of the wreck clearly shows that the ship did break in two, as some eyewitnesses reported at the time.

Before reaching the perpendicular when at an angle of 50 or 60 degrees, there was a rumbling sound which may be attributed to the boilers leaving their beds and crashing down on to or through the bulkheads. She became more perpendicular and finally absolutely perpendicular, when she went slowly down.

After sinking as far as the after part of the Boat deck she went down more quickly. The ship disappeared at 2.20 a.m

This account of the sinking led the official inquiry to make several observations about what caused the ship to sink once the damage had been inflicted. It is clear that the length of the rip down the side of the vessel had exposed too many of the bulkheads to the sea, and that once the flooding started there was virtually nothing that could be done to save the stricken ship.

Observations

I am advised that the *Titanic* as constructed could not have remained afloat long with such damage as she received. Her bulkheads were spaced to enable her to remain afloat with any two compartments in communication with the sea. She had a sufficient margin of safety with any two of the compartments flooded which were actually damaged.

In fact any three of the four forward compartments could have been flooded by the damage received without sinking the ship to the top of her bulkheads.

Even if the four forward compartments had been flooded the water would not have got into any of the compartments abaft of them though it would have been above the top of some of the forward bulkheads. But the ship, even with these four compartments flooded, would have remained afloat. But she could not remain afloat with the four forward compartments and the forward boiler room (No. 6) also flooded.

The flooding of these five compartments alone would have sunk the ship sufficiently deeply to have caused the water to rise above the bulkhead at the after end of the forward boiler room (No. 6) and to flow over into the next boiler room (No. 5), and to fill it up until in turn its after bulkhead would be overwhelmed and the water would thereby flow over and fill No. 4 boiler room, and so on in succession to the other boiler rooms till the ship would ultimately fill and sink.

It has been shown that water came into the five forward compartments to a height of about 14 feet above the keel in the first ten minutes. This was at a rate of inflow with which the ship's pumps could not possibly have coped, so that the damage done to these five compartments alone inevitably sealed the doom of the ship.

The damage done in the boiler rooms Nos. 5 and 4 was too slight to have hastened appreciably the sinking of the ship, for it was given in evidence that no considerable amount of water was in either of these compartments for an hour after the collision. The rate at which water came into No. 6 boiler room makes it highly probable that the compartment was filled in not more than an hour, after which the flow over the top of the bulkhead between 5 and 6 began and continued till No. 5 was filled.

It was shown that the leak in No. 5 boiler room was only about equal to the flow of a deck hose pipe about 3 inches in diameter.

The leak in No. 4, supposing that there was one, was only enough to admit about 3 feet of water in that compartment in 1 hour 40 minutes.

Hence the leaks in Nos. 4 and 5 boiler rooms did not appreciably hasten the sinking of the vessel.

The evidence is very doubtful as to No. 4 being damaged. The pumps were being worked in No. 5 soon after the collision. The 10 inch leather special suction pipe which was carried from aft is more likely to have been carried for use in No. 5 than No. 4 because the doors were ordered to be opened probably soon after the collision when water was known to be coming into No. 5. There is no evidence that the pumps were being worked in No. 4.

The only evidence possibly favourable to the view that the pipe was required for No. 4, and not for No. 5, is that Scott, a greaser, says that he saw engineers dragging the suction pipe along 1 hour after the collision. But even as late as this it may have been wanted for No. 5 only.

The importance of the question of the damage to No. 5 is small because the ship, as actually constructed, was doomed as soon as the water in No. 6 boiler room and all compartments forward of it entered in the quantities it actually did.

It is only of importance in dealing with the question of what would have happened to the ship had she been more completely subdivided.

It was stated in evidence that if No. 4 had not been damaged or had only been damaged to an extent within the powers of the pumps to keep under, then, if the bulkheads had been carried to C deck, the ship might have been saved. Further methods of increased subdivision and their effect upon the fate of the ship are discussed later.

Evidence was given showing that after the watertight doors in the engine and boiler rooms had been all closed, except those forward of No. 4 group of boilers, they were opened again, and there is no evidence to show that they were again closed. Though it is probable that the engineers who remained below would have closed these doors as the water rose in the compartments, yet it was not necessary for them to do this as each door had an automatic closing arrangement which would have come into operation immediately had a small amount of water come through the door.

It is probable, however, that the life of the ship would have been lengthened somewhat if these doors had been left open, for the water would have flowed through them to the after part of the ship, and the rate of flow of the water into the ship would have been for a time reduced as the bow might have been kept up a little by the water which flowed aft.

It is thus seen that the efficiency of the automatic arrangements for the closing of the watertight doors, which was questioned during the enquiry, had no important bearing on the question of hastening the sinking of the ship, except that, in the case of the doors not having been closed by the engineers, it might have retarded the sinking of the ship if they had not acted. The engineers would not have prevented the doors from closing unless they had been convinced that the ship was doomed. There is no evidence that they did prevent the doors from closing.

The engineers were applying the pumps when Barrett, leading stoker, left No. 5 boiler room, but even if they had succeeded in getting all the pumps in the ship to work they could not have saved the ship or prolonged her life to any appreciable extent.

British wreck commissioner's final report

So these were the official reasons for the sinking of the ship. The human story is best told by those who witnessed the disaster at first hand, many of whom were called to give evidence at the US or British inquiries.

The following narratives reflect the memories of crew members who were on board the *Titanic* and involved at key moments from initial strike to eventual rescue by the *Carpathia*, and include accounts from the engine room, radio room and various passenger decks. The first narrative was given by George J. Rowe to the historian Walter Lord. Rowe had signed up as a lookout on 25 March 1912 in Belfast and joined the vessel at Southampton on 6 March 1912. As someone responsible for keeping watch on the night of the tragedy, he was a key eyewitness and was summoned to give evidence at the inquiries in both the USA and Britain. He was stationed on the aft docking bridge at the stern of the ship, and at around the time of the strike noted that he saw an iceberg glide past, though at first he thought it was a large sailing ship. He was also aware of a curious movement of the ship, though at that time did not realise its significance and continued with his duties.

Rochdale
47 Bursledon Road
Bittesne
Southampton
England

Mr Lord
Dear Sir

I am in receipt of your letter of June 12th by which I can see you have the major details but I hope the forthcoming will be to your satisfaction.

I was on watch on the poop in the First Watch (8PM till midnight) on the night of April 14 1912. The night was pitch black, very calm and starry around about 11PM I noticed that the weather was becoming colder and what we call Whiskers round the Light were noticeable, that is very minute splinters of ice like myriads of coloured lights. I had to call the Middle Watch at 11.45 (midnight till 4AM) but about 11.40PM I was struck by a curious movement of the ship it was similar to going alongside a dock wall rather heavy. I looked forward and saw what I thought was a Windjammer (sailing-ship) but as we passed by it I saw it was an iceberg. Now as our own boat's davits were 80 feet from the waterline I estimated the height of the berg as about 100 feet. The engines were going astern by this time so I pulled in the long-line, and by my last reading at 10PM I made out we had been doing about 21 knots. I did __not__ think the collision was serious. In a short time the ship was hove to where shortly after I saw a boat being lowered on the starboard side and I went up on to the after bridge and phoned the fore bridge if they knew about it. I could not recognize the voice but he asked me who I was I told him the after quartermaster he asked me if I knew where the distress rockets were stowed I told him I did he then told me to bring as many as I could on to the fore bridge, I went below one deck to a locker and got a tin box with I think 12 rockets in it (they were fairly heavy), I carried them along the boat deck where there was a bit of confusion clearing away and turning out boats. As I

Rochdale
47 Basildon Road
Battersea
Southampton
England

Mr Lord
Dear Sir

I am in receipt of your letter of
of June 12th by which I can see you have the major
details but I hope the following will be to your
satisfaction

I was on watch on the poop as the First Watch
(8 PM till midnight) on the night of April 14 - 1912
The night was pitch black, very calm and starry
around about 11 PM. I noticed that the weather
was becoming colder and what we call Whiskers
round the Light were noticeable, that is very
minute splinters of ice like myriads of coloured
lights. I had to call the Middle Watch (midnight to 4
AM) but about 11-40 PM. I was struck by a curious
movement of the ship it was similar to going
alongside a dock wall rather heavy. I looked
forward and saw what I thought was a
Windjammer (sailing ship) but as we passed by it
I saw it was an iceberg. Now as our boats davits
were 80 feet from waterline I estimated the
height of the berg about 100 feet. The engines
were going astern by this time so I pulled in
the log-line, and by my last reading at 10 PM
I made out we had been doing about 21 knots
I did not think the collision was serious. In
a short time the ship was hove to, when shortly
after I saw a boat being lowered on the starboard
side and I went up on to the after bridge and
phoned the fore bridge if they knew about it

I could not recognize the voice but he asked
me who I was I told him the after Quarter-master
he asked me if I knew where the distress rockets
were stowed I told him I did he then told
me to bring as many as I could on to the
fore bridge. I went below one deck to a locker
and got a tin box with I think 12 rockets
in it (they were fairly heavy), I carried them
along the boat deck where there was a bit
of confusion clearing away and turning out
boats. As I passed over the saloon I heard
the band playing but I could not distinguish
the tune. On reaching the bridge Capt Smith
asked me if I had the rockets I told him yes
and he said fire one and fire one every
five or six minutes. After I fired about 8
Capt Smith asked me if I could Morse I
replied I could a little, he said call that
ship up and when she answers, tell her that
we are the Titanic sinking please have all
your boats ready. I kept calling her up in
between the rocket firing but we never got
a reply though we could see her white light
quite plain. After a while I said to Capt Smith
there is a light on the starboard quarter he looked
through his glasses and told me he thought it
must me a planet then he lent me his glasses
to see for myself then said the Carpathia
is not so far away during this time they
were turning out the SS Englehart raft under
the direction of Chief Off Wilde and when it
was full he was shouting out to know who
was in charge then Capt Smith turned to me
and told me to go and take charge that was

Letter to Walter Lord from George J. Rowe, quartermaster aboard *Titanic*. Continued
on pages 137 and 138.

passed over the salon I heard the band _playing_ but I could not distinguish the tune. On searching the bridge Capt. Smith asked me if I had the rockets I told him yes and he said fire one and fire one every five or six minutes. After I fired about 3 Capt Smith asked me if I could Morse I replied I could a little, he said call that ship up and when she answers, tell her that we are the Titanic _sinking_ please have all your boats ready I kept calling her up but never got a reply though we could see his white light quite plain After a while I said to Capt Smith there is a light on in the starboard quarter he looked through his glasses and told me he thought it must be a planet then he lent me his glasses to see for myself then said the Carpathia _is_ not far away during this time they were timing out the Std Englehart raft under the direction of Chief Off Wilde and when it was full he was shouting out to know who was in charge then Capt Smith turned to me and told me to go and take charge that was the last I heard Capt Smith say. We had great difficulty in lowering as the ship was well down by the head and she took a list to port it was then that I saw Mr Ismay and another gentleman (I think he was a Mr Carter) in the boat. The chief officer shouted to me and told me when you get clean go to the others and tell them to come back, that was the last I [saw]of Mr Wilde. When we were clean of the ship I said what's the best thing to do Mr Ismay he replied you're in charge we could see nothing only this white light so I told them to pull away. Mr Ismay on one oar Mr Carter on another and the 4 of the crew one each and one I steered with 7 oars. We had been pulling for about 10 minutes when we heard a noise like an immense heap of gravel being tipped from a height then she *disappeared. We pulled on but seemed to make no headway gradually dawn came and soon we could make out some boats and more ice. It must have been between 7 and 8AM when we saw a ship which was the* Carpathia *there were several boats between us and the ship we were picked up about 9AM.*

saw no more of Mr Ismay or Mr Carter after they got out of the boat nor did either of them speak I did ask one of the ship's officers how Mr Ismay was he said he was indisposed and would not leave his cabin.

*And now Mr Lord I hope you will forgive my wretched writing and spelling my hand's not so steady as it was, and I hope and trust you have every success with your book [*A Night to Remember*] if you think there is anything I have overlooked or if there is anything you wish to know do not hesitate to write as I shall only be too pleased to help. Believe me.*

Yours Truly

G. J. Rowe

P.S.

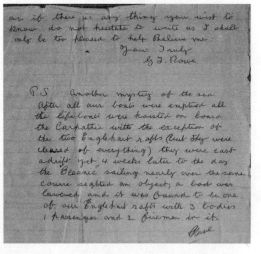

Another mystery of the sea After all our boats were emptied all the lifeboats were hoisted on board the Carpathia *with the exception of the two Englehart rafts (but they were cleaned of everything) they were cast adrift yet 4 weeks later to the day* Oceanic *sailing nearly over the same course sighted an object, a boat was lowered and it was found to be one of our Englehart rafts with 3 bodies 1 passenger and 2 firemen in it.*

G Rowe

National Maritime Museum LMQ/7/2/21

The heartbreaking postscript shows that not all the casualties perished on the night of the sinking. Some unfortunate souls had managed to escape the sinking ship, and stay alive long enough to clamber onto the Englehart rafts cast back adrift after their occupants had been brought on board the *Carpathia*. You can imagine the relief these three people must have felt slowly turning to despair once rescue failed to materialise, before finally being overcome with cold, fatigue and starvation.

Rowe also informed the British wreck commissioner's inquiry that there had been problems with lowering the lifeboat, given the angle of the ship as it sank: 'The rub strake kept on catching on the rivets down the ship's side, and it was as much as we could do to keep off. It took a good five minutes, on account of this rubbing, to get down' (British wreck commissioner's final report). A detailed description of how the iceberg strike was reported in the radio room comes from Harold Bride, who wrote about the tragedy within days of arrival in New York, with particular reference to the working of the Marconi equipment on board the ship. He was actively involved in passing messages to and from Captain Smith and the vessels that picked up their distress calls, working closely alongside his colleague Jack Phillips, who died during their attempt to flee from the ship; Bride survived, but suffered from badly frozen feet which were also crushed during his escape and prolonged exposure to the cold in the open water. Intriguingly, he notes that Captain Smith dived from the bridge of the *Titanic* as it finally sank beneath the sea.

294 West 92nd Street
New York City NYK
April 27th, 1912

W.R. Cross Esq.

Dear Sir,

Hearing of the conflicting reports concerning the loss of the Titanic, *which are being spread around, I think it is advisable for me to give you, to the best of my ability, a true account of the disaster, so that the Marconi Company may be in full possession of all the facts.*

I regret to say my memory fails me, with regard to the time of the occurrence, or any of the preceding incidents but otherwise I am sure of all my statements.

The night before the disaster, Mr Phillips and myself had had a deal of trouble owing to the leads from the Secondart of the Transformer, having burnt through, inside the casing and making contact with certain Iron Bolts holding the woodwork and frame together, thereby earthing the power to a great extent.

After binding these leads with rubber tape we once more had the apparatus in perfect working order but not before we had put in nearly six hours' work, Mr Phillips being of the opinion that, in the first place, it was the Condensers which had broken, and these we had had out and examined before locating the damage in the Transformer.

Owing to this trouble I had promised to relieve Mr Phillips on the following night at midnight instead of the usual time, 'two o'clock', as he seemed very tired.

During Sunday afternoon, towards five o'clock I was called by the Californian (call letters M.W.L.) with an ice report, but I did not immediately answer, as I was writing up the Abstracts, and also it used to take us some considerable time to start up the Motor and Alternator, it not being advisable to leave them working, as the Alternator was liable to run hot.

I however acknowledged the receipt of the report when M.W.L. transmitted it to the Baltic, and took it myself to the Officer on watch on the Bridge.

Neither Mr Phillips or I, to my knowledge, received any further ice reports.

About nine p.m. I turned in, and woke on my own accord just about midnight, relieving Mr Phillips, who had just finished sending a large batch of telegrams to Cape Race.

Mr Phillips told me that apparently we had struck something, as previous to my turning out he had felt the ship tremble and stop, and expressed an opinion that we should have to return to Belfast.

I took over the Telephone from him and he was preparing to retire when Captain Smith entered the cabin and told us to get assistance immediately.

Mr Phillips then resumed the phones, after asking the Captain if he should use the regulation distress call CQD.

The Captain said 'Yes' and Mr Phillips started in with CQD, having obtained the Latitude and Longitude of the Titanic.

The Frankfurt *was the first to answer. We gave him the ship's position which he acknowledged by 'OK, stdbi [standby]'*

The second answer was from the Carpathia *who immediately responded with his position and informed us, he was coming to our assistance as fast as possible.*

These communications I reported myself to the Captain who was, when I found him, engaged in superintending the filling and lowering of lifeboats.

The noise of escaping steam directly over one cabin cause a deal of trouble to Mr Phillips in reading the replies to our distress call, and this I also reported to Captain Smith who, by some means, managed to get it abated.

The Olympic *next answered our call but as far as I know Mr Phillips did not go to much trouble with her, as we now realized the awful state of affairs, the ship listing heavily to Port and Forward.*

The Captain also came in and told us, she was sinking fast and would not last longer than half an hour.

Mr Phillips then went outside to see how things were progressing and meanwhile I established communication with the Baltic, *telling him we were in urgent need of assistance.*

This I reported to Mr Phillips on his return but suggested M.B.C. [Baltic] was too far away to be of any use.

Mr Phillips told me, the forward well deck was underwater, and we got our lifebelts out, and tied them on each other, after putting on additional clothing.

Again Mr Phillips called CQD and S.O.S. and for nearly five minutes got no reply, and then both the Carpathia *and the* Frankfurt *called.*

Just at this moment the Captain came into the Cabin and said, 'You can do nothing more, look out for yourselves.'

Mr Phillips again resumed the phones and after listening for a few seconds jumped up and fairly screamed 'The – fool, he says 'What's up old man?'

I asked 'Who?' Mr Phillips replied 'The Frankfurt,' and at that time it seemed perfectly clear to us that the Frankfurt's operator had taken no notice or misunderstood our first call for help.

Mr Phillips' reply to this was, 'You fool, stdbi and keep out.'

Undoubtedly both Mr Phillips and I were under a great strain at this time but though the committee enquiring into the facts on this side are inclined to censor that reply, I am still of the opinion that Mr Phillips was justified in sending it.

Leaving Mr Phillips operating I went to our sleeping cabin and got all our money together, returning to find a Fireman or Coal Trimmer gently relieving Mr Phillips of his lifebelt.

There immediately followed a general scrimmage with the three of us.

I regret to say, we left too hurriedly in the end to take the man in question with us, and without a doubt he sank with the ship in the Marconi Cabins as we left him.

I had up to this time kept the P.V. entered up intending when we left the ship, to tear out the lot and each to take a copy, but now we could hear the water washing over the boat deck, and Mr Phillips said, 'Come, let's clear out.'

We had nearly the whole time been in possession of full power from the ship's Dynamo, though towards the end the lights sank, and we were ready to stand by with emergency apparatus and candles, but there was no necessity to use them.

Leaving the cabin we climbed on top of the houses comprising the officers' quarters, and our own, and here I saw the last of Mr Phillips for he disappeared walking aft.

I was now assisted in pushing off a collapsible lifeboat, which was on the port side of the forward funnel, onto the boat deck. Just as the boat fell, I noticed Captain Smith dive from the bridge into the sea.

Then followed a general scramble down on to the boat deck, but no sooner had we got there than the sea washed over. I managed to catch hold of the boat we had previously fixed up and was swept overboard with her.

I then experienced the most exciting three or four hours anyone could reasonably wish for and was in due course, with the rest of the survivors, picked up by the Carpathia.

As you have probably heard I got on the collapsible boat, a second time, which was as I had left it, upturned. I called Phillips several times but got no response, but learnt later from several sources that he was on this boat, and expired, even before we were picked off by the Titanic's *[sic Carpathia's] boats.*

I am told Fright and Exposure was the cause of his death.

As far as I can find out, he was taken on board the Carpathia *and buried at sea from her, though for some reason the bodies of those who had died were not identified before burial from the* Carpathia, *and so I cannot vouch for the truth of this.*

After a short stay in the hospital of the Carpathia, *I was asked to assist Mr Cottam the operator who seemed fairly worn out with his work.*

Hundreds of telegrams from survivors were waiting to go as we could get communications with shore stations.

Regarding the working of the Carpathia.

The list of survivors, Mr Cottam told me had been sent to the Minnewaska, *and the* Olympic.

When we established communication with the various Coast stations all of which had heavy traffic for us in some cases running into hundreds of messages, we told them we could only accept service and urgent messages, as we knew the remainder would be press and messages enquiring after someone on the Titanic.

It is easy to see we might have spent hours receiving mges [messages] enquiring after some survivors, while we had mges waiting from that survivor for transmission.

News was not withheld by Mr Cottam or myself with the idea of making money, but because as far as I know the Captain of the Carpathia *was advising Mr Cottam to get off the survivors' traffic first.*

Quite seventy-five percent of this we got off.

On arrival in New York Mr Marconi came on board with a

reporter of the New York Times. *Alas Mr Sammis was present and I received $500 for my story which both Mr Marconi and Mr Sammis authorized me to tell.*

I have forgotten to mention that the U.S. Govt sent out a ship, as they said to assist us, named the Chester.

Several images passed between the Commander of that vessel and the Carpathia *and resulted in the Captain telling us to transmit the names of the third-class passengers to the* Chester.

Though it has since been reported that the most expert operator in the U.S. Navy was on board the Chester, *I had to repeat these names, nearly three hundred in all, several times to him, taking up nearly a couple of hours of valuable time, though I sent them in the first place slowly and carefully.*

I am now staying with relatives and waiting orders from the Marconi Company here, who have been most considerate and kind, buying me much-needed clothes and looking after me generally.

I am glad to say I can now walk around, the sprain in my left foot being much better, though my right foot remains numbed from the exposure and cold, but causes me no pain [or] inconvenience whatever.

I greatly appreciate the cable the Company so kindly sent me, and thank them for the same.

Trusting this report will be satisfactory until my return to England.

I beg to remain
Yours obediently
Harold S. Bride

National Maritime Museum ref. LMQ/7/1/12

Bride spent some time in hospital, returned to England and continued working as a wireless operator on ships. He married in 1919, raised a family of three children and eventually moved to Scotland to escape the unwelcome attention that his role in the tragedy brought. He died in 1956.

Equally interesting is the perspective of crew members attending to passengers at the time of the accident. This letter, once more written to Walter Lord, comes from James Witter, who was a steward in the second-class smoke room, where evening entertainment would be held. When the ship struck ice, Witter was asked by passengers to investigate what had happened. He survived by chance, falling into a descending lifeboat while trying to assist a lady passenger.

Mr J. Witter,
The Lodge,
2 Obelisk Road,
Woolston,
Southampton,
Hampshire,
England.

9th July 1955

Dear Mr. Lord,

May I express my profound apologies for the delay in answering your very kind letter. As you will appreciate I am advancing in years and of late I have not been in the best of health.

I have done my best in the following letter to recall as much as possible of the Titanic *disaster.*

It was a beautiful, clear but very cold evening, the sea was like a sheet of glass, while I, duty smoke room steward, was clearing up the 2nd class smoke room, (11.40) ready for closing at midnight. All was very quiet, the orchestra on that evening was playing the 1st class room. There were about 40 people in the room, many of them just talking, but there were about three tables of passengers playing cards. This was very unusual as it had been the rule of the White Star Line that there should be no card playing on Sundays, and that the smoke room should be closed at 11 o'clock. On that particular Sunday I had been instructed by the Chief Steward to allow them to play cards and to close the smoke room at midnight. Then suddenly there was a jar, the ship shuddered slightly and then everything seemed normal, my first impressions were that we had shipped a heavy sea, but, knowing the condition of the weather at that time I immediately dismissed the idea. Several of the passengers enquired of me the cause of the jar, and I explained that it may be due to the fact that she had dropped a blade (I had a similar experience in my previous ship). To enlighten them I said I would go below and find out the real cause of the trouble. I went below and returned some fifteen to twenty minutes later and informed the passengers that we had hit an iceberg. At that time there were still two groups of passengers playing cards, but on hearing my explanation they immediately got up and left the smoke room without any sign of panic whatsoever. After they had all departed I locked up the smoke room and no one returned to it.

I then proceeded to my quarters encountering several groups of people talking in the working alleyway, discussing the accident. As I was about to turn in to my cabin I met the carpenter, Mr Hutchinson, who remarked 'The bloody mail room is full.' I knowing where the mail room was situated (Nearly f'ward) decided it was time to do something. Before I could proceed any further I encountered Steward Moss, who was going around the glory holes calling out the staff. He remarked, 'It's serious, Jim.' Eventually I got to my cabin where there were about thirty-two men turned in, in their bunks, I told them all to get out as the situation was serious, but they all ridiculed me. Not taking any more notice of them I opened my trunk and filled my pockets with cigarettes, and also taking the cowl from my first child, which I always carried with me. As I left the men were beginning to scramble out of their bunks, I saw none of them again.

On my way to the upper deck I met the 2nd purser, who told me to clear the cabins of passengers and ensure that they all had lifebelts, this I did then carried on to the upper deck and stood by No. 11 boat where I assisted the women and children to get on board. As the boat was about to be lowered a hysterical woman tried to clamber in to the boat, so I stood on the guard rail to assist her in, as she half fell in to the boat I went in with her, the boat was then being lowered.

We were instructed to lay off but not to pull away. The boat was very full with 50 women, 9 babes in arms, 4 male passengers and the rest crew, a total of 71 persons, as we could be of no more assistance, and thought it unnecessary to sacrifice 71 more lives we did pull a short way from the ship.

The boat was hushed except for the occasional whimper of one of the babes in arms, there was really very little sign that the people were witnessing one of the greatest tragedies of the sea.

It was about two o'clock in the morning when the Titanic finally sank, there were two terrific explosions and several loud screams as she went down bows first. As she sank the lights gradually faded as if someone was slowly turning off the current. There was a deathly silence in the boat, and even then no one realized the great loss of life. We pulled away in silence.

The morale of the people in the boat was excellent at all times, and was greatly assisted by the endeavours of a Mrs Brown, who sang and joked with everyone, she carried with her a little Toy Pig which played a little melody when its tail was turned, this amused the passengers immensely.

We pulled around hopefully when, with a great feeling of elation we sighted a ship at about six o clock, at first we all thought that it was the Olympic, but when she finally closed on us we distinguished her as the Carpathia. With thanks to God we boarded her. We were saved.

In the narrative above I have tried to give as much information as I can possibly remember, and I do hope that it will be of great assistance to you.

I enclose my paying off sheet for the Titanic as requested.
The best of luck in completing your story successfully.

Yours Sincerely
J. Witters

Mr. Lord.
25 East 38th Street
New York 16.
N.Y. U.S.A.

National Maritime Museum LMQ/7/2/45

Mrs. Henry B. Harris

Sunday afternoon, April 14, Mrs. Harris was drafted
to fill in at a poker game in one of the B-Deck suites with
a private promenade. Can't remember host's name but says
he was an Englishman. Mr. Harris asked Mrs. Harris to join
the group because they already had seven and were suspicious
that the most likely eightth among their crowd was a card
sharp. This was a way to keep him out.

The game went along at a table out on the enclosed deck.
Stakes were a dollar-a-chip, and as the afternoon went by,
Mrs. Harris did very well. Shortly after five she was ahead
by $90, when she decided to go below to her stateroom for
a minute. Going down the main stairs from "B" to "C", she
slipped on a little piece of cream cake that some one had
dropped at tea, which was just over. She took a header and
broke her arm.

The ship's doctor looked it over, but the break seemed
bad enough to call in Dr. Freuenthal, great at bones, who
was a fellow passenger. He finally set it, doubled up.

Reputed card sharp later saved and was one of first
people who came up to Mrs. Harris on Carpathia. His greeting:
"God's will be done." She told him to go away.

One who wasn't saved, or even on the passenger list, was
George Rosenshine, a friend apparently from New York. He was
travelling with a girl named Maybelle Thorne, and they were
going under the name "Mr. and Mrs. G. Thorne."

Life on the _Titanic_, as might be expected, was expensive
and gay. But Mrs. Harris doesn't remember any dancing at all.
Thinks it was before the day of casual dancing -- the Castles
and the foxtrot were just beginning to come in. On the other
hand, if there had been dancing, she probably wouldn't have
known it anyhow. The Harrises belonged to a set that loved to
play cards all the time.

(Interview, 5/31/64)

Transcript of an interview between historian Walter Lord and Mrs Henry B. Harris.

Twenty-year-old Alfred Pugh was able to give an account of the sinking from the perspective of the third-class accommodation, where he was working as a steward. At the time of the accident he was playing cards, but everyone stopped when they felt the collision; his initial thoughts were remarkably similar to those of Witter, assuming that the *Titanic* had merely dropped a propeller, and he returned to his game. He only realised there was something amiss when the order to muster came through, and assisted with the general evacuation in the lifeboats. He was asked to row a lifeboat away from the sinking ship, and on hearing no further orders to help women and children on other parts of the vessel, took his place and was thus saved. His brother, sadly, was not so lucky and went down with the ship.

'Ferndown'
Rownhams Lane
Rownhams
Southampton
England

20.7.1955
To Mr Lord

Dear Sir,

Thank you for your letter of June 12th. I must apologise for not writing before this, but I have just returned from a long vacation. Anyhow, I will try and recall some of the happenings on the night of April 15th 1912. At the time she struck the Ice-Berg I and some more of us were playing Cards in our room naturally everybody said 'What's that?' I said she had dropped a Propeller, as that [was] what it felt like to me. We continued playing for quite a while until the Order came to muster at the boats. On arriving on the Crew Deck I saw a Steward with a large lump of Ice in his hands. Also a lot of 3rd Class passengers who were all making their way to the Boat Deck. On arriving at the Boat Deck I met the 6th Officer 'Mr. Moody'. Knowing each other he called to help him to get the Passengers in the Lifeboats. We filled up No 18 boat, then did the same to No 16 boat. We met the 5th Officer there (Mr. Lowe). After filling the boat, Mr Moody remarked that he would go and see if he could be of help elsewhere. Telling me to stand by, Mr Webb then detailed the crew to man the Boat and asked me if I could manage the oars (being large and me very small). I said yes, as I had already done so at Boat Drill before leaving Southampton. Right he said jump in, and he followed taking charge. We cleared the ship all right and up to then there was no Panic. I had not heard the Band Playing, but in the distance I could hear people singing 'For Those in Peril on the Sea'. After a while Mr Webb got all the Lifeboats to keep together as he said there was a better chance to be seen. We transferred our 58 passengers to the other boats, and then started to search for any survivors after the ship had disappeared. Before she sank we could see her well down at the Fore port and her stern well out of the water. Some lights were still showing and continued to do so till she took the final plunge.

It was at day break when we saw the Carpathia *and eventually we were taken on Board. It was some days before I could realise what had happened, especially as I found that my Brother had gone down with the ship.*

Well Sir, I hope these few incidents will be of some use to you. Wishing you every success with your Book.

*I remain
Yours Sincerely
A. Pugh
PS – many thanks for menu Card.*

National Maritime Museum ref. LMQ/7/2/13

Notable about these accounts is the relative calm that greeted the initial realisation that something was wrong with the ship after the strike was first felt. This may be due to the fact that they were written several decades later, when the terror had somewhat dissipated. Nevertheless, the impression that panic only began to grip the passengers at the end is echoed by other versions of events, written days after the sinking. It is one of the myths of the *Titanic* – probably derived from the Hollywood film of 1997 – that there was pandemonium on board. This does not appear to have been the experience of many survivors, at least not in the first hour or so.

This was not quite the case for those caught up in the struggle to save the ship, and it is from the heart of the vessel – the engine rooms – that the next account comes. At the time of the accident Greaser Walter Hurst was asleep, but was immediately awakened by the sound of a crash – though no one seemed alarmed until news started to filter down that an iceberg was involved. Hurst describes the growing chaos on deck and the fact that shots were fired as the realisation began to grow that most of the boats had already gone. Vain hopes that the ship wouldn't sink gave way to a fight for survival. He describes the final moments of the ship and the calm role played by Second Officer Lightoller, and gives other snippets of information, such as a first-class passenger, Sir Cosmo Duff-Gordon, later handing out five-pound notes to the crew of the lifeboat he had been rescued in.

5 Granville St
Southampton

Mr Lord

I was serving on Titanic *as Engine Oiler or as what we British call Greaser it was at 11-20 PM on the 14th when I was awakened by a Grinding crash along the starboard side no one was very much alarmed but knew we had struck something my Father in Law was in the same room he ran up on deck and back at once with a large lump of Ice threw it in my bunk and told me to get up as we had hit a berg at that moment a messenger from the bridge told us to put on our warmest Clothes anterin the Mess Room and as a precaution put on Lifebelts. Later we went to the Fore Well Deck we were met by a Quarter Master who told us not to come on Boat Deck until later on I could plainly see a Ship's Riding Light away on the port side and Our Ship was sending up Rockets but got no Reply we could see that they were lowering boats and I saw the First one away No 1 Starboard Boat going into the water there were PG in the stern at The Tiller 4 Crew on the Oars and about 4 Passengers So we all began to go up to the boat deck, my Station was No 13 Boat but it was gone, there was a crowd around some other Boats but no one seemed to have got scared yet as they had great confidence in the Ship I stood watching the band playing in the Smoke room some in Blue Uniforms and Others in their White waiting jackets not knowing much about music I could not Identify the tunes but it seemed something fine a Lady and two Gents were by me and I heard them say 'She cannot possibly sink she has too many air-tight compartments' and I advised one man to get her into a boat if possible as I could see the ship was Sinking I said if She can stay afloat till morning we may be all right as the Marconi would get help and that certainly cheered him up some. All the boats were gone by now except No 9 and there was a bit of Trouble there the Chief officer was threatening someone and fired 2 revolver shots shouting now will you get back I was not near enough to see if anyone was shot after No 9 had left the Chief Officer shouted any crew here and about 7–8 stepped forward and he said hurry men up there and put that boat adrift it was a collapsible on Top of the Smokeroom we got it down to the deck but could not overhaul boats falls [sic] as they were hanging down shipside in water. The Ship's bows were now under Water there was a Group of Officers in a corner of the bridge and I never saw one move from there a man just in front of me jumped overboard and I without a thought did the same. The Ship's lights were still on from The Emergency dynamo. There came a terrible crashing of machinery falling forward and one propeller fell off the after funnel fell in the sea near me and I was half blinded by soot and water then came the raft we had cut adrift it fell within a dozen feet of me and some men were clinging to it as I swam to it there were terrible screams all round and one I plainly heard screaming 'Save one Life' I've never forgotten that. I saw the 2nd Officer get on to the raft and he at once took charge cut away an oar that was lashed* on and told me to use it to try and get the raft clear before it got overcrowded but I could do nothing about it there was one man quite near us he had the voice of authority kept cheering us with 'Good Boy, Good Lads' I reached the oar out to help him but he was too far gone as it touched him he turned about like a cork and was silent. There was a Gent Talking to the Officer I am sure he was a big Shot and he was complaining that his head was so cold a man nearby offered them a drink from a flask but they declined and told him to give me a drink I took the bottle thought it was brandy and took a good pull but it was Essence of peppermint nearly choked me but I am sure it did me good. The Wireless Man was on the raft the Officer asked what ships he had contacted he said Caledonia and Carpathia would be on the spot at 4 AM which was when she [was] sighted we began to shout but the Officer said she is four miles away save your breath. On board Carpathia Duff Gordon sent for his boat's crew and I saw Five Pound Note he gave to each one I took the liberty to tell one he would be sorry he had it.

I can state Definitely Captain Smith did not reach The Raft but I always had the idea he was the man that spoke to us in the water but I could not be sure.

Home in Southampton they gave us an Exam to see what we knew about it all and I have in front of me now a summoned to appear
  at the Court of Wreck Commissioners
  at Westminster London
  3rd of May 1912
  The White Star Line stopped new pay the day ship sank but gave us a small Bonus nothing for our Loss of Sea Kit and I am looking at my Pay Off Paper £2.16.0.
  Had it not been for the Generosity of The Seamen's Mission in New York I would have come home half naked as my clothes were put to dry in Carpathia's Engine Room and got lost.

  PS I went to London on The Enquiry but was not called. I am sure it was because I spoke of The Boats Leaving half Empty.
  I don't know whether you can make anything of this but it's best

I can do so wishing you good luck with it.
I remain Yours Sincerely
Walter Hurst

National Maritime Museum ref. LMQ/7/1/44

Note Hurst's claim that his criticism of the evacuation procedure meant that he was not called to give evidence at the official inquiry. Claims that more could have been done to practise lowering the lifeboats, and that despite the best efforts of the crew there was a certain amount of chaos when the boats were launched, continued to be raised both during and after the inquiry – criticisms levelled at the owners of the ship.

Another engineer, Alfred White, narrates the attempts made in the engine rooms to keep the ship afloat and restart the engines. Under the decks and probably largely unaware of the severity of the situation, when instructed to head up to see what was going on, White was shocked by the danger they were in and how fast the ship was sinking. He was lucky to escape with his life.

Dear Sir,
I am truly sorry that I could not answer your letter before as I have been very ill and have been unable to do anything at all. I knew Mr. Parr very well for the short time we were together. I was with him nearly till the last, that was at twenty to two on the 15th April in the main-light room of the Titanic. *You are asking me if he was on deck when the ship went down. I can honestly say that he was not and all the rest of the engineers were below. That was the last I saw of them. At one o'clock Mr. Parr and Mr. Sloan came below. I was on watch at that time and he said to me 'We are going to start one more engine.' I generally did that. They went to the main switch-board to change over. We knew that the ship had struck something but took no notice. Work was going on as if nothing had happened. When at twenty to two the ship seemed as if she had started again and flung us off our feet Mr. Sloan & Mr. Parr said to me 'Go up and see how things are going on and come and tell us.' Telling you the truth Sir, I had a job*

to get up the engine room ladder. I had to go up the dummy tunnel, there is a doorway there. The sight I saw I can hardly realise it. The second funnel was under water and all the boats had left the ship. I could not get back as the boat was sinking fast. We did not know they were all at boat stations. I am sure that that was where Mr. Parr was and so would I have been if they had not sent me up. That is all I can tell you. I must close this letter and I am truly sorry for Mr. Parr's wife and all his friends.

I remain yours truly,
Alfred White

June 21st 1912

3 Southampton Place
East Stub, Southampton

To the Revd Mr Langley,
National Maritime Museum LMQ/7/2/39

A far more detailed account of events, recalled forty years later in a letter to Walter Lord, came from George Kemish, who was assisting in No. 5 boiler room when the bulkhead separating it from No. 6 boiler room collapsed. He faced a struggle to escape, before making his way to the decks and out onto a lifeboat.

14 Begonia Rd. Bassett
Southampton
England
19th June 1955

Sir

I have received yours of 12th June. I am not a very good writer, but I will try to tell you what few incidents I remember as regards the wreck of the Titanic. It happened so long ago, it certainly could not be a thing easily forgotten, but at my age now at 65½ years my memory is not too good but I will try to give you a few truths of the

Disaster. The Titanic *was a brand new Ship, and a grand Ship too in those days. She was a Sister ship to the S.S.* Olympic *except she was a ship within a ship – a distance of about three feet between the two shells and believed to be unsinkable. In those days the White Star Line ran a weekly service to New York from Southampton – two ships always at sea – one Homeward – and one outward bound, and one in So'ton – one in New York. Being such a fine new Ship all the best ('cream') of Southampton seamen and Engine Room Department men were anxious to join her, yes the thick of So'ton went in her. We sailed from there on the 9th April 1912 for N.Y. She had six boiler rooms (stokeholds) each boiler room had its own pump room for bilge pumping and Boiler feed Etc. and five Boilers abreast in each Boiler room, 53 Firemen, 22 coal trimmers and five leading firemen on each watch. I was on the 8–12 watch. Being a new Ship on her maiden voyage (everything clean) she was a good job in the stokeholds (not what we were accustomed to in other old ships – slogging our guts out and nearly roasted with the heat). Even so the* Titanic *would have burned over three thousand tons of coal on each trip. Well being what I have called a good job – we just had to keep the furnaces full and <u>not</u> keep on working the fires with slice bars pricker-bars and rakes. We were sitting around on buckets – trimmers' iron wheel barrows Etc. I had just sent a trimmer up to call the 12–4 watch – it was 11.25 P.M. 14th April when there was a heavy thud and grinding tearing sound. The telegraph in each section signalled down Stop. We had a full head of steam and were doing about 23 knots per hour. We could have given much more steam pressure had it been required. We had orders to 'box up' all boilers and put on dampers to stop steam rising and lifting safety valves (steam). Well the trimmer came back from calling the 12–4 watch and he said 'Blimme we've struck an ice-berg.' We thought that a joke because we firmly believed that she had gone aground off the banks of Newfoundland. Well then some of them went up on Deck and came down again and told us – Yes the trimmer is right – She has struck a berg. Now counting Boiler sections No 1 started from forward, No 2 next and so on until you came to number 6 and then came the*

Engine-room. From No 1 there was a long tunnel which took us to a winding (spiral) stairway that led up to our quarters – rooms Etc. After climbing about 60 steps we came to the 12–4 room, another 30 steps up the 4–8 room another flight up the 8–12. Leading Fireman & Greasers. You then came out on the forward Well Deck and Rec. room for crew. Engineers came up and ordered all Firemen down below to draw all fires, because excessive steam pressure was blowing joints Etc. – All bulkhead watertight doors were closed so we had to go along what they called the working alleyway and down over the tops of the Boilers and escape ladders. We certainly had a Hell of a time putting those fires out.

The grimness of the fight below decks is clear. Water was not the only danger; fires and steam explosions were just as likely to maim or kill the engineers and firemen.

When we went to our quarters again the 12–4 men were packing their bags and dragging their beds up on to the recreation Deck because their rooms were flooded. Oh we thought this a huge joke and had a good laugh. We went down below again to see everything was alright. Engineers were very busy with valves Etc. I saw one Engineer slip and break his leg (for obvious reasons I won't give you his name) we placed him in a pump-room and did everything we could to help the other Engineers. Ships' Carpenters were constantly taking soundings. They may have known, but no one else (except Skipper Smith) that things were going to happen. About 12.45 A.M. 15th April (Sunday) we got news 'Captain has ordered all hands Boat Stations.' The ship was as steady as if she had been in dry-dock, going down very steadily forward but even at that time it was hardly notice-able. The Boat Deck was thronged with people. Many women and children had to be forcibly put in the Boats. They felt much more safe on the Decks of the Big Liner than in the small boats about 90 FT above the water line. Therefore the Boats that got away first did not take half the number of people they could have done, and then later when we realised things were really serious the boats getting

*away later were very much overloaded. The Band had stopped playing
by now, about the last person I took particular notice of was W.T.
Stead (novelist) calmly reading in the First Class Smoke room. It
looked as if he intended stopping where he was whatever happened.*

William Thomas Stead was a well-known author and journalist, writing
extensively on contemporary issues to highlight some of the main social
problems of the age, and actively campaigning against the Boer War (1899-
–1902). During his period as editor of the *Review of Reviews*, in 1892 a
fictional story was published concerning a White Star Line vessel with a
clairvoyant on board who sensed a disaster to a ship that collided with
an iceberg. Perhaps even more remarkably, he had published an article
in 1886 about the loss of a mail steamer in the mid-Atlantic after a collision with another vessel, in which the large loss of life was blamed on
the shortage of lifeboats. His editorial comment was, 'This is exactly what
might take place and will take place if liners are sent to sea short of boats.'

*One boat – I think it was either No 9 or No 11 – was being lowered
but 5 or 6 ft. from the water line it was on a very uneven keel, one
end of the Boat falls had caught up somehow. I imagined they were
trying to cut the entangled falls which I found out they eventually
did do because they could not unhook the tackle, they were shouting
and screaming that there were no members of the crew aboard. But
they managed to free it. I saw how desperate the situation was by
now, all boats were away. We had been throwing deck-chairs and
anything movable overboard. I took a flying leap intending to grab
the dangling boat falls and slither down them to the water – but I
missed them (I reckon a parachute would have been handy in that
drop). I swam until I got aboard that No 9 or No 11 boat I don't
know to this day what boat it was. A Deck hand named Paddy
McGough took charge of her. She was overloaded dangerously. Picking
up one or two more persons from the water would probably have
meant drowning about 80, that was the number in her.*

These terrible life-or-death decisions faced every overloaded boat.

It was extremely cold now and terrible for the women and kids. What few boats that were in view then tried to keep together, we were rowing aimlessly our hands froze on the oars and we lost sight of the others. It had been fairly light (moon) until now, but mercifully clouds covered the moon and it became very dark. When the Titanic *took her final plunge there was a noise I shall never forget – shouting, screaming and explosions. A hundred thousand fans at a Cup Final could not make more noise. Well we drifted about until it started getting daylight. We could just see the Berg it had drifted on to the sky line with the help of the bump we gave it. There was a low ice field practically all around us. Paddy McGough suddenly gave a great shout – 'Let us all Pray to God for there is a ship on the horizon and 'tis making for us,' some of our crowd had already passed out, but those who were still able did pray and cry. The old S.S.* Carpathia *picked us up about 7A.M on the 15th April. She took us to New York (took about 4 days I think). Quite a few survivors died on the* Carpathia. *The first night aboard there quite a few died from exposure and frost-bite. An officer asked me to go to the mortuary, four had died – he had an idea one of them was a member of the* Titanic *crew and 'perhaps I could identify him'. I jibbed, it may have been one of my mates. I had had enough.*

Here is another element in the tragedy – that many people died even after they had been taken on board the *Carpathia*. Hypothermia, shock and exposure were the principal causes of death.

Reporters (Newspaper Etc.) were waiting right outside Nantucket Light-Ship. There were hundreds of River Boats. Nobody was allowed on board. We were even under guard when we got up to New York. West Street (11th Avenue) and 10th Avenue was packed with people, but we didn't get the chance to make a few dollars. Us-members of the Titanic *crew were escorted to Wright's Seamens' Mission in West St. were measured up – got two suits of clothes – 2 pairs of boots, 2 shirts 2 suits of underwear. Ties socks Etc. Gee I looked a typical*

*Yank when I got home. We came home in the Red Star Line ship
Lapland. Were landed at Plymouth. All kinds of Officials took our
depositions for the Board of Trade Inquiry in London. We were to
remain in Southampton while the Inquiry was on, to receive five
shillings a day, if called to London another 3/6 per day. I was home
for three months and then went to sea again. All we got out of it
was – what would have been the normal trip's pay – 23 days, our
money then was only £5 per month. Our Seamens' Union gave us
£3 for loss of Kit. A 'promise' from the White Star Line of a job for
life. I have never had anything from them. I have had long un-
employment at times, and some very hard times, at present I work
as a Fitter's Mate – when I can get work. Never mind I suppose I
am lucky to be here at all.*
   Yours Faithfully George Kemish

National Maritime Museum LMQ/7/1/49

George Kemish, like so many of the ordinary seamen who survived, went
back to sea and continued serving on ships throughout his working life.

An account of the last moments of Thomas Andrews, the naval
architect, is provided by stewardess Mary Sloan, who spent a fair degree
of time in his company during the last hours. In a letter to her sister
she describes him as a true hero, escorting women and children to the
lifeboats and meeting his end with courage. It is a moving account,
giving an insight into his final thoughts.

S.S. Lapland, April 27th.

My dear Maggie,

*I expect you will be glad to hear from me once more and to know I
am still in the land of the living. Did you manage to keep the news
from mother, I trust she is well. Well, we are now nearing England
in the Lapland. They are very good to us here, and we have had a
lovely passage home. About that dreadful night, I won't go into details
now, I shall tell you all when I see you. I hope you got the cablegram*

all right. I shall never forget Mr. Shannon's friends in New York. They I mean Mrs. M'Williams came on board the Lapland *on Friday morning accompanied by a Mr. Robb, president of the telephone in N.Y. Mr. Robb sent off the cable, and Mrs. M'Williams took me to Brooklyn, gave me money and clothes. Mr. and Mrs. Robb came at night and Mr. Robb made me take a 10 dollar bill. Young Mr. Bryans a 5 dollar bill. Did you ever hear of such kindness from strangers. Of course I took them on condition I would pay them back again. You must write to them and thank them as I will also. The ladies of New York Relief Committee came on board the* Lapland *with changes of underclothing, But I was at Brooklyn. You will be glad to know that dreadful night I never lost my head once. When she struck at a quarter to twelve and the engines stopped I knew very well something was wrong. Doctor Simpson came and told me the mails were afloat. I knew things were pretty bad. He brought Miss Marsden and I into his room and gave us a little whiskey and water. I laughed and asked him if he thought we needed it, and he said we should. Miss Marsden was crying, he was cross with her. He asked me if I was afraid, I replied I was not. He said well spoken like a true Ulster girl. He had to hurry away to see if anyone was hurt. We helped him on with his greatcoat, I never saw him again. I felt better after, then I saw our dear old Doctor Laughlin, I asked him to tell me the worst. He said, child, things are very bad. I indeed got a life belt and got on deck. I went round my rooms to see if my passengers were all up and to see if they had life belts on. Poor Mr. Andrews came along, I read in his face all I wanted to know. He saw me knocking at some of the passengers' doors, he said that was right, told me to see if they had life belts on and to get one for myself and go on deck. He was a brave man. Last time I saw and heard him was about an hour later helping to get the women and children into the boats, imploring them not to hesitate, but to go when asked as there was no time to be lost, so Mr. Andrews met his fate like a true hero realizing his great danger, and gave up his life to save the women and children of the* Titanic. *They will find it hard to replace him, and I myself am terribly cut up about him. I was talking to him on the Friday night previous as he was going into dinner. The dear old doctor was waiting for him on the stair landing, and calling him by his christian name Tommy, Mr. Andrews seemed loth to go, he wanted to talk about home, he was telling me his father was ill, and Mrs. A. was not so well. I was congratulating him on the beauty and perfection of the ship. He said the part he did not like the* Titanic *was taking us further away from home every hour. I looked at him and his face struck me at the time as having a very sad expression. He is one of the many who can be ill spared. Well, I got away from all the others and intended to go back to my room for some of my jewellery, but I had not time at the last. I went on deck the second time, one of our little bill boys recognized me, and pointing to a crowded boat said, Miss Sloan, that's your boat No. 12. I said, child, how do you know, I will wait for another, so it pushed off without me. I was still standing when I saw Captain Smith getting excited, passengers would not have noticed I did. I knew then we were soon going the distress signals then were going every second, so I thought if anyone asked me again to go I should do so, there was a big crush from behind me, at last they realized their danger, so I was pushed into the boat. I believe it was one of the last boats to leave. We had scarcely got clear when she began sinking rapidly. The rest is too awful to write about. We were in the boats all night. I took a turn to row. The women said I encouraged them, I was pleased. We picked up 30 men. Standing on an upturned boat, among them was one of our Officers, Mr. Lightoller, we then took charge until the* Carpathia *picked us up about 7 in the morning. I only hope I shall never have a like experience again. Mr. Lightoller paid me the compliment of saying I was a sailor. We are arriving about midnight on Sunday night. I don't know what the White Star people are going to do with us, I shall wait and see. I have lost everything. I will stay in Marland Terrace, so you can write me there.*

Should love to see you all and talk to you.

We are arriving on the Lapland, *I think I told you this before. Trusting this will find you all safe and well.*

Your loving Sister
May.

Give my love to Mrs. Brown, Willie and Joe. Let Lizzie read this as the paper is short here.

National Maritime Museum LMQ/7/2/28

One of the most lucid accounts of the events immediately following the initial iceberg strike is provided by Mrs Charlotte Collyer. She recalled a conversation with a stewardess who informed her after dinner on Sunday evening that they were heading into dangerous waters, but curiously this had a reassuring effect as she assumed the crew would be all the more vigilant for icebergs.

'Do you know where we are' she said pleasantly, 'we are in what is called the Devil's Hole.' 'What does that mean?' I asked. 'That is a dangerous part of the ocean,' she answered. 'Many accidents have happened near there. They say that icebergs drift down as far as this. It's getting to be very cold on deck so perhaps there is ice around us now.' She left the cabin and I soon dropped off to sleep, her talk about icebergs had not frightened me, but it shows that the crew were awake to the danger.

Mrs Collyer vividly remembered the moments after the ship had struck the iceberg:

As far as I can tell we had not slackened our speed in the least. It must have been a little after ten o'clock when my husband came in and woke me up. He sat and talked to me for how long I do not know, before he began to make ready to go to bed. And then the crash! The sensation to me was as if the ship had been seized by a giant hand and shaken once, twice then stopped dead in its course. That is to say there was a long backward jerk, followed by a shorter one. I was not thrown out of my berth and my husband staggered on his feet only slightly. We heard no strange sounds, no rending of plates and woodwork, but we noticed that the engines had stopped running. They tried to start the engines a few minutes later but after some coughing and rumbling there was silence once more.

Her account continued with people beginning to realise they might be in danger. The reassurances of the officers on deck were undermined by the appearance of stokers fleeing onto the deck from the boiler rooms – clearly something serious had happened. For the first time the possibility arose that the ship could sink. This was followed quickly by a sense of denial that the unthinkable might happen.

Suddenly there was a commotion near one of the gangways and we saw a stoker come climbing up from below. He stopped a few feet away from us. All the fingers of one hand had been cut off. Blood was running from the stumps and blood was spattered over his face and over his clothes. The red marks showed very clearly against the coal dust with which he was covered. I went over and spoke to him. I asked him if there was any danger. 'Danger,' he screamed at the top of his voice, 'I should just say so! It's hell down below, look at me. This boat will sink like a stone in ten minutes.' He staggered away and lay down fainting with his head on a coil of rope. At this moment I got my first grip of fear – awful sickening fear. That poor man with his bleeding hand and his speckled face brought up a picture of smashed engines and mangled human bodies. I hung on to my husband's arm and although he was very brave, and not trembling, I saw that his face was as white as paper. We realised that the accident was much worse than we had supposed, but even then I and all the others about me of whom I have any knowledge did not believe that the *Titanic* would go down.

Mrs Collyer also described the heartbreaking moment that so many women and children endured when she was ushered into a lifeboat with her daughter Marjorie, leaving her husband Harvey behind to his fate. The despair of separation and the knowledge that this would be the last time she would see him alive is vividly related.

The third boat was about half full when a sailor caught Marjorie in his arms and tore her away from me and threw her into the boat. She was not even given a chance to tell her father goodbye! 'You too!' a man yelled close to my ear. 'You're a woman, take a seat in that boat or it will be too late.' The deck seemed to be slipping under my feet. It was leaning at a sharp angle for the ship was then sinking fast, bows down. I clung desperately to my husband. I do not know what I said but I shall always be glad to think that I did not want to leave him. A man seized me by the arm then another threw both his arms about my waist and dragged me away by main strength. I heard my husband say 'Go, Lotty, for God's sake be brave and go! I'll get a seat in another boat.' The men who held me rushed me across the deck and hurled me bodily into the lifeboat. I landed on one shoulder and bruised it badly. Other women were crowding behind me, but I stumbled to my feet and saw over their heads my husband's back as he walked steadily down the deck and disappeared among the men. His face was turned away so that I never saw it again, but I know that he went unafraid to his death.

Mrs Collyer was also witness to the desperate attempts made by some men to escape. One incident particularly stands out, as she pleaded for the life of a youth who tried to join their lifeboat as it was released from the davits.

The boat was practically full and no more women were anywhere near it when Fifth Officer Lowe jumped in and ordered it lowered. The sailors on deck had started to obey him when a very sad thing happened. A young lad hardly more than a schoolboy, a pink cheeked lad, almost small enough to be counted as a child, was standing close to the rail. He had made no attempt to force his way into the boat though his eyes had been fixed piteously on the Officer. Now when he realised that he was really to be left behind his courage failed him. With a cry he climbed upon the rail and leapt down into the boat. He fell among us women and crawled under a seat. I and another woman covered him up with our skirts. We wanted to give the poor lad a chance, but the Officer dragged him to his feet and ordered him back onto the ship. We begged for his life. I remember him saying that he would not take up too much room but the Officer drew his revolver and thrust it into his face. 'I give you just ten seconds to get back onto that ship before I blow your brains out,' he shouted. The lad only begged the harder and I thought I should see him shot where he stood. But the Officer suddenly changed his tone. He lowered his revolver and looked the boy squarely in the eyes. 'For God's sake be a man!' he said gently. 'We have got women and children.' The little lad turned round eyed and climbed back over the rail without a word. He was not saved. All the women about me were sobbing and I saw my little Marjorie take the Officer's hand. 'Oh, Mr Man don't shoot, please don't shoot the poor man!' she was saying and he spared the time to shake his head and smile.

> Donald Hysop, Alastair Forsyth and Sheila Jemima,
> *Titanic Voices: Memories from the Fateful Voyage*
> (Southampton: Sutton Publishing, Ltd, 1997)

Bertha Watt was able to escape the ship with her friends Charlotte and Marjorie Collyer, and described a similarly traumatic experience when writing to Walter Lord years later. Part of her account reflects anger that Ismay escaped the ship whilst women and children were left behind, a charge that was to recur during the recriminations and finger-pointing when blame for the accident was being assigned in the weeks after the ship had sunk. It is also an important account because she refers to the ship breaking in two before it finally sank, something that was rejected by the official boards of inquiry and only verified when the wreck was discovered and investigated after 1985.

We had a happy four days, met so many nice people and everything went along fine. Sunday evening I was allowed to stay up later, we had attended a sort of hymn service put on by the Rev. Ernest C.

Carter after which we had an evening snack . . .

Following the supper I was off to bed, mother had taken a little longer to come down & then was reading when the ship hit. I was asleep so mother partly dressed & went on deck to see what happened. One officer she spoke to replied 'Go back to bed we will soon be under way.' But she wasn't satisfied with that so when she saw other people coming on deck, they sort of stood around to see what was happening. After some little time Mr. Collier [sic] came along & advised her to go and get me up as he had seen the 1st Class lifeboats going off. So they both came down the stairs, no elevator operating that night, the steward was just at my door to awaken me when mother arrived. I pulled on stockings & tucked my nightie into my panties & put my coat on, it was fur lined thank goodness. By the time we got on deck the Colliers [sic] were there and a few other folk but no big crowd. We stood talking in a group, the Collyers, Marion Wright, who was coming out to be married in 'The Little Church around the Corner' in N.Y., my uncle gave her away. She now lives in Oregon & we have been life long friends. Then there were two young men who also sat on our table, if I remember the one was John Ashby & the other Dr. Pain. While standing there Mr. Hoffman came up with his two little boys & finished dressing them on deck (Hoffman was an assumed name, their real surname was Navratil). Many stories were published about them because he had stolen them from their divorced mother in France and was heading for the US & I guess a new wife. He had been a tailor and the little boys were models of fashion although both were very young, maybe 4 & 6. Shortly a call was made 'Women & children this way' so we all went over to the starboard side, one boat was on the way down and one was hanging on its davits overboard & full of men, looked as if they were steerage passengers & we heard that they had more or less charged this boat so they left them hang[ing] there until after our boat left. The master at arms was standing with a gun at that point. One boat went down ahead of us. Then we loaded in to the next, no order, some people in first seemed to be sitting with feet up on seats while some of us stood all night. When we women folk got in we all said to the men, 'Come on, there's plenty room,' but the officer in charge of loading said, 'Women and children first.' We waited a few minutes and none came so we were let down, all thought we would stop at another deck and pick up some more women, but no we didn't and I'll never forget the sight of these 3 or 4 men standing looking over the side. One other boat was loading as we left and the one that was hanging, that was the last. Our boat was in charge of a fine old Irish seaman who did his best to keep folk in line and he told us we were almost the last boat off. Shortly after leaving we heard shots, were told these were fired to make the men come out of that boat. By the time we got out just a little way the Titanic was really going down by the nose, so Paddy, as we called him, said row for all your worth or we would be drawn down by the suction. Two stewards were rowing but didn't look too experienced. Paddy asked others to help. We heard cries for help but couldn't see too well where they were. We possibly were out ¾ hour when the ship seemed to break in the middle and went in nose & stern and in what seemed minutes not a vestige of her could be seen. Then all was calm & dark, up until then the lights of the ship gave some help, but as she sank lower & lower, row after row of lights would go out. We were near the stern of our boat and Paddy talked to me a great deal, told me about the stars etc., but said they had no compass & no rudder in this boat so all we could do was row a little and hope we would see something coming. We had been told before we left the ship that this was all precautionary measures & the Olympic would be along shortly to pick us all up. So after quite a while I saw a light away in the distance and called to Paddy. He answered that it wasn't a ship but one of our own boats who must be lucky to have a light. I wanted to know how he could tell and he said from the light above the water. How this has always been a point of anger for me over the years, it's hard to explain. In one enquiry Ismay stated he was in the only boat with a light, that boat was picked up by the Carpathia a good 2–3 hrs ahead of us. Mr Ismay was all tucked away in bed in a cabin long before half of us were landed on the Carpathia. Now they try to tell people how brave he was and how he helped women

too well were they were We possibly were out 3/4 hour
when the ship seemed to break in the middle and
went in nose & stern and it
what seemed minutes not a
vestage of her could be seen. Then all was calm
& dark, up until then the lights of the ship gave
some help, but as she sank lower & lower, row
after row of lights would go out. We were near
the stern of our boat and Paddy talked to me a
great deal, told me about the stars etc but said they
had no compass & no rudder in this boat so all we
could do was row a little and hope we would see
something coming. We had been told before we left the
ship that this was all precautionary measures & the
Olympic would be along shortly to pick us all up.
So after quite a while I saw a light away in
the distance and called to Paddy. He answered that
it wasn't a ship but one of our own boats who must
be lucky to have a light. I wanted to know how he could
tell and he said from the height above the water. How this
has always been a point of anger for me over the
years, its hard to explain. In one enquiry Ismay
stated he was in the only boat with a light, that boat
was picked up by the Carpathia a good 2-3 hrs
ahead of us. Mr Ismay was all tucked away in bed
in a cabin long before half of us were landed on the
C— now they try to tell people how brave he was and
how he helped women into boats & only went into
the last boat under pressure, well we never saw him
and we knew some of the people in the last
boat off & he wasn't there either. so no one will ever
white wash him to me. Our boat had either

Letter from Bertha Watt, *Titanic* survivor, to Walter Lord, dated 10 April 1963.

into boats & only went into the last boat under pressure, well we never saw him & we knew some of the people in the last boat off & he wasn't there either. So no one will ever white wash him to me. Our boat had either 46 or 47 in it. All boats had printed on them 75 min 100 max. We had 1 box of dry biscuits, no water, light or compass. Never had a boat drill or assigned a special boat to go to.

We left the ship about 1am or close there and arrived aboard the Carpathia *about 9.30am, how good that ship looked to all of us. I climbed up the rope ladder without any belt affair around me, had always been good at athletics in school & I think that morning I could even have climbed a single rope. But the Capt. was very angry. We were all given hot Toddy & a blanket & some slept wherever they found a spot. At our table on* Titanic *was a very fine couple, Mr. & Mrs. Leopold Weisz. He was a sculptor & had been established in Montreal but went home to Belgium to bring his wife out, he was one who never came home. That first day on the* Carpathia *she was in a bad way & was bound to jump, my good mother must have walked miles with her up & down the decks. . . Well Mom finally got her calmed down and got her interested in helping a whole big table full of mothers & children who could not speak English. Madame Weisz could speak 7 languages so sat at this table every meal and ordered for the folk. A great tribute should be paid her for the patience & help when her own heart was breaking. The last we saw of her she was being taken away by some Catholic sisters. He had done a beautiful drawing in my autograph album, but alas that went down with all other things . . .*

Those few days before we landed in N.Y. were a life all their own. Tragedy affects people in so many different ways. We slept down on straw bags in the crew quarters. These men had given up their cabins for us but some wouldn't have anything to do with the place. Mother said as long as the engines kept booming away she could sleep anywhere. People slept on tables & under them & every corner was filled up on the small ship. How lucky we were to be alive and even fed. But many were very fussy & annoying & stealing was really bad. Seemed everyone lost things both the regular passengers & any who brought anything with them. Mother made dresses for Margery Collyer & me out of a blue blanket and #50 thread sewing them by hand. Kept us warm but we sure looked funny, now as I look back . . .

The things I saw are as plain in my mind as if they were printed on my brain. Guess I was very lucky having the kind of mother I had, for she was a tower of strength to lots who were sort of falling apart and a most practical psychologist in her own way. I know now that I learned a great deal of the fundamentals I have built a happy life on, such as faith, hope & charity, just in one short week of my life, listening to people talk and hearing answers my mother gave to me & others and later thinking how some behaved. Mother took me to Boston or rather Fall River by boat just two weeks after. She probably didn't think much of it at the time, but what a good thing it was.

National Maritime Museum LMQ/7/2/37

Bertha remained in America after her rescue, married a doctor from Vancouver, Leslie Marshall, in 1923 and moved to British Columbia, where she spent the rest of her days before her death in 1993.

Another account of the sinking is provided by Mary Hewlett, a second-class passenger on her way to visit one of her sons in South Dakota. She gives the impression that there was a degree of chaos when trying to release the lifeboats, and that their craft was nearly crushed in attempts to launch another boat.

On board the Cunard
R.M.S. Laconia

May 30th, 1912

My dear Marica

Now that I have recovered from the nervous breakdown I had after the horrors of the shipwreck, I will try to write you a little about it. I was in bed and asleep & I did not feel the shock of the collision with the iceberg & no one called me. I awoke & finding the engines had stopped I got out of bed & looked into the alleyway & saw the steward – he assured me there was no danger & that I need not dress unless I liked. Then I heard him go to the stewardess's cabin & say 'Hurry up' so I got on my underclothes & my furlined coat & a hat & went on deck & there an officer was ordering people to climb up a ladder on to the upper deck so I went with the crowd & when I reached the top there were eight or ten stewards there who said I must get into a boat that was on the davits – but I begged not to go – however they insisted and I was put into boat No. 13 – with about 50 people – mostly men of the unemployed class – & stokers, stewards & cooks – not one real seaman. Amongst these there were only about 12 women in the boat & no compass, lanterns or water. When the boat finally reached the water there was no one who under-stood how to release it from the ropes & so there we were until a knife could be found and the ropes cut. In the meantime No. 14 boat was descending on the top of us & we had great difficulty in making them stop lowering that boat until we were free. Then we pulled out from the Titanic somehow as the men at the oars did not know how to row – could not keep time – & did not know starboard from port!!!

We got about a mile & a half away before the ship finally went down & then we stopped there in the dark with the icebergs all around us & the other life boats (also without lights) rowing about near us. I had some long letters (I had written to my girls) in my handbag and I gave them to be burned sheet by sheet as signals. The dawn came about 4.30 & then we saw dozens of icebergs & the new moon in a pink haze. It was a most wonderful sight & soon after that, about five o'clock we saw the mast lights of the Carpathia on the horizon – & then the headlights – & then the portholes & then we knew we should be saved. We had to go up on a rope ladder on the side of the Carpathia (I don't know how I did it), and then we were taken on board & given coffee & brandy – but as our boat was about the sixteenth or eighteenth to arrive all the berths were given away before I reached there & so I had to stay in the Library for the four days & nights before we reached New York – & there were no brushes or combs to be had – nor toothbrushes as these were all sold in a minute.

The Carpathia *is a small ship & how she found room for seven hundred people besides her own passengers seems marvellous. Of course the scenes on board were very harrowing – as so many people had lost their dear ones – there were 150 widows. Thank God – Jumbo was not with me – so that I only lost my clothes & presents for my family in America. When I landed in New York my son Frank was not there to meet me – he did not get my letter until after the accident so I had to stay in New York alone for three days till he came. I had no dress on & no luggage, but the people at the hotel were very kind when I said I had been on the* Titanic *& the housekeeper lent me a nightie and wrapper – until I could get some things from the shops. I had some money in a little bag on my corsets as well as my best jewellery. So I was very fortunate. I went out West with Frank but the place did not agree with me & I found great difficulty in breathing. So returned to Chicago where Jumbo met me & we are now on our way back to England for the summer.*

Despite her ordeal, Mary had recovered sufficiently to overcome whatever nerves she might have felt to admire the furnishings of the *Laconia*.

This is a very excellent boat. There is a gymnasium where one can ride & row & pull weights & do Indian clubs & ride bicycles & do all sorts of exercises. Jumbo and I spend an hour there every morning. There is a boat with a sliding seat & imitation oars. I wish you were here to practise with me. I shall be in London for the July sales as I must get some clothes, so if you want any shopping done just let me know & I will send out anything you require. Address

c/o Mrs Groves
6 The Avenue
Brondesbury
London – N.W.

Now I expect you are tired of all this rigmarole so I will say goodbye with love to yourself & Miss Nan – & kind regards to Col. Thompson

& the rest of the R.A.M.C. that I know.

Yours affectionately

Mary Hewlett

National Maritime Museum LMQ/7/1/42

A moving account comes from Celiney Decker, a bride of only 50 days, who lost her husband, Antoni. She describes their moment of parting – his attempts to join her in the lifeboat, followed by her struggles to get back on board the sinking *Titanic* to be reunited with him.

June 15, 1955

Dear Mr. Lord:

In reply to your letter concerning my experiences on the Titanic, *I will try to answer your questions to the best of my knowledge.*

I was a bride of 50 days. My husband and I were on our way to America to make it our home. He had been to America before where he had a business.

When I first realized that something was wrong, it was 11 o'clock at night and I was fast asleep. Suddenly I heard a tremendous noise and immediately I knew the ship had been hit hard. It almost threw me off the bed. The motor stopped at once. My husband and I jumped up and ran to see what had happened. We went to the engine room and saw the crew trying to repair parts of the ship. We were still wearing our nightclothes.

We rushed back to our rooms and put on our life preservers and then went up on deck.

Later we returned to our rooms to try to get our clothes, money, and jewelry, but we found our room to be flooded with water. We went back on deck and we all started praying. We thought we could never be saved.

All the life boats were being lowered. There were only 14 life boats. My husband and I headed for the life boats. He put me on and as he tried to join me, two policemen grabbed him as they wanted to save all the women and children first. I began yelling and crying as I wanted to join him on the sinking ship. The boat was paddled away from the Titanic *so fast that I couldn't jump off to be with my husband.*

We were about five minutes away from the ship, but we could still see it as the lights stayed on until the Titanic *sank. The people still on the* Titanic *were yelling and crying as it was slowly sinking.*

When the ship sank it made a tremendous noise that I will never forget. The impact of the sinking was so great, it shook the waters and we thought our life boat would sink too. Everyone screamed.

After the sinking, which was right at midnight, we were without any lights.

As our boat was being paddled in the dark, everyone prayed.

I had fainted and I was very depressed. (There were 14 people aboard our lifeboat.)

The next morning we saw a big ship. We were all taken aboard one by one with a rope and a board. On this ship, I met my sister who was also on the Titanic *and had been put on one of the other life boats. We were given hot tea, blankets and clothes.*

After four days, we arrived in New York. I was ill and was taken to the hospital where I stayed for a week. After a week, I was united with my father. My name was Celiney Yazbeck.

Hope this information helps you in writing your book.

Sincerely,
Mrs. Celiney Decker

National Maritime Museum LMQ/7/1/24

George Rheims's letter to his wife contains an insight into one of the enduring mysteries of the *Titanic* – whether one of the officers committed suicide after shooting a male passenger who had tried to scramble into a lifeboat ahead of women and children. The identity of the officer is unclear, and Rheims does not give a name, though he does at least indicate that the incident occurred. His account is disturbing in other ways, since he was among those without a seat in a lifeboat and was left to await his death. He praises the wonderful calm with which his companions met their ends, yet even at the last the will to survive drove him and others to continue looking for a way off the ship, only to face the horrors of the open ocean and those slowly freezing to death.

On Sunday night I had dinner with Joe* in the restaurant and went to bed, when around 11 o'clock, being in the front part of this ship, I felt a strong shock and a noise like steam escaping from the machinery; really terrifying. I thought there had been an accident in the machinery. About a quarter of an hour later, we were told that we had hit an iceberg, but that there was no danger and that we should go back to bed!! As I could see that the ship was listing, I did nothing of the sort. Soon Joe came to join me and we did not leave each other until the end. Around 11.30, all the passengers had gotten out of their cabins. The ship was listing more and more. An officer came to tell us to put on our life-belts. You can imagine what pleasant news that was!

I went back to my cabin and put on my belt and some warm clothes. Joe did likewise and we met again on deck where there was now quite a gathering. They started lowering the lifeboats (16 lifeboats from 3000 people!) It was forbidden for the men to get in them; a few of them, cowards, did not hesitate however and jumped in the boats, but in general, most people's attitude was admirable. It took about an hour to lower all the lifeboats. A few of them were only half full. When the last boat was leaving, I saw an officer shoot with his revolver a man who was trying to get in. As there was nothing left to be done, the officer said: 'Gentlemen, each one for himself. Good-bye!' He gave a military salute and shot himself in the head. That's what I call a man!!!

We remained then, about 1500 persons, with no way to escape. It was sure death for all of us. I cannot say enough about the wonderful calm with which each one contemplated it. We said good-bye to all our friends and each one prepared himself to die decently. Joe took both my hands and said: 'George, if you survive, look after my babies. If I live, you will not have to worry about Marie!' We then separated for a minute. I went back to my cabin to get your picture, then went up on deck again to meet Joe. We undressed, keeping on only our shirts and shorts.

I did not lose my head one minute, I had decided to jump off the boat and try to escape swimming. I cannot describe to you the horrible things I saw at that moment. The ship headed down and an explosion threw me on the floor where I found myself entangled in chairs and ropes. I managed to extricate myself. Joe wanted to go up all the way to the rear of the ship. I told him that that would be sure death and that he should come with me; he said he did not know how to swim well enough. So I took a running start and jumped overboard. It seemed to me that the fall would never end; then suddenly, and icy cold and a long dive. When I came up to the surface again, I started swimming vigorously to get away from the ship in order not to get caught in the suction. It was horribly cold. Suddenly, I saw the Titanic go down, straight up, with horrible explosions and excruciating screams. All the passengers were sticking like flies to the stern. There was then a huge swirl, then silence. Suddenly rose a dismal moaning sound which I won't ever forget; it came from those poor people who were floating around, calling for help. It was horrifying, mysterious, supernatural. It lasted about an hour; then it all ceased. The poor people, they had all drowned.

I was swimming alone in the night, when suddenly I saw far away a sort of raft, half submerged, loaded with people. It took me I guess about half an hour to reach it. At first they would not let me get on, but I succeeded never the less. We were about twenty people there, men and women, with water up to our thighs. We had to balance ourselves, from left to right, to prevent the raft from turning over. I remained there six hours, in my shirt, freezing to death. I almost let myself go and fall into the water two or three times, but the thought of you prevented me from doing it. I got my courage back, and for I don't know what reason, I took command of the raft. What a horrible night that was! We had to push back about a dozen fellows who wanted to get on the raft: we were loaded to the limit. Eight persons died during the night, from cold or from despair! I will spare you the details, which were horrible. (I had the joy however of saving a poor fellow's life, a father of nine children who asked me for my photograph, with dedication, as if I were the king of England!) At eight o'clock in the morning, a life-boat from the Titanic *came to rescue us and took us on board the* Carpathia *where we were wonderfully taken care of.*

I found everyone on the dock. I find it difficult to walk, my feet being slightly bruised. Here I am settled at Harry's** place and I think that a few days' rest will do me a lot of good.

I admit that I am a little tired and you must excuse me if I end this letter here, a little abruptly.

19 East fifty-second street
April 19th 1912

* Joe Loring was my uncle's brother-in-law.
** Harry was my uncle's brother.

National Maritime Museum LMQ/7/2/16

A disproportionate number of those in third-class accommodation died, leading to a popular belief that not sufficient attempts were made to rescue them. This was tackled by the inquiries, and largely discounted. However, testimony from Anna Kincaid suggests that third-class passengers received no particular help from the crew.

1405 South 5th Street
Tacoma, Washington
July 18, 1955

Mr. Walter Lord
25 East 38th Street
New York 16, New York

Dear Sir:

Re – Information requested covering
some details of Titanic *disaster*

I will try to answer as fully as I can remember, the questions you asked me in your recent letter of July 10th, 1955.

Q. You asked how I learned what was happening.
A. A young Danish boy came to the part of the Third Class where I was. He was looking for his sweetheart, who was also there. He gave us lifebelts. I could understand him quite well, but although he and his girlfriend wanted and urged me to go up with them I just couldn't believe that this wonderful ship could possibly be in real trouble. I was so seasick that all I wanted was to be left alone so I could lie down. I was fully clothed and now had a lifebelt. I am sorry but I do not know the names of either of these two young people.

Q. Why I finally decided to go up on deck?
A. I finally could hear the commotion overhead increasing and the ship did not move ahead, so I decided to go up, even though I still felt so very ill. So some after midnight, about 12.30 a.m. I did go up. There I saw practically everyone on their knees praying. At this time I met a young school friend of mine, Alfred Wicklund, from my own home country. He helped me get into the lifebelt. He told me he was going back down as he felt he would rather die in bed. I never saw him again.

Q. Why was it difficult for the Third Class people to get to life boats?
A. The stairway was closed. It seems that those in charge were sure that the ship would be saved, and I suppose did not think it best to have more people above than necessary. After Alfred went back downstairs I got to talking to a young Swedish girl who was with two friends who had been 'home' and were returning to the United States. They knew about an emergency stairway and showed us where it was, and so that is how I got up to where the life boats were; the girl too.

Q. You asked about my thoughts as I passed the Banquet Hall?
A. We were quite awed at the splendor there. The tables were so beautifully set and all the furniture, and everything about this huge room was out of this world to both of us. We even thought of going in and helping ourselves, but decided we might have to pay, so didn't.

Q. Did Third Class passengers have same chance as others to reach safety?

A. Just shortly after the Swedish girl and I got above, by using the emergency stairway, the main stairway doors were opened and those below could then get up. Until then there was no help of any kind accorded to Third Class passengers. So, it was only in the very last desperate moments that Third Class passengers were given any chance to reach safety.

A few other observations and things I remember:

On the Carpathia I saw the Danish boy's sweetheart. He was the one I mentioned giving me a lifebelt. She was simply frantic and hysterical as she had become separated from her boy friend. She later lost her mind and she was sent back to Denmark.

I saw a Swedish couple and their five children kiss each other goodbye, and then they all jumped overboard. (This was while I was still on the Titanic.)

After we were in lifeboats, those who had papers or any article that could burn, lit these, thus making flares. In this way the lifeboats kept going in the same direction, and not getting scattered in various directions. In the morning we were sighted by the Carpathia, and were taken aboard her in the early hours, about 8.30 a.m. I might also add that, though the ocean was quite calm, two lifeboats did overturn – at least that is all I saw capsize.

It seems strange to me now, but all I could think of while all this was happening was that I must get to America. After we were safe, and on the Carpathia, I was very upset, and no doubt, in a case of shock, from the experience I had just come through.

I have had this information typed by a stenographer, and her fee will be $10.00.

Sincerely,

Anna Kincaid

National Maritime Museum LMQ/7/2/27

A more structured account of the disaster is provided by Karl Howard Behr, a first-class passenger who wrote a book about his life, and included a chapter about the *Titanic*. It is a more reflective piece, compiled from memory and with hindsight, but contains an interesting account of an encounter with Ismay, and his actions during the evacuation.

CHAPTER XIV

TITANIC DISASTER

I boarded the *Titanic* at Cherbourg. Helen, Mr. and Mrs. Beckwith and Mr. and Mrs. Kimball boarded it in England. We were the same group who had been together on the delightful voyage on the *Cedric* to the Mediterranean less than two months before.

The first morning at sea, Helen and I walked all over this beautiful but to us too enormous ship. Naturally, with Helen on board I enjoyed every minute of our calm voyage until the fateful night of the catastrophe. During the first few days I went to the main office twice to locate the Squash Court and was misdirected each time. Evidently the two men in the office were too ignorant regarding this new ship to know where the Squash Court was located. I mention this incident simply because it indicated, which later was more tragically shown, that the officers and crew had started on this maiden voyage without adequate familiarity with the ship.

Behr's interest in racket sports is understandable, given he was men's doubles runner-up at Wimbledon in 1907 with his partner, Beals C. Wright.

After dinner on the evening of the sinking of the *Titanic*, our small party, including a Mr. Compton (later lost) remained in the smoking room unusually late, being among the last to leave for our cabins. Only a few minutes after I reached my own cabin in the stern on Deck D the ship suddenly trembled all over, not as violently, however, as had the small vessel on my return from Porto [*sic*] Rico each time its screw came out of the water during the hurricane as previously described.

My first thought was that we had broken a shaft. I stood still for over a minute and noticing the engines continuing to run, realized it could not have been the shaft, yet the trembling had not been violent enough to indicate a collision. Putting my collar, vest and cutaway coat back on, I opened the door and looked along the gangway. Not a person was in sight. I therefore concluded nothing serious had happened and very nearly started to undress for bed. As I pondered for a few moments the engines stopped, and some premonition urged me to go to Helen's cabin just to be sure all was right.

I started along the gangway for her cabin in the bow on E deck and, as I recall met no passengers on this long trip, possibly half the length of the ship. Arriving at Helen's cabin, I found all of our party, still dressed, outside their cabins somewhat disturbed as ice had gathered in the port-holes of their starboard cabins. A number of other passengers also were out in this gangway. After talking to Dick Beckwith (Helen's stepfather), we decided that he should go below forward, and I to the top deck to see what we could find out.

Helen put on her heavy coat and she and I went up to the Boat Deck. Passing through the main lobby we saw one or two officers and some sailors, but can recall no passengers. We walked the length of the deserted Boat Deck. It was very cold, but I could notice no list on the ship's part and there was no apparent activity.

When we got back to our party on E Deck, Dick Beckwith had just returned and reported water in the Squash Court. We then urged everyone to put on all their clothes and heavy coats, feeling we should go up to the Boat Deck where [we] would be in the proper place in case there should be serious trouble after all. After some minutes' discussion, we all proceeded up the main stairs to the Boat Deck. We met the Captain coming down the stairs alone. He said nothing to us, undoubtedly not yet realizing the extent of the damage.

Arriving on the Boat Deck, we found a few small groups of

passengers, all talking and wondering like us what had happened. It was not much over ten minutes later, when a group of sailors with some officers came along and commenced to unlash some life boats. Shortly a tall civilian arrived who we recognized as Mr. Ismay, the Chairman of the White Star Line. He approached a group of passengers near us and told them that they should get into the life boats. This was our first intimation that something serious may have occurred.

One life boat was comfortably filled when Ismay walked over to us and calmly told us that we should get into a second life boat which was being filled. It was swung over the side flush with the deck. No one in our group however was anxious to obey. The prospect of being lowered some eighty feet or more to the ocean in the dark was not alluring, and we all still felt that nothing so far warranted such a risk; to our minds the idea of the *Titanic* sinking was preposterous. It should be remembered that we had read about many of the features of this great new ship, of which not the least emphasised was its unsinkability. No one therefore moved to obey Ismay as he walked off. I could still see no sign of any list on looking down the deck.

In a few minutes, Ismay noticed us still standing together; he again walked over and with considerably more emphasis told us we must follow instructions and get into the life boat – we were the last passengers on the deck. I told Mrs. Beckwith I thought we should do what he said, and she finally led the way to the boat. Stopping in front of Ismay, she asked if all her party could get into the same life boat and he replied, 'Of course Madam, every one of you.'

We got into the boat in which all were standing up, and there we hung for probably five minutes, during which Ismay was apparently waiting for more people. An officer finally came up to him and said there were no more passengers on the Boat Deck. Ismay then told this officer to take charge of the boat, telling four or five more sailors to get in, he then said 'Lower away' and walked off.

We apparently were among the last passengers to come up to

the Boat Deck. It afterwards was disclosed that all First Cabin passengers had been ordered to A Deck below, and the stairs to the Boat Deck had been roped off. This was a dreadful error. A Deck was a covered deck, and the life boats lowered to it could only be filled by passengers being helped through its square windows. This created confusion, much wasted time and difficulty of control. Many life boats, not being readily visible from this deck except through these windows were apparently lowered half full or less. One of the tragedies of this maiden voyage was as already intimated, lack of familiarity with the ship on the part of officers and crew. Had the First Cabin passengers been ordered to the Boat Deck, hardly any should have been lost.

We rowed slowly away from the ship in quite calm water. Our little group was congregated in the stern of the life boat. Dick Beckwith and I took turns rowing one of the large sweeping oars. Helen, who stood next to me, leaned over after some ten minutes or more and quietly said, 'The boat is leaking badly, I am standing in water.'

My first thought was of the stop-cock, which our officer had shouted to a sailor to close as we were being lowered from the ship. The stop-cocks are left open on life boats aboard ship to drain off rain water. It was almost directly under Helen, and I felt all around it but could notice no leak. I then got some blankets, put them on top of the stop-cock, and Helen stood on them during the rest of the night. The leakage, which ultimately increased to at least six or more inches in depth, was undoubtedly due to the unswollen dry seams of this new boat.

It was about this time that we became convinced the *Titanic* might sink. The ship was fully lighted and we could see from the lines of her port-holes that she was slowly going down by the bow. It is difficult to estimate time after so long a period, but I should say we had now been in the life boat at least twenty-five minutes, and had rowed some distance from the ship, probably five hundred yards in company of the life boat which had preceded us. Each of these life boats had at least a half dozen extra sailors, due to lack of available passengers on the Boat Deck – already referred to. They were, I believe, the only two life boats lowered from the starboard Boat Deck. I have no knowledge of what happened on the port side.

By now, for the first time, we were hearing noise and shouting from the *Titanic* and in a few more minutes we could see her going down slowly by the bow still fully lighted. Quite suddenly it seems to me now, her bow started to slide under and her stern rise as her lights went out. We heard with anguish the screams and moaning of those plunged into the icy water.

Within a very few minutes all shouting and noise over the water had ceased, and our two boats continued to row along side by side. I was resting after a turn at rowing and was rubbing Helen's wet stocking feet to get them warmer when someone nudged me. I straightened up to see a man next to me concealing in his hand a nickel-plated revolver, or so it seemed in the dim light. Leaning over he whispered in my ear, 'Should the worst come to the worst, you can use this revolver for your wife, after my wife and I have finished with it.' He was in no wise panicky. I thanked him, and it now appears strange how natural his courtesy seemed under the circumstances. Later he came up to me on the *Carpathia* and referred to this incident in the life boat. He was an attractive-looking middle aged man but I do not recall his giving me his name, and I never spoke to him again owing to my absorbing work on that ship during the return journey.

None of us in the life boat knew whether any rescue ship had been reached by the *Titanic's* radio. All during the night we saw lights around us but they proved only to be the flashlights of other life boats. It was shortly after daybreak when we saw the *Carpathia* coming towards us in the distance. We immediately started rowing towards her and were along side within perhaps half an hour. All around us other life boats were converging towards this welcome ship.

We climbed up rope ladders to one of her lower decks where we were met by stewards and stewardesses and told to go to the First Cabin Dining Saloon. Here hot coffee and food were waiting for us. Captain Rostron and his crew had worked throughout the night preparing in every way to serve the rescued should the *Carpathia* be fortunate enough to locate us. Rostron had driven his ship at almost full speed in the pitch dark through the ice floes to this magnificent rescue. He was fully deserving of the future honours bestowed on him for his daring and brilliant service.

Those of us who had been so fortunate as to leave the *Titanic* from the Boat Deck in the earliest lifeboats launched, I am thankful to say, had no close contact with the tragedy and horror of the actual sinking. All six of our party and our friends Mr. and Mrs. George Harder, who had followed us to the Boat Deck, were safe on the *Carpathia*, where however, we were to witness for four days the suffering and sorrow of others. It was a dreadfully sad and nerve-wracking experience. Families were split up, some lost fathers, brothers, sisters or wives.

Under Captain Rostron's instructions all First Cabin passengers were asked to meet in the large saloon after lunch on the first day to select a committee to assist in caring for the rescued. I became a member of this committee of seven. We were occupied mainly with the steerage passengers; obtaining clothing, blankets and arranging places for them to sleep. It was harrowing to talk with these despairing people from whom I had to get names, home addresses and the names of lost relatives. These lists were radioed to New York.

I was fast asleep fully clothed, on top of a table in the Small Smoking Room forward on our second night. Suddenly there was a terrific crash. I jumped off the table, sure we had collided with another ship or iceberg. I rushed out the door onto the deck, starting for Helen. As I hit the deck it was pouring rain – suddenly a flash of lightning almost knocked me down. It was followed by another crash of thunder. I turned back to the Smoking Room; never before had a violent thunder-storm been more welcome.

It was on the *Carpathia* that I first met Dick Williams. He had a harrowing experience, being plunged into the water, finally reaching a crowded life raft. His father was lost in the sinking of the *Titanic*.

Captain Rostron had turned his ship back to New York after sailing slowly around for some hours looking for more life boats or rafts. We were practically surrounded by small ice but I saw no large icebergs. The *Carpathia* finally started through this icy water at full speed on her way back to New York, maintaining this speed for four days and nights until our arrival in New York harbour.

Due to my committee work, I saw Captain Rostron every day. When we neared Sandy Hook he told me he had been receiving wireless requests from the press asking permission to board the *Carpathia* at Sandy Hook. He was opposed to having survivors interviewed and asked my views. I told him I agreed that the *Carpathia* was no place for newspaper reporters at that time. None were allowed aboard, and passengers were urged not to reply to the megaphone calls from the numerous press boats which accompanied us down the harbour in the dark of early evening.

When we finally went down the gang plank to the crowded dock, with its frantic waiting crowd, one of my friends, I am ashamed not to recall who, shouted to me to follow him down the dock. I soon saw Herman, Margaret and Gertrude. They led me to Father; he was sitting in a chair, wrapped in a blanket. His face appeared to have shrunk to half its size; I shall never forget the indelible imprint of suffering. He was too feeble my vigorous Father, to get up to greet me. He just held out his arms, the tears streaming down his face.

I was to learn later of the country-wide consternation over this greatest peace time sea disaster. Two of my classmates had spent a night on the steps of the White Star Line until my name had come through as rescued, and an office boy had gone to Father's apartment to answer the numerous telephone enquiries.

The wonderful spirit of your mother during this whole episode, her calmness and courage, were further revelations of her grand character.

K. H. Behr, excerpt from an account of his
life written for his family and some friends,
National Maritime Museum LMQ/7/1/5

Behr had only joined the *Titanic* because he was enamoured with Helen Newsom, who had been taken on a grand tour of Europe by her mother to discourage Behr's interest and was on the ship. The couple were married in 1913.

The passengers lost from first class included the great and the good of the age, among them Colonel John Jacob Astor, the millionaire hotel owner, who was returning to America with his new young second wife, Madeline. She survived, and her tale was recounted in a letter from W. H. Dobbyn to Robert Ferguson, both employees of the Astors.

22 West Twenty-Sixth Street

May 15th, 1912
Dear Mr. Ferguson,

I have wished many times during the past four weeks that you were here to help me with your advice and your presence. I will not attempt to thank you for your letter – it means a great deal to me and I shall treasure it, as I do the Colonel's own words in his will, which are as much to me as what he left me. The last word I had from him was a telegram asking me to meet him when he arrived in New York. Mrs. Astor told me the Sunday the Titanic *struck he had prepared a wireless to send me on the following day, but that day never came for him. You, who were his friend and whom he trusted, for you were very close to him, you will know how I feel now that I shall not see him again. He was a reticent man, but there have been times when he spoke of you to me when he showed how he trusted you and what a really deep feeling of friendship he had for you and how much he appreciated your years of work with him. Vincent spoke to me the other day in a way which showed me that he, too, knows how his father felt toward you.*

Although it is only a little over four weeks since the Titanic *struck it seems as many months or years to me. You can well understand the awful dread and anxiety of the first week when, day and night, we haunted the offices of the White Star Line and the Associated Press, hoping always to find a name that never appeared among the survivors. At first, when we thought that nearly all were saved and the* Carpathia *was bound for Halifax, Vincent and I arranged to go to Halifax, and we changed our plan only one hour before the train left, as we found the* Carpathia *was coming direct to New York. Then followed days of suspense – then the certain news that the Colonel was not on the* Carpathia *and that none of the other boats in the vicinity of the wreck had saved anyone. I shall never forget the night the* Carpathia *got in. Vincent, Mr. Biddle, Miss Force and I were at the Cunard dock with Mr. Kimball and Dr. Craquin and a trained nurse and ambulance. We had had no word from Mrs. Astor, and the papers stated that she was very ill. The great pier was packed with people. They were very quiet – there was no noise – no confusion. They were admitted by ticket only, and the police regulations were perfect. I happened near a window, heard a gun fired, and looking out saw the red lights of the* Carpathia *as she was slowly turning in, bringing with her what sad and dreadful news. For up to that time we had heard no details. There was an ominous stillness as the gang-way was made fast, and then as the people came off such scenes as one can never forget. It was several minutes before Vincent, who had received permission to go on board, could force his way through the crowd, but he finally got on the ship where he found Mrs. Astor waiting, and brought her down. She could walk, and we had no need of the ambulance. I never saw a sadder face or one more beautiful, or anything braver or finer than the wonderful control she had of herself. We avoided the crush by taking her down one of the freight elevators at the foot of which stood our automobile. She stopped to see her father on 37th street. You know he is crippled and he could not go to meet her. Then she went to 840 Fifth.*

She has since told me the story of that terrible night. She had not been feeling well that afternoon and had retired early. She was awakened by the shock, rather slight, of the Titanic's *striking and by the engines stopping. She spoke to the Colonel who said it was nothing, and that the engines would soon start again. They did, but stopped. He then looked out the window, or port hole, and said there was* ice about. The air was bitterly cold. He dressed immediately and hurried up to the bridge to see the Captain, who told him it was serious. He then took Mrs. Astor to the deck, where I believe she got some warmer clothing, and he secured a chair for her. He put on a life belt, which she helped fasten, and afterward he got some man to tie it tighter about him. He was perfectly cool and collected, his only thought being for her comfort. When, at last, an officer ordered her to a boat, she did not want to go without him, and the officer took her arm and made her go, the Colonel reassuring her that he would go with her. (He did, I am sure, only to get her to go.) She got in the boat, thinking he would follow for there were a number of vacant places, and the deck about them deserted. He asked the officer if he might go with her, and was refused. She was terribly frightened when she found herself alone, and the boat being lowered. She remembers his calling to her if she was alright or if she was comfortable, and that he asked the officer the number of the boat, and he said something she could not hear. Her boat had gone but a little way when the Titanic sank. She thought she heard him calling, and she stood up and cried that they were coming, but the people in the boat made her stop, and apparently they made no effort to go back toward those cries for help. There was no light in her boat, and anyone in the water, only a few feet away, could not see them. You would be terribly sorry for her if you could see her and hear her tell the awful tragedy. She is so young and she cared so much for him.

The Colonel's funeral was in the village church in Rhinebeck. You have doubtless read about it. It was a beautiful service, simple and unostentatious. The choir, 29, from Trinity Chapel sang. The three songs were 'Hark, Hark, My Soul', 'Peace, Perfect Peace', (a song the Colonel selected for his Mother's funeral), and 'Saviour, Blessed Saviour'. He was buried here in Trinity Cemetery . . . It's late & I must close, but not before saying that the more I learn of this fearful disaster, the more I admire the Colonel's quiet bravery, and his gentle care of his wife, in the face of what he knew was death. I am glad that the last few months of his life were so happy . . .

With deep appreciation of your letter and of the friendship it expressed and with all good wishes for you and yours,

Yours sincerely

W. H. Dobbyn

National Maritime Museum, ref. LMQ/7/1/2

While Astor's behaviour seems to have been honourable, some other first-class survivors attracted criticism. In particular, Sir Cosmo Duff-Gordon, erstwhile member of the British fencing team from the 1908 Olympics, was on board the ship with his wife – booked under the names Mr and Mrs Morgan. He was in a lifeboat that contained only twelve people, and it would appear that the decision was made not to go back to help their struggling fellow passengers. Sir Cosmo vigorously defended himself at the British inquiry against accusations that he bribed the crewmen not to return to help the drowning, stating that money was indeed paid but only in gratitude and to compensate the crew members in the boat for their loss of pay since the ship had gone down. This is corroborated by Walter Hurst's recollections of what happened on board the *Carpathia*. The following account is recorded by Lady Duff-Gordon's secretary, Laura Mabel Francatelli, who accompanied the couple on the *Titanic* and was in the same lifeboat.

Ritz-Carlton Hotel
Madison Avenue & Forty Sixth Street
New York

Sunday 28th '12

My darling Mary Ann,
Over a week I have been trying to write to you, but had to tear each one up, ink impossible, so scribbling in bed with pencil. Never in my life, can I say how happy it made me to get your darling letter,

wishing me a happy birthday, just after our arrival here, and after our terrible experience, it seemed like a voice from home, which I thought I should never hear again. Oh darling, you cannot know, what I have passed through, not bodily, as I am strong, but mind & nerves, it is a wonder we are not all grey-headed – it is impossible for me to describe the horrors of it all, it was about ¼ to 12, when the crash came. I was just getting into bed. Madame & Sir Cosmo had been in bed sometime, they were up on A deck the top, and I on E, the bottom deck for saloon passengers, it was a marvelous boat, like a floating huge Hotel, in fact I have not seen an Hotel so grand. The collision shook me, as well as everything else in my room. I immediately slipped on my dressing gown, & opened my door, saw several people come out of their rooms in night attire, two Gentlemen came up, & spoke to me, & told me not to be frightened, but go back to bed, we had run into an iceberg, but we were quite safe, however the engines were making a terrific noise. I still stood there quite 20 minutes, or more, saw all the officers come down, to inspect the damage, & then starting screwing down the iron doors outside my bedroom, presently a man came rushing up, saying all the Hold & luggage & Mail had gone, so I thought I shall fly on a few things, & go & tell Madame. When I left my room the water was on my deck, coming along the corridor. We were 20 feet above the water level, so we had already sunk 20 feet, but of course I did not realise this till afterwards. Everybody I passed assured me, I was safe, but to my terrible surprise, I found all the people running up & down the stairs.

When I reached Madame's room, she was already out of bed, & put two dressing gowns on for warmth, Sir Cosmo was dressing. The next minute a man came along & said 'Captain's orders,' <u>all to put life preservers on</u>, and the next instant they were putting one on Madame, & I, Oh Marion that was a sickening moment, I felt myself go like Marble, but Madame & I prayed together, for God to look after us, & keep us safe, if it was his will. Sir Cosmo then took us up on top deck. Crowds were up there, & they were already lowering the lifeboats filled with women & children, I looked over the side of the boat, & tried to penetrate the blackness, & noticed that the water was not such a long distance away from us, as we had always remarked what a height it was, I said to Sir Cosmo, I believe we are sinking, he said, Nonsense come away. We then walked more to the bow of the boat, near the bridge several lifeboats had been lowered, they were preparing the last two, on that side of the ship, the Starboard side. They cried out, 'Any more women,' saw us, & came to try & drag Madame & I away from Sir Cosmo, but Madame clung to Sir Cosmo, & begged him not to let them take her, or separate her, she said, I will go down with you, and I clung to Madame, I would not leave them, it would have been too awful to have been alone.

After all the lifeboats had gone, everybody seemed to rush to the other side of the boat, & leave ours vacant, but we still stood there, as Sir Cosmo said, we must wait for orders, presently an officer started to swing off a little boat called the 'Emergency' boat, quite an ordinary little rowing boat & started to man it, he saw us & ordered us in, they were then firing the rockets beside us, we had to be nearly thrown up into this boat, two other American gentlemen jumped in, & seven stokers, they started to lower us. We had not gone a few yards when our little boat got caught up by a wire rope on my side, and in a few minutes we should all have been hurled into the sea, had it not been for that brave officer still up on deck. He shouted Cut it with a knife, but nobody had one, & we were all in black darkness, hanging in midair, he shouted Mind your heads, & threw a piece of heavy iron which shook our boat, & so set it free, we then went rapidly down to the water.

The dear officer gave orders to row away from the sinking boat at least 200 yards, he afterwards, poor dear brave fellow, shot himself. We saw the whole thing, and watched that tremendous thing quickly sink, there was then terrible, terrible explosions, and all darkness, then followed the awful cries & screams of the 1600 dear souls, fighting for their lives in the water. Oh never shall I forget, that awful night, floating about the ocean in this little boat, freezing cold, & listening to this terrible suffering, we all prayed all night long, that help may come to us all, & how I thought of all my darlings, & all those dear to me. I knew you were all safe and none of you knew what we were going through.

It is marvelous how brave one can be, when facing the greatest danger, God gives us strength to bear these things. We floated about all that long night, were terribly cold, & the men rowing, got so cold they began to drop oars & lay at bottom of boat. I sat on one man's feet, to try & make them a little warm & tried to rub another one's hands, but I was so cold myself, I had not much power to rub.

Oh at daybreak, when we saw the lights of that ship, about 4 miles away, we rowed like mad, & passed icebergs like mountains, at last about 6.30 the dear Carpathia *picked us up, our little boat was like a speck against that giant. Then came my weakest moment, they lowered a rope swing, which was awkward to sit on, with my life preserver round me. Then they hauled me up, by the side of the boat. Can you imagine, swinging in the air over the sea, I just shut my eyes & clung tight saying 'Am I safe,' at last I felt a strong arm pulling me onto the boat. I was so chattering could say nothing, they gave Madame & I lots of hot brandy, I cannot go on, it was all too terrible the scenes, & sadness we lived in for the next four days & nights on the darling* Carpathia. *Oh but they were so kind to us, everybody lent us everything, & their beds, but of course, all had to sleep on tables, floors, or anywhere.*

Since being safe on land, I am afraid I am a coward, my nerves had gone, but I do not show it, as I am constantly battling with it, as poor Madame gets worse, every day since we have been here, but she was so brave, & calm all through it, I have never imagined anybody so wonderful, but now unfortunately the reaction, so you see, we have not seen anything of New York, hardly been out of the bedrooms & Sitting room of the Hotel. Miss Margaret is a darling, has lent me underclothes & a skirt and blouse, fancy dear, I haven't a stitch left, or a penny in the world, everything went down, Miss Celia's trunk, Florence's Costume she lent me, & Lady Tiverton's musquash coat, they insisted on me taking, besides everything of mine. It worries me, but I cannot trouble about a thing, I seem numbed to all wordly things. They count so little, when you have been through all we have. Madame hasn't a stitch but her dressing gown, & Moleskin coat we threw round her, at the last minute, & lost all her jewelry, she landed in N.Y. in her dressing gown, & we haven't troubled about clothes. I have only seen Max twice for a few minutes, with Miss Margaret, he sends me sweet letters, & wants to help me in every way. We hope to come home, as quickly as possible. Sir Cosmo is trying to fix up all the business quickly, so as soon as it is decided, I will let you know. I only wish we could get home, without crossing that stretch of water, naturally we shall feel nervous, & feel we shall not sleep a wink the whole time. I know I shall not undress. Sir Cosmo & Madame have been so kind to me. I cannot say how much, fancy, it is nearly 3 o/c, & I know I cannot go to sleep but must put my light out. Will you dearest send me a list of addresses, of the girls, so I can send them cards as promised, but I will not say I shall write letters, & dear, I am never away from Madame & have nothing to write. I have only the wreck on my mind. I wonder how they were at home, & if they heard at once that I was saved, so they did not suffer much anxiety about me. I received a cable from them, but no letter so far, but I have had such nice letters from lots of people. Miss Celia sent me a lovely letter, also Miss Lowles, Mrs Tweedie, Mrs Haig, & girls from the Paris office. Wasn't it sweet of them. Now darling, bye bye, give my fond love to dear little Mabel, Connie, & Hilda & Winnie, also love to my friend Ada, & Miss Amy, Mrs Wright, & dear, all the girls I love.

I will hurry home to you dear one. Kindest thoughts to all your Family dear, & lots of fondest love for dear self.

Yours always,
Franks

Copy of a letter from Laura Mabel Francatelli to Mary Ann Taylor, National Maritime Museum, ref. LMQ/7/1/28

Many people were convinced that abandoning ship was not a wise move, especially as there were rumours that not only the *Carpathia* was on its way, but also the *Olympic*. In a letter to Walter Lord, Alice Cleaver (subsequently Mrs Alice Williams), nursemaid to the Allison family, recounted her memories of what people were saying as the ship was about to sink.

46 Millbrook Road
Southampton
Hants
England

Sept 13th '55

Mr. Walter Lord
25 East 38th Street
New York NY

Dear Mr. Lord

In answer to your letter re: Titanic. The information Mr. Crowle gave you is quite correct. I was acting as nurse to the two children of Mr. & Mrs. Allison having taken the position two weeks before we sailed as their nurse decided not to go at the last moment.

Lorraine was 3 years old at the time and Trevor 10 months. There is not much I can tell you in a letter. I had some difficulty in persuading Mr. Allison to get up and go to see what had happened after the crash, which they did not hear at all & thought it was my imagination. Some long time after the engines had stopped he decided to go and find out the trouble. While he was away I was warned we would have to leave the ship, so prepared the children & Mrs. Allison, but she became hysterical & I had to calm her. About that time an officer came round to close the cabins & advised us to go on deck. We met Mr. Allison outside the cabin but he seemed too dazed to speak. I handed him some brandy & asked him to look after Mrs. Allison & Lorraine & I would keep Baby. The child I managed to get off the ship, some confusion occurred outside as to which deck we should go & that is how we became separated & afterward I heard from one of the staff that Mrs. Allison was hysterical again & that Mr. Allison had difficulty with her & I can only surmise that is how they lost their lives, as there was plenty of room in the lifeboats, because people refused to leave thinking it was safer on the ship.

I am afraid this will not be much help to you, but if I can help

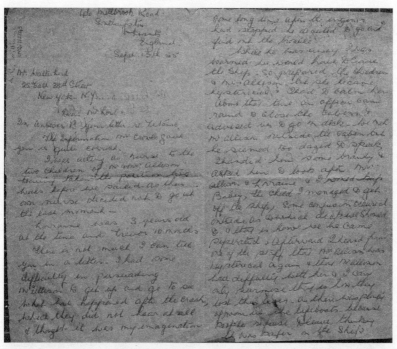

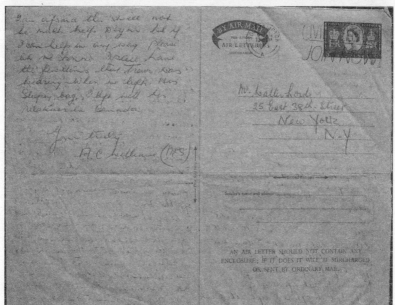

Letter to Walter Lord from Alice Williams (née Cleaver), nurse to the Allison family.

in any way please let me know. I still have the few items that Trevor was wearing when we left. His sleeping bag I left with his relatives in Canada.

Yours truly,
A C Williams (Mrs)

National Maritime Museum, ref. LMQ/7/2/43

A *Titanic* collapsible recovered in the Bahamas. Photo sent from Mr Hill to Walter Lord, accompanying the letter on pages 200 and 202.

The cries of the drowning are vividly described by Lawrence Beesley to Walter Lord in a reflective and haunting account of the immediate aftermath of the final moments of the *Titanic*.

Any attempt to describe the cries of those drowning after the Titanic *sunk must depend on the reliability of those who were rescued in the boats, and the question must arise whether they were in such a state of excitement or fear of danger – in fact so disturbed in mind as to be unable to give a calm & collected judgement of the volume & intensity of those cries for help. Did we, for example, magnify their* amount and horror as they reached us, because our minds were already disturbed? Apparently not. Referring to the 'Loss of the Titanic' I have there spoken of the conditions in which we found ourselves, as being calm, collected, and free from any sense of alarm. The sailor's remark – 'It seems like a blooming picnic' sums up the situation very well. The dead calm, the boat at rest on the quiet, phosphorescent sea, the brilliance of the stars all conduced to create a peaceful atmosphere far removed from the imminent tragedy awaiting its culmination a few hundred yards away.

At the same time it must not be forgotten that before the cries began, the stupefying crash of the machinery falling from its bed, and with the cargo and contents tearing its way through the steel bulkheads, one by one, might be deemed to cause alarm in the boats standing by. How far did that affect us, in that it may have warped our judgement of the cries that arose after the ship disappeared?

It was certainly a terrible and awe inspiring sound in the middle of the silent night, but a sound connected with the ship only, not with its living contents. We had no knowledge of the number of boats available, how many had got away in the boats, and, in fact, no reason to doubt that every one on board had, in some way, a chance of safety. There was therefore no forewarning of the tragedy, no anticipation of peril for our fellow passengers as we saw the Titanic glide slowly down to her doom. The ship had gone but the passengers were, in all probability, safe, waiting only as we did, for the dawn to bring the rescuing ships. Therefore the terrible nature of the cries, which reached us almost immediately after the Titanic sank, came upon us entirely unprepared for their terrible message. They came as a thunderbolt, unexpected, inconceivable, incredible. No one in any of the boats standing off a few hundred yards away can have escaped the paralysing shock of knowing that so short a distance away a tragedy, unbelievable in its magnitude, was being enacted, which we, helpless, could in no way avert or diminish.

The cries came to us in full volume along the surface of the level sea as though only a few yards away, carrying with them every possible *emotion of human fear, despair, agony, fierce resentment & blind anger mingled – I am certain of this – with notes of infinite surprise, as though each one were saying, 'How is it possible that this awful thing is happening to me? That I should be caught in this death trap?'*

The mere volume of cries was shattering. Consider that 1500 passengers and crew lost their lives that night of horror. Thrown into the icy sea, some proportion would perish immediately. . . and some killed accidentally in the sinking or trapped in cabins that would not open. Five hundred might be accounted for in these ways, leaving perhaps as a minimum, a thousand alive, struggling in the water, buoyed up by lifebelts (which, though designed for their safety, served only to prolong their despair), seeking some kind of support from wreckage, and all the time calling for help from any boats which might be near.

National Maritime Museum, ref. LMQ/7/3/B

Many lifeboats nevertheless attempted to save as many people from the water as possible. Clearly still upset many years after the event, Lillian Bentham (subsequently Mrs John Black) recalled her experience in the boats, and how she blew a whistle to attract the attention of those struggling in the cold water.

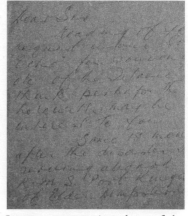

I have always avoided publicity. The Titanic *disaster is very vivid, even today – the years have not dimmed the dreadful experience. I am not as brave today as I was then. I am sure I will see the picture [A Night to Remember], but I will be emotionally*

Letter accompanying photo of the *Titanic* collapsible sent to Walter Lord. Continued on page 202.

(upset) disturbed. There was eleven in my party, returning from England and only three of us saved. One died several years ago and the other lady died July 8th, Miss Emily Rugg of Wilmington, Delaware. We were in life-boat #12 and it has quite a record. We saved several men who were on an upturned boat – I had the privilege of helping to pull the men in our boat. If you recall it was a whistle that saved the lives of the men and I have the honor of being the proud possessor of the whistle, also five pieces of silver taken from the pocket of a man who died in our boat (given to me by a steward).

To Geoffrey G. Martin, Rank Films, 23 July 1958, National Maritime Museum, ref LMQ/7/1/7

Yet clearly, given the capacity of the boats and the number of people who were actually saved, not all the lifeboats were anywhere near full. Indeed, tragic to relate, even those who did make the safety of a boat were not guaranteed survival. The following letter (and accompanying photograph) came from Herbert Hill, who discovered a missing boat from the *Titanic* a full eighteen months after the disaster, adrift in the Caribbean.

Some 18 months after the disaster I was serving aboard the RMS Port Kingston *of Elder Demposter Ltd on voyage to Kingston in Jamaica. Approaching Turk's Island at the entrance to the Caribbean Sea we sighted and embarked a lifeboat, ex-*Titanic, *finally taking it home to Avonmouth, where this photograph was taken. Eventually I heard it was preserved in Bristol. The period of drift approximately would mean a voyage of some 2,000 miles, a remarkable thing to accomplish at sea. I kept a fragment of the lifeboat, but am sorry I cannot find it, which reminds me I am aged, but I have very poignant memories of the disaster perhaps too, because I have been adrift myself three times and lived to tell the tale to my grandson.*

Letter to William McQuitty, subsequently given to Walter Lord, National Maritime Museum, ref. LMQ/1/12/5

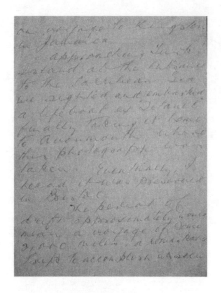
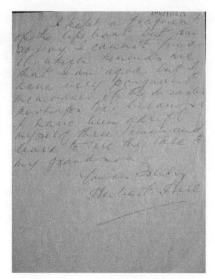

The *Carpathia's* frantic attempts to rescue the *Titanic's* stricken passengers were outlined in full by Captain Rostron at the US official inquiry. The transcripts reveal the time he first received the distress signal, the dangers he faced in speeding to the scene in icy waters, the number of icebergs that he saw and the specific challenges involved in picking up so many lifeboats. Details of the medical attention his crew were able to provide are also given, as well as the state of the people hauled on board and the flotsam and jetsam in the water, all that remained to mark the passing of the great ship.

> *We backed out from the dock at noon on Thursday. We proceeded down the river, the weather being fine and clear, and we left the pilot at the pilot boat and passed the Ambrose Channel Lightship about 2 o'clock p.m . . . From that up to Sunday midnight we had fine, clear weather, and everything was going on without any trouble of any kind. At 12.35 a.m. on Monday I was informed of the urgent distress signal from the* Titanic *. . . The wireless operator had taken the message and run with it up to the bridge, and gave it to the first officer who was in charge, with a junior officer with him, and both ran down the ladder to my door and called me. I had only*

just turned in. It was an urgent distress signal from the Titanic, *requiring immediate assistance and giving me his position. The position of the* Titanic *at the time was 41° 46' north, 50° 14' west . . . Immediately on getting the message, I gave the order to turn the ship around, and immediately I had given that order I asked the operator if he was absolutely sure it was a distress signal from the* Titanic. *I asked him twice . . .*

The whole thing was absolutely providential. I will tell you this, that the wireless operator was in his cabin, at the time, not on official business at all, but just simply listening as he was undressing. He was unlacing his boots at the time. He had this apparatus on his ear, and the message came. That was the whole thing. In 10 minutes, maybe he would have been in bed, and we would not have heard the messages . . .

In the meantime I was dressing, and I picked up our position on my chart, and set a course to pick up the Titanic. *The course was north 52 degrees west true 58 miles from my position. I then sent for the chief engineer. In the meantime I was dressing and seeing the ship put on her course. The chief engineer came up. I told him to call another watch of stokers and make all possible speed to the* Titanic, *as she was in trouble. He ran down immediately and told me my orders would be carried out at once. After that I gave the first officer, who was in charge of the bridge, orders to knock off all work which the men were doing on deck, the watch on deck, and prepare all our lifeboats, take out the spare gear, and have them all ready for turning outboard. Immediately I had done that I sent for the heads of the different departments, the English doctor, the purser, and the chief steward, and they came to my cabin, and then I issued my orders . . . We carry an English doctor, an Italian doctor, and a Hungarian doctor. My orders were these:*

- *English doctor, with assistants, to remain in first class dining room.*
- *Italian doctor, with assistants, to remain in second class dining room.*
- *Hungarian doctor, with assistants, to remain in third class dining room.*

- *Each doctor to have supplies of restoratives, stimulants, and everything to hand for immediate needs of probable wounded or sick.*
- *Purser, with assistant purser and chief steward, to receive the passengers, etc., at different gangways, controlling our own stewards in assisting* Titanic *passengers to the dining rooms, etc.; also to get Christian and surnames of all survivors as soon as possible to send by wireless.*
- *Inspector, steerage stewards, and master at arms to control our own steerage passengers and keep them out of the third class dining hall, and also to keep them out of the way and off the deck to prevent confusion.*
- *Chief steward: That all hands would be called and to have coffee, etc., ready to serve out to all our crew.*
- *Have coffee, tea, soup, etc., in each saloon, blankets in saloons, at the gangways, and some for the boats.*
- *To see all rescued cared for and immediate wants attended to.*
- *My cabin and all officials' cabins to be given up. Smoke rooms, library, etc., dining rooms, would be utilized to accommodate the survivors.*
- *All spare berths in steerage to be utilized for* Titanic's *passengers, and get all our own steerage passengers grouped together.*
- *Stewards to be placed in each alleyway to reassure our own passengers, should they inquire about noise in getting our boats out, etc., or the working of engines.*
- *To all I strictly enjoined the necessity for order, discipline and quietness and to avoid all confusion.*
- *Chief and first officers: All the hands to be called; get coffee, etc. Prepare and swing out all boats.*
- *All gangway doors to be opened.*
- *Electric sprays in each gangway and over side.*
- *A block with line rove hooked in each gangway.*
- *A chair sling at each gangway, for getting up sick or wounded.*
- *Boatswains' chairs. Pilot ladders and canvas ash bags to be at each gangway, the canvas ash bags for children . . . (the canvas*

ash bags were of great assistance in getting the infants and children aboard).

- *Cargo falls with both ends clear; bowlines in the ends, and bights secured along ship's sides, for boat ropes or to help the people up.*
- *Heaving lines distributed along the ship's side, and gaskets handy near gangways for lashing people in chairs, etc.*
- *Forward derricks, topped and rigged, and steam on winches; also told off officers for different stations and for certain eventualities.*
- *Ordered company's rockets to be fired at 2:45 a.m. and every quarter of an hour after to reassure* Titanic.

As each official saw everything in readiness, he reported to me personally on the bridge that all my orders were carried out, enumerating the same, and that everything was in readiness. This was at 3:45. That was a quarter of an hour before we got up to the scene of the disaster. The details of all this work I left to the several officials, and I am glad to say that they were most efficiently carried out . . . It took us three and a half hours . . .

At 2:40, I saw a flare, about half a point on the port bow, and immediately took it for granted that it was the Titanic *itself, and I remarked that she must be still afloat, as I knew we were a long way off, and it seemed so high. However, soon after seeing the flare I made out an iceberg about a point on the port bow, to which I had to port to keep well clear of. Knowing that the* Titanic *had struck ice, of course I had to take extra care and every precaution to keep clear of anything that might look like ice. Between 2:45 and 4 o'clock, the time I stopped my engines, we were passing icebergs on every side and making them ahead and having to alter our course several times to clear the bergs . . .*

It was in the night time. I can confess this much, that if I had known at the time there was so much ice about, I should not [have run under a full head of steam]; but I was right in it then. I could see the ice. I knew I was perfectly clear. There is one other consideration: Although I was running a risk with my own ship and my

own passengers, I also had to consider what I was going for . . . I
had to consider the lives of others . . . Of course it was a chance, but
at the same time I knew quite what I was doing.

. . . At 4 o'clock I stopped. At 4:10 I got the first boat alongside.
Previous to getting the first boat alongside, however, I saw an iceberg
close to me, right ahead, and I had to starboard to get out of the
way. And I picked him up on the weather side of the ship. I had to
clear this ice . . .

We picked up the first boat, and the boat was in charge of an
officer. I saw that he was not under full control of this boat, and
the officer sung out to me that he only had one seaman in the boat,
so I had to manoeuvre the ship to get as close to the boat as possible,
as I knew well it would be difficult to do the pulling. However, they
got alongside, and they got them up all right.

By the time we had the first boat's people it was breaking day,
and then I could see the remaining boats all around within an area
of about 4 miles. I also saw icebergs all around me. There were about
20 icebergs that would be anywhere from about 150 to 200 feet high
and numerous smaller bergs; also numerous what we call "growlers".
You would not call them bergs. They were anywhere from 10 to 12
feet high and 10 to 15 feet long above the water. I manoeuvred the
ship and we gradually got all the boats together. We got all the boats
alongside and all the people up aboard by 8:30. I was then very close
to where the Titanic must have gone down, as there was a lot of
hardly wreckage but small pieces of broken-up stuff nothing in the
way of anything large.

At 8 o'clock the Leyland Line steamer Californian hove up, and
we exchanged messages. I gave them the notes by semaphore about
the Titanic going down, and that I had got all the passengers from
the boats; but we were then not quite sure whether we could account
for all the boats. I told them: 'Think one boat still unaccounted for.'
He then asked me if he should search around, and I said, 'Yes, please.'
It was then 10:50.

I want to go back again, a little bit. At 8:30 all the people were
on board. I asked for the purser, and told him that I wanted to hold

a service, a short prayer of thankfulness for those rescued and a short burial service for those who were lost. I consulted with Mr. Ismay. I ran down for a moment and told them that I wished to do this, and Mr. Ismay left everything in my hands. I then got an Episcopal clergyman, one of our passengers, and asked him if he would do this for me, which he did, willingly.

While they were holding the service, I was on the bridge, of course, and I manoeuvred around the scene of the wreckage. We saw nothing except one body . . . with a life preserver on. That is the only body I saw . . . It appeared to me to be one of the crew. He was only about 100 yards from the ship. We could see him quite distinctly, and saw that he was absolutely dead. He was lying on his side like this (indicating) and his head was awash. Of course he could not possibly have been alive and remain in that position. I did not take him aboard. For one reason, the Titanic's passengers then were knocking about the deck and I did not want to cause any unnecessary excitement or any more hysteria among them, so I steamed past, trying to get them not to see it. From the boats we took three dead men, who had died of exposure . . . Another man was brought up – I think he was one of the crew – who died that morning about 10 o'clock, I think, and he, with the other three, were buried (at sea) at 4 o'clock in the afternoon . . . One of my own officers and the Titanic's officers identified the bodies, as far as possible, and took everything from them that could be of the slightest clue or use. Nothing was left but their clothes . . .

There were several ladies in the boats. They were slightly injured about the arms and things of that kind, of course; although I must say, from the very start, all these people behaved magnificently. As each boat came alongside everyone was calm, and they kept perfectly still in their boats. They were quiet and orderly, and each person came up the ladder, or was pulled up, in turn as they were told off. There was no confusion whatever among the passengers. They behaved magnificently – every one of them. As they came aboard, they were, of course, attended to . . .

As the people came out, we left the boats alongside. Of course lots of gear had been knocked out of the boats and thrown out of the way of the people as they were getting up; so, while they were holding this service and while I was cruising around, I had had all of my boats swung out, ready for lowering over, and while they were getting all the people aboard from the boats, I got the spare men and some of my officers, and swung my boats inboard again, and landed them on their blocks and secured them, and swung the davits out again, disconnected the falls again, and got up the Titanic's *boats. While I was cruising around, I was also getting these boats up. I got seven of the* Titanic's *boats up in our davits, and six up on the forecastle head with the forward derricks; so that is 13 boats in all . . .*

I came right around for New York immediately, and returned to New York . . . The first and principal reason was that we had all these women aboard, and I knew they were hysterical and in a bad state. I knew very well, also, that (the US) would want all the news possible. I knew very well, further, that if I went to Halifax, we could get them there all right, but I did not know how many of these people were half dead, how many were injured, or how many were really sick, or anything like that. I knew, also, that if we went to Halifax, we would have the possibility of coming across more ice, and I knew very well what the effect of that would be on people who had had the experience these people had had. I knew what that would be the whole time we were in the vicinity of ice. I took that into consideration. I knew very well that if we went to Halifax it would be a case of railway journeys for these passengers, as I knew they would have to go to New York, and there would be all the miseries of that. Furthermore, I did not know what the condition of the weather might be, or what accommodation I could give them in Halifax, and that was a great consideration – one of the greatest considerations that made me turn back.

Testimony of Captain Rostron, US board of inquiry, day 1

The official boards of inquiry were convened to determine how the ship had sunk, and how the attempts to save the ship, the eventual

The Café Parisienne on 'B' Deck was a luxurious addition to *Titanic* that *Olympic* had not featured before.

The gymnasium on the *Titanic* was full of the most up-to-date equipment, and Mr T. W. McCawley in the white flannels, was employed as a physical educator to show passengers how to use the machinery. McCawley, from Aberdeen, was sadly lost in the tragedy.

The swimming pool on the *Olympic*, which was identical to that on the *Titanic*.

Artist's impression of the first-class electric elevators.

First-class suite bedroom number B59.

Artist's impression of a second-class state room, used by the White Star Line to promote the ship.

Artist's impression of a first-class en-suite bathroom.

Photo of the *Titanic*'s officers. Back row left to right: Chief Purser Herbert McElroy, 2nd Officer Charles Lightoller, 3rd Officer Herbert Pitman, 4th Officer Joseph Boxhall, 5th Officer Harold Lowe. Front row left to right: 6th Officer James Moody, Chief Officer Henry Wilde, Captain Edward Smith, 1st Officer William Murdoch.

Titanic's two wireless officers Jack Phillips (left) and Harold Bride. This photo was taken by Father Browne on a previous voyage on the *Adriatic*. Phillips stuck to his post tirelessly in the early hours of 15 April 1912, summoning other ships to the *Titanic*'s rescue.

Lord Pirrie of Harland
and Wolff and Bruce Ismay
of the White Star Line
inspecting the hull of the
Titanic prior to launch.

Thomas Andrews, the naval architect
who designed the *Titanic*.

First-class
passengers
awaiting the
departure of
the boat train
from London
Waterloo to
Southampton
Docks.

Passengers on the White Star Wharf at Queenstown, Ireland awaiting the tenders to take them to the ship.

Passengers disembarking from the tender *America* at Queenstown, taken by Father Browne who disembarked at Ireland.

Mail being loaded onto the Royal Mail Steamship *Titanic*.

Artist's impression of the *Titanic* sinking. Eyewitnesses described how calm the sea was and how brilliantly lit the ship was up until the last few moments.

Father Browne's last picture
of the departing *Titanic*.

Photo taken by a passenger onboard the *Carpathia* of *Titanic* survivors in
lifeboats being rescued after a long night floating aimlessly on the Atlantic.

Anxious relatives awaiting news of survivors outside the White Star Line offices in Southampton. Lists of names were put up outside the offices daily when news of the fate of passengers and crew had been sent from New York.

The first *Titanic* survivors photographed on their arrival back to Southampton Docks.

evacuation, and the rescue had been conducted. After evidence had been gathered from survivors and the rescue teams sent out to find and recover anyone still adrift after the *Titanic* had sunk, the following reports were compiled and published.

The British report contained a detailed description of the attempts to rescue as many people, and the launching of the lifeboats, along with an assessment of why so many people failed to be saved. When reading the numbers contained in the report, it is worth bearing in mind the number of people who set sail – over 2,200. It is also worth noting the lack of blame attached to anyone in authority at any point.

Account of the Saving and Rescue of Those Who Survived Boats

The *Titanic* was provided with 20 boats. They were all on the Boat deck. Fourteen were lifeboats. These were hung inboard in davits, seven on the starboard side and seven on the port side, and were designed to carry 65 persons each. Two were emergency boats. These were also in davits, but were hung outboard, one on the starboard side and one on the port side, and were designed to carry 40 persons each. The remaining four boats were Englehardt or collapsible boats. Two of these were stowed on the Boat deck and two on the roof of the officers' quarters, and were designed to carry 47 persons each. Thus the total boat accommodation was 1,178 persons. The boats in davits were numbered, the odd numbers being on the starboard side and even numbers on the port side. The numbering began with emergency boats which were forward, and ran aft. Thus the boats on the starboard side were numbered 1 (an emergency boat) 3, 5, 7, 9, 11, 13 and 15 (lifeboats), and those on the port side 2 (an emergency boat), 4, 6, 8, 10, 12, 14 and 16 (lifeboats). The collapsible boats were lettered, A and B being on the roof of the officers' quarters, and C and D being on the Boat deck; C was abreast of No. 1 (emergency boat) and D abreast of No. 2 (emergency boat) . . .

In ordinary circumstances all these boats (with the exception of 1 and 2) were kept covered up, and contained only a portion of their equipment, such as oars, masts and sails, and water; some of the remaining portion, such as lamps, compasses and biscuits being stowed in the ship in some convenient place, ready for use when required. Much examination was directed at the hearing to show that some boats left the ship without a lamp and others without a compass and so on, but in the circumstances of confusion and excitement which existed at the time of the disaster this seems to me to be excusable.

Each member of the crew had a boat assigned to him in printed lists which were posted up in convenient places for the men to see; but it appeared that in some cases the men had not looked at these lists and did not know their respective boats.

This is a clear indication that discipline on board was not what it should have been, and that the attitude to safety was lax. There is also evidence that insufficient tests and training drills had been conducted.

There had been no proper boat drill nor a muster. It was explained that great difficulty frequently exists in getting firemen to take part in a boat drill. They regard it as no part of their work. There seem to be no statutory requirements as to boat drills or musters, although there is a provision (Section 9 of the Merchant Shipping Act of 1906) that when a boat drill does take place the Master of the vessel is, under a penalty, to record the fact in his log. I think it is desirable that the Board of Trade should make rules requiring boat drills and boat musters to be held of such a kind and at such times as may be suitable to the ship and to the voyage on which she is engaged. Boat drill, regulated according to the opportunities of the service, should always be held.

It is perhaps worth recording that there was an inspection of the boats themselves at Southampton by Mr. Clarke, the emigration officer; and that, as a result, Mr. Clarke gave his certificate that the boats were satisfactory. For the purpose of this inspection two of the boats were lowered to the water and crews exercised in them.

The collision took place at 11.40 p.m. (ship's time). About midnight it was realized that that the vessel could not live, and at about 12.5 the order was given to uncover the 14 boats under davits. The work began on both sides of the ship under the super-intendence of five officers. It did not proceed quickly at first; the crew arrived on the Boat deck only gradually, and there was an average of not more than three deck hands to each boat. At 12.20 the order was given to swing out the boats, and this work was at once commenced. There were a few passengers on the deck at this time. Mr. Lightoller, who was one of the officers directing operations, says that the noise of the steam blowing off was so great that his voice could not be heard, and that he had to give directions with his hands.

Before this work had been begun, the stewards were rousing the passengers in their different quarters, helping them to put on lifebelts and getting them up to the Boat deck. At about 12.30 the order was given to place women and children in the boats. This was proceeded with at once and at about 12.45 Mr. Murdoch gave the order to lower No. 7 boat (on the starboard side) to the water. The work of uncovering, filling and lowering the boats was done under the following supervision: Mr. Lowe, the fifth officer, saw to Nos. 1, 3, 5 and 7; Mr. Murdoch (lost) saw also to 1 and 7 and to A and C. Mr. Moody (lost) looked after Nos. 9, 11, 13 and 15. Mr. Murdoch also saw to 9 and 11. Mr. Lightoller saw to Nos. 4, 6, 8, B and D. Mr. Wilde (lost) also saw to 8 and D. Mr. Lightoller and Mr. Moody saw to 10 and 16 and Mr. Lowe to 12 and 14. Mr. Wilde also assisted at No. 14, Mr. Boxhall helping generally.

The evidence satisfies me that the officers did their work very well and without any thought of themselves. Captain Smith, the Master, Mr. Wilde, the chief officer, Mr. Murdoch, the first officer, and Mr. Moody, the sixth officer, all went down with the ship while performing their duties. The others, with the exception of

Mr. Lightoller, took charge of boats and thus were saved. Mr. Lightoller was swept off the deck as the vessel went down and was subsequently picked up.

All of those in charge of the ship were thus exonerated from blame – during the evacuation, at least – and therefore the official verdict remains that, once the ship was sinking, everyone did their duty.

So far as can be ascertained the boats left the ship at the following times, but I think it is necessary to say that these, and, indeed, all the times subsequent to the collision which are mentioned by the witnesses, are unreliable.

No.	Starboard Side.	No.	Port Side.
7	At 12.45 a.m.	6	At 12.55 a.m.
5	12.55 a.m.	8	1.10
3	1.0	10	1.20
1	1.10	12	1.25
9	1.20	14	1.30
11	1.25	16	1.35
13	1.35	2	1.45
15	1.35	4	1.55
C	1.40	D	2.5

A	Floated off when the ship sank and was utilised as a raft.	B	Floated off when the ship sank and was utilised as a raft.

As regards the collapsible boats, C and D were properly lowered; as to A and B, which were on the roof of the officers' house, they were left until the last. There was difficulty in getting these boats down to the deck, and the ship had at this time a list. Very few of the deck hands were left in the ship, as they had nearly all gone to man the lifeboats, and the stewards and firemen were unaccustomed to work the collapsible boats. Work appears to have been going on in connection with these two boats at the time that the ship sank. The boats seem to have floated from the deck and to have served in the water as rafts.

The following table shows the numbers of the male crew, male passengers, and women and children who, according to the evidence, left the ship in each boat. In three or four instances the numbers of women and children are only arrived at by subtracting the numbers of crew and male passengers from the total said to be in the boat (these are in italics). In each case the lowest figures are taken:

Starboard side Boat No.	Men of crew	Men Passengers	Women and Children	Total	Port side Boat No.	Men of crew	Men Passengers	Women and Children	Total
7	3	4	20	27	6	2	2	24	28
5	5	6	30	41	8	4	-	35	39
3	15	10	25	50	10	5	-	50	55
1	7	8	2	12	2	4	1	21	26
9	8	6	42	56	12	2	-	40	42
11	9	1	60	70	14	8	2	53	63
13	5	-	59	64	16	6	-	50	56
15	13	4	53	70	4	4	-	36	40
C	5	2	64	71	D	2	2	40	44

A Utilised after the ship sank.   **B   Utilised after the ship sank.**

Totals 70   36   355   461   **Totals**   37   7   349   394
General Total:
107 men of the crew
43 men passengers
704 women and children

This shows in all 107 men of the crew, 43 male passengers, and 704 women and children, or a total of 854 in 18 boats. In addition, about 60 persons, two of whom were women, were said to have been transferred, subsequently, from A and B collapsible boats to other boats, and were rescued from the water, making a total of 914 who escaped with their lives. It is obvious that these figures are quite unreliable, for only 712 were, in fact, saved by the *Carpathia*, the steamer which came to the rescue at about 4 a.m., and all the boats were accounted for. Another remarkable discrepancy is that, of the 712 saved, 189 were, in fact, men of the crew, 129 were male passengers and 394 were women and children. In other words, the real proportion of women to men saved was much less than the proportion appearing in the evidence from the boats. Allowing for those subsequently picked up, of the 712 persons saved only 652 could have left the *Titanic* in boats, or an average of about 36 per boat. There was a tendency in the evidence to exaggerate the numbers in each boat, to exaggerate the proportion of women to men, and to diminish the number of crew. I do not attribute this to any wish on the part of the witnesses to mislead the Court, but to a natural desire to make the best case for themselves and their ship. The seamen who gave evidence were too frequently encouraged when under examination in the witness-box to understate the number of crew in the boats. The number of crew actually saved was 189, giving an average of 10 per boat; and if from this figure the 58 men of the 60 persons above mentioned be deducted the average number of crew leaving the ship in the boats must still have been at least 7. The probability, however, is that many of the 60 picked up were passengers.

The discipline both among passengers and crew during the lowering of the boats was good, but the organisation should have been better, and if it had been it is possible that more lives would have been saved.

Once again, there is a sense that more could have been done to prepare and drill the crew for an emergency situation, and that no one knew precisely what to do once the order to evacuate the ship was given. Part of this can be put down to the way events unfolded, but this does not equate to panic among the passengers or crew; merely disorganisation in terms of planning and communication.

The real difficulty in dealing with the question of the boats is to find the explanation of so many of them leaving the ship with comparatively few persons in them. No. 1 certainly left with only 12; this was an emergency boat with a carrying capacity of 40. No. 7 left with only 27, and No. 6 with only 28; these were lifeboats with a carrying capacity of 65 each; and several of the others, according to the evidence and certainly according to the truth, must have left only partly filled. Many explanations are forthcoming, one being that the passengers were unwilling to leave the ship. When the earlier boats left, and before the *Titanic* had begun materially to settle down, there was a drop of 65 feet from the Boat deck to the water, and the women feared to get into the boats. Many people thought that the risk in the ship was less than the risk in the boats. This explanation is supported by the evidence of Captain Rostron, of the *Carpathia.* He says that after those who were saved got on board his ship, he was told by some of them that when the boats first left the *Titanic* the people 'really would not be put in the boats; they did not want to go in'. There was a large body of evidence from the *Titanic* to the same effect, and I have no doubt that many people, particularly women, refused to leave the deck for the boats. At one time the Master appears to have had the intention of putting the people into the boats from the gangway doors in the side of the ship. This was possibly with a view to allay the fears of the passengers, for from these doors the water could be reached by means of ladders, and the lowering of some of the earlier boats when only partly filled may be accounted for in this way. There is no doubt that the Master did order some of the partly filled boats to row to a position under one of the doors with the object [of] taking in passengers at that point. It appears, however, that these doors were never opened. Another explanation is that some women refused to leave their husbands. It is said further that the officers engaged in putting the people into the boats feared that the boats might buckle if they were filled; but this proved to be an unfounded apprehension, for one or more boats were completely filled and then successfully lowered to the water.

At 12.35 the message from the *Carpathia* was received announcing that she was making for the *Titanic*. This probably became known and may have tended to make the passengers still more unwilling to leave the ship; and the lights of a ship (the *Californian*) which were seen by many people may have encouraged the passengers to hope that assistance was at hand. These explanations are perhaps sufficient to account for so many of the lifeboats leaving without a full boat load; but I think, nevertheless, that if the boats had been kept a little longer before being lowered, or if the after gangway doors had been opened, more passengers might have been induced to enter the boats. And if women could not be induced to enter the boats, the boats ought then to have been filled up with men. It is difficult to account for so many of the lifeboats being sent from the sinking ship, in a smooth sea, far from full. These boats left behind them many hundreds of lives to perish. I do not, however, desire these observations to be read as casting any reflection on the officers of the ship or on the crew who were working on the Boat deck. They all worked admirably, but I think that if there had been better organisation the results would have been more satisfactory.

This is a highly emotive area, both in terms of those left behind while there were clearly some empty spaces on the descending lifeboats, and of people in the water whose desperate cries for help were ignored. Yet the official verdict – once again – was that general conduct was worthy of praise.

I heard much evidence as to the conduct of the boats after the *Titanic* sank and when there must have been many struggling people in the water, and I regret to say that in my opinion some, at all events, of the boats failed to attempt to save lives when they might have done so, and might have done so successfully. This was particularly the case of boat No. 1. It may reasonably have been thought that the risk of making the attempt was too great; but it seems to me that if the attempt had been made by some of these boats it might have been the means of saving a few more lives. Subject to these few adverse comments, I have nothing but praise for both passengers and crew. All the witnesses speak well of their behaviour. It is to be remembered that the night was dark, the noise of the escaping steam was terrifying, the peril, though perhaps not generally recognised, was imminent and great, and many passengers who were unable to speak or to understand English, were being collected together and hurried into the boats.

British wreck commissioner's report

The official US report into how the ship was evacuated was similarly critical about the lack of preparation for evacuation, and why so many lifeboats were unoccupied or underutilised.

STEAMSHIP TITANIC'S LIFEBOATS CLEARED AWAY.
When Captain Smith received the reports as to the water entering the ship, he promptly gave the order to clear away the lifeboats . . . and later orders were given to put women and children into the boats. During this time distress rockets were fired at frequent intervals.

The lack of preparation was at this time most noticeable. There was no system adopted for loading the boats; there was great indecision as to the deck from which boats were to be loaded; there was wide diversity of opinion as to the number of the crew necessary to man each boat; there was no direction whatever as to the number of passengers to be carried by each boat, and no uniformity in loading them. On one side only women and children were put in the boats, while on the other side there was almost an equal proportion of men and women put into the boats, the women and children being given the preference in all cases. The failure to utilize all lifeboats to their recognized capacity for safety unquestionably resulted in the needless sacrifice of several hundred lives which might otherwise have been saved.

CAPACITY OF LIFEBOATS NOT UTILIZED.
The vessel was provided with lifeboats, as above stated, for 1,176

persons, while but 706 were saved. Only a few of the ship's lifeboats were fully loaded, while others were but partially filled. Some were loaded at the boat deck, and some at the A deck, and these were successfully lowered to the water. The twentieth boat was washed overboard when the forward part of the ship was submerged, and in its overturned condition served as a life raft for about 30 people, including Second Officer Lightoller, Wireless Operators Bride and Phillips (the latter dying before rescue), passengers Col. Gracie and Mr. Jack Thayer, and others of the crew, who climbed upon it from the water at about the time the ship disappeared.

LIFEBOAT DEVICES

Had the sea been rough it is questionable whether any of the lifeboats of the *Titanic* would have reached the water without being damaged or destroyed. The point of suspension of the *Titanic*'s boats was about 70 feet above the level of the sea. Had the ship been rolling heavily the lifeboats as they were lowered would have swung out from the side of the ship as it rolled toward them and on the return roll would have swung back and crashed against its side. It is evident from the testimony that as the list of the *Titanic* became noticeable the lifeboats scraped against the high side as they were being lowered. Every effort should be made to improve boat handling devices, and to improve the control of boats while being lowered.

CONFLICT IN LIFEBOAT REPORTS

In the reports of the survivors there are marked differences of opinion as to the number carried by each lifeboat. In No. 1, for instance, one survivor reports ten in all. The seaman in charge reports 7 crew and 14 to 20 passengers . . . The officer who loaded this boat estimated that from 3 to 5 women and 22 men were aboard . . . Accepting the minimum report as made by any one survivor in every boat, the total far exceeds the actual number picked up by the *Carpathia*.

NO DISTINCTION BETWEEN PASSENGERS

The testimony is definite that, except in isolated instances, there was no panic. In loading boats no distinction was made between first, second, and third class passengers, although the proportion of lost is larger among third class passengers than in either of the other classes. Women and children, without discrimination, were given preference.

Your committee believes that under proper discipline the survivors could have been concentrated into fewer boats after reaching the water, and we think that it would have been possible to have saved many lives had those in charge of the boats thus released returned promptly to the scene of the disaster.

CONDUCT ON LIFEBOATS

After lowering, several of the boats rowed many hours in the direction of the lights supposed to have been displayed by the *Californian*. Other boats lay on their oars in the vicinity of the sinking ship, a few survivors being rescued from the water. After distributing his passengers among the four other boats which he had herded together, and after the cries of distress had died away, Fifth Officer Lowe, in boat No. 14, went to the scene of the wreck and rescued four living passengers from the water, one of whom afterwards died in the lifeboat, but was identified. Officer Lowe then set sail in boat No. 14, took in tow one collapsible boat, and proceeded to the rescue of passengers on another collapsible lifeboat.

The men who had taken refuge on the overturned collapsible lifeboat were rescued, including Second Officer Lightoller and passengers Gracie and Thayer, and Wireless Operators Bride and Phillips, by lifeboats No. 4 and No. 12, before the arrival of the *Carpathia*. The fourth collapsible lifeboat was rowed to the side of the *Carpathia*, and contained 28 women and children, mostly third class passengers, 3 firemen, 1 steward, 4 Filipinos, President Ismay, and Mr. Carter, of Philadelphia, and was in charge of Quartermaster Rowe.

SHIP SINKING

The ship went down gradually by the bow, assuming an almost perpendicular position just before sinking at 12.47 a.m., New York time, April 15. There have been many conflicting statements as to whether the ship broke in two, but the preponderance of evidence is to the effect that she assumed an almost end-on position and sank intact.

NO SUCTION

The committee deems it of sufficient importance to call attention to the fact that as the ship disappeared under the water there was no apparent suction or unusual disturbance of the surface of the water. Testimony is abundant that while she was going down there was not sufficient suction to be manifest to any of the witnesses who were in the water or on the overturned collapsible boat or on the floating debris, or to the occupants of the lifeboats in the vicinity of the vessel, or to prevent those in the water, whether equipped with lifebelts or not, from easily swimming away from the ship's side while she was sinking.

US board of inquiry report

In relation to the treatment of third-class passengers, as alleged by various survivors, the official British report reached its own conclusions as to why proportionately fewer of them survived compared to passengers from other classes of accommodation.

Account of the Saving and Rescue of those who Survived

Third Class Passengers

It had been suggested before the Enquiry that the third class passengers had been unfairly treated; that their access to the Boat deck had been impeded, and that when at last they reached that deck the first and second class passengers were given precedence in getting places in the boats. There appears to have been no truth in these suggestions. It is no doubt true that the proportion of third class passengers saved falls far short of the proportion of the first and second class, but this is accounted for by the greater reluctance of the third class passengers to leave the ship, by their unwillingness to part with their baggage, by the difficulty in getting them up from their quarters, which were at the extreme ends of the ship, and by other similar causes. The interests of the relatives of some of the third class passengers who had perished were in the hands of Mr. Harbinson, who attended the Enquiry on their behalf. He said at the end of his address to the Court:

'I wish to say distinctly that no evidence has been given in the course of this case which would substantiate a charge that any attempt was made to keep back the third class passengers. I desire further to say that there is no evidence that when they did reach the Boat deck there was any discrimination practised either by the officers or the sailors in putting them into the boats.'

I am satisfied that the explanation of the excessive proportion of third class passengers lost is not to be found in the suggestion that the third class passengers were in any way unfairly treated. They were not unfairly treated.

Nevertheless, doubts remained. H. G. Wells, no less, was moved to comment on the plight of the third-class passengers in one of his articles in the *Daily Mail*, reported in the *Bookman* in June 1912 by E. B. French:

It was one of those accidents which happen with a precision of time and circumstance that outdoes art; not an incident in it all that was not supremely typical. It was the penetrating comment of chance upon our entire social system. Beneath a surface of magnificent efficiency was – slapdash. The ship was not even equipped to save its third-class passengers; they had placed themselves on board with an infinite confidence in the care that was to be taken of them, and most of their women and children went down with the cry of those who find themselves cheated out of life.

It was not just a general impression that third-class passengers had been let down during the rescue operation. The commissioner of the British inquiry made it quite clear that specific allegations relating to actions by passengers or crew against third-class passengers during the struggle for survival both on board the *Titanic* and thereafter in the icy waters had been made by at least two individuals. But he then decreed that these specific instances were outside the jurisdiction of his court.

The Commissioner: Now what are the issues which have been mentioned as being issues between those two gentlemen and the crew?

Mr. J. P. Farrell, M.P.: They are of the very gravest kind. Thomas McCormack alleges that when swimming in the sea he endeavoured to board two boats and was struck on the head and the hands and shoved back into the sea, and endeavoured to be drowned. That is one charge.

The Commissioner: That gentleman who did it may be guilty of manslaughter for aught I know.

Mr. J. P. Farrell, M.P.: McCormack was not drowned, my Lord.

The Commissioner: Very well, then he may be guilty of an attempt to commit manslaughter, but I cannot try that.

Mr. J. P. Farrell, M.P.: Is it not a question for investigation by this Court?

The Commissioner: I do not think so.

Mr. J. P. Farrell, M.P.: There is another charge we have about a man named McCoy.

The Commissioner: That I do not think comes within my jurisdiction at all. If any crime has been committed by some individual in connection with this unfortunate matter that has to be tried by somebody else.

Mr. J. P. Farrell, M.P.: But, my Lord, we also appear for others. We have gone to a great deal of expense.

The Commissioner: Now you know, Mr. Farrell, if you will confine yourself to what I think is possibly a legitimate position on your part, there will be no difficulty about it.

Mr. J. P. Farrell, M.P.: I will accept any suggestion with great pleasure.

The Commissioner: You want to represent, as I understand, not the representatives of two but the representatives of a great number of the passengers on board this vessel.

Mr. J. P. Farrell, M.P.: Quite so, my Lord.

The Commissioner: Third class passengers?

Mr. J. P. Farrell, M.P.: Quite so, my Lord.

The Commissioner: I can quite conceive that there may be circumstances in connection with this catastrophe which affected third class passengers and perhaps did not affect the first class and the second class, and if you or your brother, the solicitor, will take up that position and bring before me any matters that particularly affect the third class passengers I shall be very glad to be assisted by the evidence that he is able to put before me.

Mr. J. P. Farrell, M.P.: I am obliged to your Lordship.

The Commissioner: But do not turn me into a criminal judge to try charges of attempted manslaughter.

British wreck commission board of inquiry day 4

Despite being a first-class passenger, Karl Behr also fought on behalf the third-class passengers who had lost everything in the disaster, as a member of the Titanic Survivors' Committee (formed on board the *Carpathia*). In particular, he was critical of Ismay, recalling the incident at the lifeboat as evidence that he carried authority on the ship as its owner.

Some months later, at the instigation of our Titanic Survivors' Committee, suit was commenced against the White Star Line on behalf of the steerage passengers. Our case was based mainly on the contention that the *Titanic* had taken unwarranted risks in ice filled waters by refraining from slowing down; that this was due to the desire of the White Star Line that this new ship should demonstrate on its maiden voyage its great speed. The defense of course, was based upon the collision being an unavoidable accident and not due to negligence.

The case, finally tried in the United States District Court in New York, hinged to a considerable extent, on the presence on board the *Titanic* of Mr. Ismay. We contended that in effect he was the owner on board, and could have instructed the Captain to slow his ship. The defense contended he was on board solely in the capacity of a passenger. My testimony at the trial, outlining as already described, his launching of our life boats and the acceptance by the ship's officers present did much to prove that he was recognised as having authority.

The result of this litigation was the recovery of substantial damages for loss of life and baggage by the steerage passengers.

National Maritime Museum LMQ/7/1/5

Of the 2,207 souls on board the *Titanic* when it struck the iceberg, fewer than one-third – 706 – were rescued from the open ocean. Yet alongside the relief of the survivors came hope that loved ones might also be among the saved. The pain of realising that friends and family were not among the lucky ones taken on board the *Carpathia* is succinctly described by Mrs Charlotte Collyer. She had left her husband on board the ship but clung to the possibility that he had found a place in the lifeboats.

There was scarcely anyone who had not been separated from husband, child or friend. Was the last one among the handful saved? We could only rush frantically from group to group, searching the haggard faces, crying out names, and endless questions. No survivor knows better than I the bitter cruelty of disappointment and despair. I had a husband to search for, a husband whom in the greatness of my faith, I had believed would be found in one of the boats. He was not there.

Donald Hyslop, Alastair Forsythe and Sheila Jemima, *Titanic Voices: Memories from the Fateful Voyage* (Southampton: Sutton Publishing Ltd, 1997)

Part Three

The Aftermath of
the Tragedy

6

The Immediate Aftermath

Looking down over the rail we distinctly saw a number of bodies so clearly that we could make out what they were wearing, and whether they were men or women. We saw one woman in her nightdress with a baby clasped closely to her breast. Several of the women passengers screamed, and left the rail in a fainting condition.

The *Titanic* sank in the early hours of 15 April, and the *Carpathia* took the survivors to New York. It docked three days later on 18 April, and the survivors limped ashore to face an uncertain future. The British wreck commissioner's official report provided a breakdown of who was saved, according to the class of passenger and crew.

Numbers Saved

The following were the numbers saved:

1st Class

Adult males	57	out of	175	or	32.57	percent.
Adult females	140	out of	144	or	97.22	percent.
Male Children	5	All Saved				
Female Children	1	All Saved				
Total	203	out of	325	or	62.46	percent.

2nd Class

Adult males	14	out of	168	or	8.33	percent.
Adult females	80	out of	93	or	86.02	percent.

Male Children	11	All Saved				
Female Children	13	All Saved				
Total	118	out of	285	or	41.40	percent.

3rd Class

Adult males	75	out of	462	or	16.23	percent.
Adult females	76	out of	165	or	46.06	percent.
Male Children	13	out of	48	or	27.08	percent.
Female Children	14	out of	31	or	45.16	percent.
Total	178	out of	706	or	25.21	percent.

Crew Saved

Deck	43	out of	66	or	65.15	percent.
Engine Department Room Department						
Victualling Department	72	out of	325	or	22.15	percent.
(including 20 women out of 23)	97	out of	494	or	19.63	percent.

Total 212 out of 885, or 23.95 percent.

Total on board saved 711 out of 2,201, or 32.30 percent.

Passengers and Crew

Adult males	338	out of	1,167	or	20.27	percent.
Adult females	316	out of	425	or	74.35	percent.
Children	57	out of	109	or	52.29	percent.

Total 711 out of 2,201, or 32.30 percent.

British wreck commissioner's final report

By 18 April, the news had already reverberated around a stunned world, with confused reports of the names of survivors being broadcast from the moment people were brought on board the *Carpathia,* the ship's radios being used to spread information – often erroneous – concerning who had been rescued. Consequently, people were frantic with worry, and by the time the *Carpathia* docked, thousands of people were waiting to greet her.

The sense of shock in New York, when the news broke on the evening of 15 April, had been widespread. Alexander Macomb wrote to his mother the following day, recording his observations on what had happened. The offices of the White Star Line were the focus of activity, as people flocked there in search of updates on casualty lists and news of survivors.

U.S.S. Florida
Tompkinsville
New York
April 16, 1912

Dear Mother,
The terrible news of the sinking of the Titanic *reached New York at about eleven o'clock last night and the scene on Broadway was awful. Crowds of people were coming out of the theatres, cafés were going full tilt, and autos whizzing everywhere, when the newsboys began to cry 'Extra! Extra Paper!* Titanic *sunk with 1,800 on board!' You can't imagine the effect of those words on the crowd. Nobody could realize what had happened, and when they did begin to understand, the excitement was almost enough to cause a panic in the theatres. Women began to faint and weep, and scores of people in evening clothes jumped in cabs and taxis and rushed to the offices of the White Star Line, where they remained all night waiting for news. The scene in front of the steamship office was a tragedy in itself. As the list of those known to have been saved was printed on a large bulletin board, you could hear cries of joy and relief from various parts of the throng, massed in front of the office. When they started the list of those who had not been heard of cries of 'Oh! Oh, God!' could be heard everywhere, and the hysterical women seemed to fill the whole city with their screams. I have never seen anything so heart-rending in my life. Of course, you have read all about the disaster*

in the Boston papers, so I won't describe it, but the latest news here is that at least 1200 persons were drowned, and about 900 saved. The survivors are coming to this city on the Carpathia *which will arrive Thursday night, and you can imagine the scene when the vessel gets in. I wouldn't miss it for anything. It seems certain that Mr. Astor was drowned, as a wireless message reports his body picked up, but young Mrs. Astor was rescued and is on the* Carpathia. *It is rumoured that she expects an addition to the family. Isn't that sad? Vincent Astor offered any sum to the steamship company if they would give him news of his father, but nothing definite could be learned. The most appalling thing about the accident is the fact, that after all the* Titanic*'s boats were filled with passengers, there were still 1,200 people left on the ship with no means of escape, except life preservers which could not have kept them alive in that ice water for more than a few hours! In other words, the vessel didn't have half enough life boats. . . Well, I can't write about this forever. . . We leave for the Navy yard early to-morrow morning. Good-night,*

  Your affectionate Alex

        National Maritime Museum ref. LMQ/7/2/1

Almost at once the grim task of recovering bodies began, and the White Star Line chartered the Commercial Cable Company's vessel *Mackay Bennett* for the mission. On board was Frederick Hamilton, a cable engineer. He kept a diary of the proceedings, which lasted the best part of a fortnight. In total, 333 bodies were recovered during this operation.

April 17th 1912, Halifax:
At 6.50pm. Having taken in a supply of ice and a large number of coffins, cast off from the wharf en route for the position of the *Titanic* disaster. The Rev. Canon Hind of All Saints Cathedral, Halifax, accompanying the expedition. An expert embalmer also on board. Cold and clear weather prevailed until the 19th when rain began, followed by fog . . .

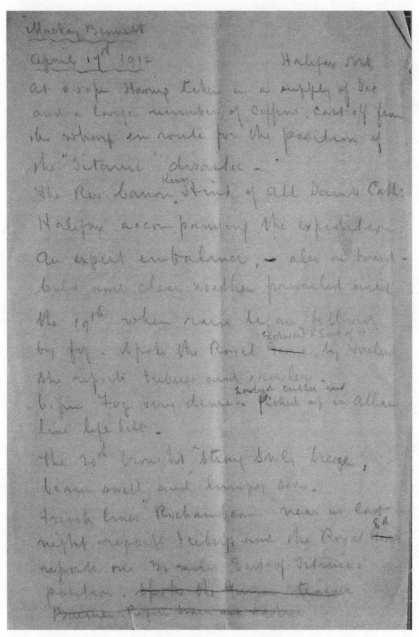

Diary of Frederick A. Hamilton, cable engineer of the recovery ship *Mackay Bennett*. Page 233 shows his sketch of boats searching for bodies.

April 20th 1912
The *Rhine* passed us in the afternoon bound west and reports
having seen bodies and wreckage. Later, about 6pm the *Bremen*
steamed past us pointing west. She also reports having sighted
an hour and a half ago wreckage and bodies. At 7pm a large
iceberg seen, faintly discernible to the north. We are now nearing
the area where the bodies were seen. Temperature of the sea at
noon was 56°. At 4pm it was found to be 32°.

April 21st:
Began picking up bodies. . . The ocean is strewn with a litter of
woodwork, chairs and bodies. . . Cutter working continuously
picking up bodies – total 51 (2 children, 3 women, 46 men). . . At
8pm the tolling of the bell summoned all hands to the forecastle
where the funeral service was conducted by the Rev. Canon Hind.
30 bodies (men) were committed to the deep. The remains were
each weighted and carefully sewn up in canvas. It was a weird scene
that gathering on the forecastle – the crescent moon shedding a
faint light on us as the ship lay wallowing in the great rollers. For
nearly an hour the words 'For as much as it hath pleased almighty
God to take unto himself the soul of our dear brother here departed
we therefore commit his body to the deep' were repeated and at
each interval came <u>splash</u> as the weighted body plunged into the
sea there to sink to a depth of about two miles.

On the 22nd we steamed close past the iceberg near which the
bodies were recovered. An endeavour was made to photograph
this arctic Cathedral but as rain was falling it is feared that the
result will not be satisfactory. Some sketches will however give a
good idea of the general features of the berg. The ship is standing
eastwards. Lowered cutter and examined a lifeboat. Found it
smashed. No name visible. Steamed through a great quantity of
wreckage, splintered woodwork, cabin fittings, mahogany parts
of drawers, carvings, all wrenched away from their fastenings,
deck chairs, and then bodies, the latter at a distance of some

fifteen miles from where
those picked up on the 21st
were found . . . At 8pm
another burial service

April 23rd:
. . . Both cutters busy all day
recovering bodies. . . At 7pm
the Allen liner *Scandinavian*
stopped near us and took
despatches from our cutter,
the fog had lifted slightly but
shut down denser than ever
soon after she signalled 'Good
night' on her flash light . . .

On the 24th . . . at noon
another burial service was held
and seventy-seven bodies followed the others. The hoarse tone of
the steam whistle reverberating through the fog, the dripping rigging,
the ghostly sea, the heaps of dead and the hard weather beaten
faces of the crew, some of whom with more or less raspy voices
sympathisingly [*sic*] joined in the Hymn, tunefully rendered by
Canon Hind 'Jesus Lover of my Soul', whilst all hands balanced
themselves against the heavy rolling of the ship as she lurched over
to the great Atlantic swell. Cold, wet, miserable and comfortless,
but what of these! Think of the far reaching wide-spread sorrow
and distress, the hopes, dread, fears, the dismay and the despair of
those whose nearest and dearest, support and comfort, pride and
hope, have been wrenched from them in this great disaster . . .

On the morning of the 26th the *Minea* joined in the work of
recovery some two to three miles to the westward of us. Her final
find we hear was the body of Mr. C. M. Hayes, President of the
Grand Trunk. At noon we steamed up to the *Minea*, sent the

cutter to her for some material, and soon afterwards set course towards Halifax. The total number of bodies picked up by the MB was 305, of which 116 were buried at sea. A large amount of money and jewels was recovered and the identification of most of the bodies established . . .

This has been an arduous undertaking for all who have had to recover, overhaul and attend to the bodies. The operation of lifting the heavy clothes & soaked remains with the cutter was not an easy task. The searching, numbering and where possible identifying each body, depositing the property found thereon in a bag marked with the number corresponding to that attached to the remains, sewing up in canvas and securing weights to those set apart for burial, entailed prolonged and patient labour. The embalmer was the only man to whom the work was pleasant, one might add without undue exaggeration – enjoyable – with him it was a labour of love, and his laudable pride in developing the subject under his skilful hands suggested the ardent photographer 'bringing up' his plate or film to the right tone . . .

Tuesday April 30th
8.25am took Pilot on board off Devil's Island and proceeded up Halifax harbour. Crowds of people thronged the wharves, tops of homes and ends of streets. Flags on ships and buildings all half-masted. Quarantine and other officials came on board near George's Island, after which ship stood in to the Navy yard and hauled in alongside. Elaborate arrangements made for the reception of the remains now ready for landing. 10am began transferring bodies to shore. A continuous procession of hearses conveyed the bodies to the Mayflower Rink.

Transcribed from pencil notes possibly in Hamilton's hand,
National Maritime Museum, ref. JOD/221/1, 2

Reports of human remains, scattered across the sea alongside floating wreckage from the ship continued to be made by ships sailing through the area for days after the tragedy. This newspaper account recalls sightings made by the steamship *Bremen* on 20 April.

FROM OUR OWN CORRESPONDENT.

NEW YORK, WEDNESDAY

More than 100 of the *Titanic's* victims were seen floating on the water by the steamship *Bremen*, which arrived today from Bremen, when, on April 20, the German liner passed over the spot where the *Titanic* went down.

Mrs. Johanna Stunke, a first-class cabin passenger on the *Bremen*, gave a vivid story of the scene from the liner's rail.

'It was between four and five o'clock on Saturday,' she said, 'when our ship sighted off the bow to the starboard an iceberg. We had been told by some of the officers that the *Bremen* was going to pass within a few miles of the position given by the *Titanic* when she sank, so when the cry went up that ice was sighted we all rushed to the starboard rail. It was a beautiful afternoon, and the sun glistening on the big iceberg was a wonderful picture, but as we drew nearer and could make out small dots floating around in the sea a feeling of awe and sadness crept over everyone, and the ship proceeded in absolute silence. We passed within a hundred feet of the southernmost drift of the wreckage, and looking down over the rail we distinctly saw a number of bodies so clearly that we could make out what they were wearing, and whether they were men or women.

'We saw one woman in her nightdress with a baby clasped closely to her breast. Several of the women passengers screamed, and left the rail in a fainting condition.

'There was another woman, fully dressed, with her arms tight around the body of a shaggy dog that looked like a St. Bernard. The bodies of three men in a group, all clinging to one steamer chair floated close by, and just beyond them were a dozen bodies of men, all in life-preservers, clinging together as though in the last desperate struggle for life. Those were the only bodies we passed near enough to distinguish, but we could see the white life-preservers of many more dotting the sea all the way to the iceberg.

'The officers told us that was probably the berg hit by the *Titanic,* and that the bodies and ice had drifted along together, but only a few miles south of their original position where the collision occurred. The scene moved everyone on board to the point of tears, even the officers making no secret of their emotion.'

Donald Hyslop, Alastair Forsythe and Sheila Jemima,
Titanic Voices: Memories from the Fateful Voyage (Southampton: Sutton Publishing Ltd, 1997)

Given that so many bodies werer recovered, it is not surprising that relatives were desperate to find out what had happened to their loved ones, often seeking the smallest piece of information.

14.5.12

5 Duke St.
Richmond

Sir

I am writing to you in reference to my dear brother Arthur Hayter who was a steward on the ill fated Titanic & was among the drowned. I heard from his wife that he had you to look after during the voyage & I thought perhaps you might be able to let us know if you saw anything of him at the last, on that fatal night. It would be a little consolation to us, his broken-hearted brothers & sisters, & to his aged parents who are 82 & 84 respectively. He was such a good brother & son. Excuse me taking the liberty of writing to you, & thanking you, Sir, for a reply.

I remain
Yours sincerely.
Louise Hayter

To: B. Ismay Esqr.
Chairman of White Star Cpy.

National Maritime Museum, ref. TRNISM/1/1

The tragedy left many families destitute, and the Titanic Disaster Relief Fund was immediately established through public subscription, with a corresponding American fund providing immediate aid to those left in their intended new homeland with all their worldly possessions at the bottom of the Atlantic – often widows with young children to support. The relatives of those who were lost at sea in the employ of White Star sought financial aid from the company, including Anne Harrison, widow of William Henry Harrison, Ismay's secretary who went down with the ship (his body was later recovered by the *Mackay Bennett*).

2 St. George's Road
Freshfield

May 11th, 1912

Dear Mr. Ismay,
Thank you very much for your kind letter, we are heart broken but asking God to give us strength to bear our trouble. My husband was such a loving man and Father. I have a little boy 13 nearly overcome with grief he has gone to a new school a Mr. Taylor's in Freshfield, he has promised to look after him, and to try to comfort him. We have taken a small house here for a year, our old home was too painful to stay in. How my husband loved his work at the office, and you for your kindness to him – he was so proud of his position as Private help to you.

I hope you will be able to do something for us, we should love to keep our home, so that we can keep together although very lonely. My daughter is not a strong girl, and not able to do much. Forgive me writing you like this, but it is my next trouble how we are going to live. My husband was insured for £500 but no Will so I get a 3rd only.

I do hope you have got over your very terrible time. Again thanking you for your kind letter
I am Yours sincerely
A. Harrison

An even more moving letter was penned by William Henry Harrison's son, William junior, revealing the extent of the grief the family felt at the loss of the principal breadwinner. The letter is particularly poignant given they had just been in receipt of the possessions William senior had on him when he died.

2 St. George's Rd
Formby

May 22nd, 1912

Dear Mr. Ismay,

I am writing to ask you if Mother and I, may come to see you some time this week or next. We called to-day but you were engaged.

Poor Mother is broken-hearted, indeed so are we all, we loved him so much. He was so good and kind.

Do forgive my asking you, but do be kind to Mother please. I myself don't mind working for my living if I can. Although my Father sheltered me so, and kept me at home doing nothing. But now he is gone it is my place to look after Mother and my little brother as best I can.

On Saturday we had sent to us the things found on Pa, what a sad little package it was too. A bunch of rusty keys, the little silver knife you gave to him, a little Diary of your engagements, a pocket-book of his own, and some money, a little gold stud. So we think he must have been in evening dress.

We are quite settled now in our new little home, I do so hope we shall be able to keep together.

Again asking you for your kindness and forgiveness in writing as I have,
I am Yours truly,
Willie Harrison

William wrote back thanking Ismay for the financial assistance he had arranged for the family shortly afterwards.

2 St. George's Rd.
Formby

May 30th, 1912

Dear Mr. Ismay,
I can't really tell you how truly thankful we are to you, for your great
kindness to us. You will never know how grateful we are, because we
can never tell you. Although our sorrow is still as big, we are so
relieved to know that we can live comfortably all together. Poor
Mother is quite bright to-night, and looks more like herself. Tommy
was so pleased with his things, and became quite excited, when we
told him, from whom they came.
   Again thanking you very very much
   I remain yours,
   Very Sincerely,
   William Harrison

National Maritime Museum, ref TRNISM/3/1

The White Star Line had the task of informing the next of kin of their
employees that they had died. The family of George Arthur Beedum,
steward on the *Titanic* who had written to them only days before the
ship sank, received this letter.

White Star Line
Trafalgar Chambers
Southampton
May 2nd 1912

Madam,
We regret to inform you that G. A. Beedem [sic] 'Steward' has not
been cabled to us amongst the list of survivors.

   Yours truly,
   John Bartholomew,
   Victualling Superintendent

   Condolences continued to be sent to the bereaved family.

Manchester
Thursday

My dear Mrs. Beedham [sic],
I want to send you my word of sympathy in this your dark hour of saviour & suffering. In this trying time it is impossible to do more than endeavour to share one another's sorrows, 'the heart knoweth its own bitterness.'
    I will say little, but assure you of my prayerful sorrow for you in your bereavement & loss – perhaps the silent sympathy is the best.
    May He who alone can comfort the needy comfort <u>you</u> & may He minister to your heart's sorrow in the passing hours.
    I am glad Mrs. Dickinson called to see you. My wife will call and I return on Saturday. If I can be of any service please command me. Meanwhile I would assure you of our prayers on your behalf.
    Believe me
    Yours very truly,
    Frank Vaughan

Paperwork was required to obtain financial assistance.

White Star Line
Trafalgar Chambers
Southampton
May 4th 1912

Mrs. Beedum
185, Victoria Road,
Southsea.

Dear Mrs. Beedum,
I shall be obliged if you will fill me in the attached form respecting compensation as soon as possible and return to me, when I will have it passed to our Solicitors.
    Yours faithfully,
    Geo. Bartholomew
    Victualling Superintendent

Yet the sums involved were not great, and in the meantime people such as Mrs Beedum were directed to apply for charitable donations.

May 20th '12

Dear Mrs. Beedem [sic],
My husband has asked me to send you a line to ask if you will send him a receipt for the £5 as you did before – there is no hurry about it – but just so that we keep his a/c of this very straight.
We hope you have applied to the Daily Telegraph Fund & that you will hear from them.
My husband asked Mr. Hardy about your dear one & he said he was on the deck helping the women & children when he last saw him. If we ever hear any information, we will let you know at once. I hope your little boy is better. We have so often thought of you in your great trouble,
With kindest regards,
Yours sincerely,
J. Bartholomew

National Maritime Museum, ref. LMQ/7/3/B

Media attention settled on Ismay as soon as he set foot in America, and in particular focused on his role in the accident – not just whether he had encouraged or ordered Captain Smith to sail faster through the ice field, but the fact that he had found space in a lifeboat while women and children had perished. His wife, though, was simply relieved to hear that he was alive:

Sandheys,
Mossley Hill,
Liverpool

My darling Bruce,
It seems an eternity since last Monday night when I first heard that the Titanic *had met with an accident. We reached Fishguard about*

6.30 & there got telegrams from the Officer & from Margaret saying that there was a report that the ship had struck an iceberg, but no lives lost, & that she was proceeding with 2 other liners to Halifax. Of course I was full of sorrow at the thought of the splendid vessel but felt no real anxiety until the next wire about 10.30. That was followed by another at 3.30 which made me terrified for your safety. Words fail to describe the horror and anxiety of the hours that followed. It seemed an eternity. Oh darling what that time must have been to you. When I think of the anguish you must have been through it makes me tremble even now. Thank God. Thank God that you have been spared to us. My life would have been over if you had not been saved. For me there never has been & never could be any man but you & I feel I can never express the gratitude & thankfulness that fills me for your escape. Only a week ago today that I watched that magnificent vessel sail away so proudly. I never dreamt of danger as I wished her God speed. I have wished many times since Monday night that I had gone with you, I might have helped you in this awful hour. I know so well what bitterness of spirit you must be feeling for the loss of so many precious lives & the ship itself that you loved like a living thing. It must have been ordained by Providence as every precaution human skill & care could devise had been done. We have both been spared to each other, let us try to make our lives of use in the world. My dearest if I have you I feel no trouble or sorrow can be unbearable, & that these last 48 hours that we can never forget may yet in some unknown way be turned into good. I intend sailing on the Caronia *on Saturday to come back with you if you will be long enough on shore to make this possible. I am sending a few things by the* Adriatic *as I am sure you will like your own clothing better than anything you can get in New York.*

In spite of all the horrors of the tragedy it makes one feel very proud of their fellow creatures when one thinks how heroic they can be in the face of an awful death. The children were nearly distracted when they feared that you might not have been spared to us. Take care of yourself for all our sakes my dear one. I would sail on the Adriatic *tomorrow only Mr. Sanderson advises me to wait and hear what you are going to do, as I don't want to run any chance of passing you on the ocean. Lottie & Margaret & Tom all came to me at once, and are here now. We are hoping so earnestly that Mr. Harrison, Fry and Dodd are among the saved. Margaret has been twice to see Mrs. Fry today & says she is wonderfully brave & composed.*

Jimmy has been very ill with pneumonia, 2 Nurses & Mr. Rich staying at Iwerne, & yesterday Bower was sent for; but today he has taken a turn for the better. Of course he knows nothing of the disaster to the Titanic.

God Bless you my darling & may we be together very soon. All my love goes with this.

Always yours,
Florence
April 17th
Liverpool

The issue of Ismay's presence in the lifeboat arose during the US inquiry into the disaster when crew member George Rowe provided testimony about what he had seen.

Senator Burton: Now, tell us the circumstances under which Mr Ismay and that other gentleman got into the boat.
Mr Rowe: When Chief Officer Wilde asked if there were any more women and children, there was no reply, so Mr Ismay came into the boat.
Senator Burton: Mr Wilde asked if there were any more women and children? Can you say that there were none?
Mr Rowe: I could not see. but there were none forthcoming.
Senator Burton: You could see around there on the deck, could you not?
Mr Rowe: I could see the fireman and steward that completed the boat's crew, but as regards any families I could not see any.
Senator Burton: Were there any men passengers besides Mr Ismay and the other man?

Mr Rowe: I did not see any, sir.

Senator Burton: Was it light enough so that you could see anyone near by?

Mr Rowe: Yes, sir.

Senator Burton: Did you hear anyone ask Mr Ismay and Mr Carter to get in the boat?

Mr Rowe: No, sir.

Senator Burton: if Chief Officer Wilde had spoken to them would you have known it?

Mr Rowe: I think so, because they got in the after part of the boat where I was.

US Senate inquiry, p. 519

Further information was given by Second Officer Lightoller, who was convinced that Ismay was genuinely distressed by the fact that he had survived while women and children had remained on board the sinking ship.

> I may say that at that time Mr. Ismay did not seem to me to be in a mental condition to finally decide anything. I tried my utmost to rouse Mr. Ismay, for he was obsessed with the idea, and kept repeating, that he ought to have gone down with the ship because he found that women had gone down. I told him there was no such reason; I told him a very great deal; I tried to get that idea out of his head, but he was taken with it; and I know the doctor tried, too; but we had difficulty in arousing Mr. Ismay, purely owing to that wholly and solely, that women had gone down in the boat and he had not.

Ismay issued a statement to the press once he arrived in New York, having been made aware of the US government's intention to hold an immediate inquiry into the causes of the accident and receiving a summons to attend – little knowing that his personal conduct would be part of the focus of the inquiry. In this statement, he clearly stated that he had been on board as a passenger only, and gave no command for Captain Smith to speed through the ice field.

Copy of statement made to press and on landing from *Carpathia*.

The following statement was issued by Mr J. Bruce Ismay today.

When I appeared before the Senate Committee Friday morning I assumed the purpose of the enquiry was to ascertain the cause of the sinking of the *Titanic* with a view to determining whether additional legislation was required to prevent the recurrence of so horrible a disaster.

I welcomed such an enquiry and appeared voluntarily, without subpoena, and answered all questions put to me by the members of the Committee to the best of my ability, with complete frankness and without reserve. I did not suppose the question of my personal conduct was the subject of the enquiry, although I was ready to tell everything I did on the night of the collision.

As I have been subpoenaed to attend before the Committee in Washington tomorrow, I should prefer to make no public statement out of respect for the Committee, but I do not think that courtesy requires me to be silent in the face of the untrue statements made in some of the newspapers.

When I went on board the *Titanic* at Southampton on April 10th, it was my intention to return on her. I had no intention of remaining in the United States at that time. I came merely to observe the new vessel, as I had done in the case of other vessels of our lines.

During the voyage I was a passenger and exercised no greater rights or privileges than any other passenger. I was not consulted by the commander about the ship, her course, speed, navigation, or her conduct at sea. All these matters were under the exclusive control of the Captain. I saw Captain Smith only occasionally, as other passengers did; I was never in his room; I was never on the bridge until after the accident; I did not sit at his table in the saloon;

I had not visited the engine room nor gone through the ship, and did not go, or attempt to go, to any part of the ship to which any other First Class passenger did not have access.

It is absolutely and unqualifiedly false that I ever said that I wished that the *Titanic* should make a speed record or should increase her daily runs. I deny absolutely having said to any person that we would increase our speed in order to get out of the ice zone, or any words to that effect.

As I have already testified, at no time did the *Titanic*, during the voyage, attain her full speed. It was not expected that she would reach New York before Wednesday morning. If she had been pressed she could probably have arrived Tuesday evening.

The statement that the White Star Line would receive an additional sum by way of bounty, or otherwise, for attaining a certain speed, is absolutely untrue. The White Star Line receives from the British Government a fixed compensation of £70,000 per annum for carrying mails, without regard to the speed of any of its vessels, and no additional sum is paid on account of any increase in speed.

I was never consulted by the Captain or any other person nor did I ever make any suggestions whatever to any human being about the course of the ship. The *Titanic*, as I am informed, was on the southernmost westward track of trans-Atlantic steamships. The tracks, or lanes, were designated many years ago by agreement of all the important steamship lines, and all Captains of the White Star Line are required to navigate their vessels as closely as possible on these tracks, subject to the following standing instructions:

'Commanders must distinctly understand that the issue of these Regulations does not in any way relieve them from responsibility for the safe and efficient navigation of their respective vessels, and they are also enjoined to remember that they must run no risk which might by any possibility result in accident to their ships. It is to be hoped that they will ever bear in mind that the safety of the lives and property entrusted to their care is the ruling principle that should govern them in the navigation of their vessels, and that no supposed gain in expedition or saving of time on the voyage is to be purchased at the risk of accident. The Company desires to maintain for its vessels a reputation for safety, and only looks for such speed on the various voyages as is consistent with safe and prudent navigation.

'Commanders are reminded that the steamers are to a great extent uninsured, and that their own livelihood, as well as the Company's success, depends on immunity from accident; no precaution which insures safe navigation is to be considered excessive.'

The only information I received on the ship that other vessels had sighted ice was by a wireless message received from the *Baltic*, which I have already testified to. This was handed to me by Captain Smith without any remark as he was passing me on the passenger deck on the afternoon of Sunday, April 14th. I read the telegram casually and put it in my pocket. At about 10 minutes past seven, while I was sitting in the Smoke Room, Captain Smith came in and asked me to give him the message received from the *Baltic* in order to post it for the information of the Officers. I handed it to him and nothing further was said by either of us. I did not speak to any of the other officers on the subject.

If the information I received had aroused any apprehension in my mind – which it did not – I should not have ventured to make any suggestion to a commander of Captain Smith's experience. The responsibility for the navigation of the ship rested solely with him.

It has been stated that Captain Smith and I were having a dinner party in one of the salons from 7.30 to 10.30 Sunday night and that at the time of the collision Captain Smith was sitting with me in the saloon.

Both of these statements are absolutely false. I did not dine with the Captain nor did I see him during the evening of April 14th. The Doctor dined with me in the Restaurant at 7.30, and I went direct to my stateroom and went to bed at about 10.30. I was asleep when the collision occurred. I felt a jar, went out into the passageway without dressing, met a steward, asked him what was the matter and [he] said he did not know. I returned to my room. I felt the ship slow down, put on an overcoat over my pyjamas and went up on the bridge deck and on the bridge. I asked Captain Smith what was the matter and he said we had struck ice. I asked him whether he thought it serious and he said he did. On returning to my room, I met the Chief Engineer and asked him whether he thought the damage serious and he said he thought it was.

I then returned to my room and put on a suit of clothes. I had been in my overcoat and pyjamas up to this time. I then went back to the boat deck and heard Captain Smith give the order to clear the boats. I helped in this work for nearly two hours as far as I can judge. I worked at the starboard boats helping women and children into the boats and lowering them over the side. I did nothing with regard to the boats on the port side. By that time every wooden life boat on the starboard side had been lowered away and I found that they were engaged in getting out the forward collapsible boat on the starboard side. I assisted in this work and all the women that were on this deck were helped into the boat. They were all, I think, Third-Class passengers. As the boat was going over the side, Mr. Carter, a passenger, and myself got into it.

At that time there was not a woman on the boat deck, nor any passengers of any class, so far as we could see or hear. The boat had between 35 and 40 in it, I should think, most of them women. There were perhaps four or five men, and it was afterwards discovered that there were four Chinamen concealed under the thwarts in the bottom of the boat. The distance that the boat had to be lowered into the water was, I should estimate, about 20 feet. Mr. Carter and I did not get into the boat until after they had begun to lower it away. When the boat reached the water I helped to row it, pushing the oar from me as I sat. This is the explanation of the fact that my back was to the sinking steamer. The boat would have accommodated certainly six or more passengers in addition if there had been any on the boat deck to go. These facts can be substantiated by Mr. E. E. Carter, of Philadelphia, who got in at the time that I did and was rowing the boat with me. I hope I need not say that neither Mr. Carter nor myself would for one moment have thought of getting into the boat if there had been any women there to go in it, nor should I have done so if I had thought that by remaining on the ship I could have been of the slightest further assistance.

It is impossible for me to answer every false statement, rumour or invention that has appeared in the newspapers. I am prepared to answer any questions that may be asked by the Committee of the Senate, or any other responsible person. I shall, therefore, make no further statement of this kind, except to explain the messages that I sent from the *Carpathia*. These messages have been completely misunderstood. An inference has been drawn from them that I was anxious to avoid the Senate Committee's inquiry, which it was intended to hold in New York. As a matter of fact when dispatching these messages I had not the slightest idea that any inquiry was contemplated and I had no information regarding it until the arrival of the *Carpathia* at the Cunard dock in New York on Thursday night, when I was informed by Senators Smith and Newlands of the appointment of the Special Committee to hold the inquiry. The only purpose I had in sending these messages was to express my desire to have the crew returned to their homes in England for their own benefit at the earliest possible moment, and I also was naturally anxious to return to my family, but left the matter of my return entirely to our representatives in New York.

I deeply regret that I am compelled to make my personal statement when my whole thought is on the horror of the disaster. In building the *Titanic* it was the hope of my associates and myself that we had built a vessel which could not be destroyed by the perils of the sea or the dangers of navigation. The event has proved the futility of that hope. The present legal requirements have proved inadequate. They must be changed; but whether they are changed or not this awful experience has taught the steamship owners of the world that too much reliance has been placed on water-tight compartments and on wireless telegraphy, and that they must equip every vessel with life boats and rafts sufficient to provide for every soul on board, and sufficient men to handle them.

Apl. 21, 1912.

National Maritime Museum TRNISM/1/1

However, the US authorities were reluctant to permit Ismay to return to Britain, and insisted he stayed until their inquiry was complete:

Washington, D.C., April 25, 1912
Mr. J. BRUCE ISMAY
Willard Hotel, Washington, D.C.
Sir: Replying to your letter of this date, just received, permit me to say that I am not unmindful of the fact that you are being detained in this country against your will, and, probably, at no little inconvenience to yourself and your family. I can readily see that your absence from England at a time so momentous in the affairs of your company would be most embarrassing, but the horror of the Titanic *catastrophe and its importance to the people of the world call for scrupulous investigation into the causes leading up to the disaster, that future losses of similar character may, if possible, be avoided. To that end, we have been charged by the Senate of the United States with the duty of making this official enquiry, and, so far as I am concerned, nothing will be left undone which may in any matter contribute to this end. As I said to you in New York on Friday evening last, when you asked to be permitted to return home, and again on Saturday night, when you made the same request, I shall not consent to your leaving this country until the fullest enquiry has been made into the circumstances surrounding the accident. This information can be fully detailed by yourself and other officers of your country and the officers and crew of your ship. I am working night and day to achieve this result, and you should continue to help me instead of annoying me and delaying my work by your personal importunities.*

> *Trusting that you will receive this letter in the spirit in which it
> is written, I am,*
> *Very respectfully,*
> WM. ALDEN SMITH,
> *Chairman Senate Subcommittee Investigating Titanic Disaster*
> National Maritime Museum LMQ/7/2/22

H. G. Wells was among the many unconvinced by Ismay's protestations.
He wrote a damning article in the *Daily Mail*, later published in the
Bookman in June 1912, contrasting Ismay's actions with those of the unher-
alded stewards and crew who either perished on board or risked life and
limb to rescue passengers while Ismay found sanctuary in a lifeboat.

> In the unfolding record of behaviour it is the stewardesses and
> bandsmen and engineers – persons of the trade union class – who
> shine as brightly as any. And by the supreme artistry of Chance it
> fell to the lot of that tragic and unhappy gentleman, Mr Bruce
> Ismay, to be aboard and to be caught by the urgent vacancy in the
> boat and the snare of the moment. No untried man dare say that
> he would have behaved better in his place. But for capitalism and
> for our existing social system his escape – with five and fifty third-
> class children waiting below to drown – was the abandonment of
> every noble pretension. It is not the man I would criticise, but the
> manifest absence of any such sense of the supreme dignity of his
> position as would have sustained him in that crisis. He was a rich
> man and a ruling man, but in the test he was not a proud man. In
> the common man's realisation that such is indeed the case with most
> of those who dominate the world lies the true cause and danger of
> our social indiscipline. And the remedy in the first place lies not in
> the consciences of the wealthy. Heroism and a general devotion to
> the common good are the only effective answer to distrust.

Despite severe criticism in both the American press and back in Britain,
Ismay did receive some support, often from somewhat unexpected
quarters.

J. E. Prindle, President
Earl E. Gaines, Secretary
A.C. Smith, Vice-President

The Ismay Commercial Club
Ismay,
Montana

May 5th '12

Mr. J. Bruce Ismay,
London, England

Dear Sir:
Since the Titanic *disaster the national dailies have heaped a lot of abuse and notoriety upon you and have dragged the name of Ismay Montana into the noise and suggested that we change the name of the town because it happens to be the same as yours. We are not only going to retain the same name, but have sent copies of a reply to all the prominent daily papers stating the facts as we see them and our attitude toward you and the whole affair.*

We hope in a way to exonerate you and keep up the good name of the town of Ismay as well if they will give the article publication.
Yours very truly,
Earl E. Gaines

National Maritime Museum, ref TRNISM/1/1

7

The Inquiry

He made a mistake, a very grievous mistake, but one in which, in face of the practice and of past experience, negligence cannot he said to have had any part; and in the absence of negligence it is, in my opinion, impossible to fix Captain Smith with blame.

Unsurprisingly, given the massive loss of life and the high profile of the disaster on both sides of the Atlantic, both the US and British governments set up public inquiries into its causes in attempts to prevent a similar tragedy occurring again. The US Senate moved the most quickly, appointing Senator William Alden Smith chairman and opening proceedings on 19 April, the day after the *Carpathia* arrived back in New York with the survivors and principal witnesses. In total, the inquiry would last eighteen days, calling forward 86 individuals to give evidence that would fill over 1,000 pages of testimony. Speed was necessary, partly to obtain the freshest possible account of proceedings from passengers and crew while the events were still clear in their minds, but also to ensure that non-US citizens could give evidence before they had to be allowed to leave the country. Consequently, no one was permitted to return to Britain and other parts of the world until after 25 May, when the inquiry finished. The British wreck commissioner's inquiry was convened under the authority of the British Board of Trade, with Lord Mersey as chairman. The investigation began on 2 May 1912 and ran until 3 July, with 36 days of evidence resulting in tens of thousands of individual pieces of evidence.

The sections of the two reports relating to the construction of the ship, the fixtures and fittings relating to safety (with particular attention to lifeboat capacity), the precise circumstances surrounding the impact with the iceberg, the damage it caused, the way the ship sank and the attempts to evacuate the vessel have been reproduced already in this volume. What follows are the recommendations of the reports, with suggestions for the revision of the clearly inadequate health and safety regulations that the tragedy served to highlight, and the boards' delivering verdicts on whom or what was to blame. The British report included a section outlining what action should have been taken to avoid a collision in the first instance.

Action That Should Have Been Taken

The question is what ought the Master to have done. I am advised that with the knowledge of the proximity of ice which the Master had, two courses were open to him: The one was to stand well to the southward instead of turning up to a westerly course; the other was to reduce speed materially as night approached. He did neither. The alteration of the course at 5.50 p.m. was so insignificant that it cannot be attributed to any intention to avoid ice. This deviation brought the vessel back to within about two miles of the customary route before 11.30 p.m. And there was certainly no reduction of speed. Why, then, did the Master persevere in his course and maintain his speed? The answer is to be found in the evidence. It was shown that for many years past, indeed, for a quarter of a century or more, the practice of liners using this track when in the vicinity of ice at night had been in clear weather to keep the course, to maintain the speed and to trust to a sharp look-out to enable them to avoid the danger. This practice, it was said, had been justified by experience, no casualties having resulted from it. I accept the evidence as to the practice and as to the immunity from casualties which is said to have accompanied it. But the event has proved the practice to be bad. Its root is probably to be found in competition and in the desire of the public for quick passages rather than in the judgement of navigators. But unfortunately experience appeared to justify it. In these circumstances I am not able to blame Captain Smith. He had not the experience which his own misfortune has afforded to those whom he has left behind, and he was doing only that which other skilled men would have done in the same position. It was suggested at the bar that he was yielding to influences which ought not to have affected him; that the presence of Mr. Ismay on board and the knowledge which he perhaps had of a conversation between Mr. Ismay and the Chief Engineer [Bell] at Queenstown about the speed of the ship and the consumption of coal probably induced him to neglect precautions which he would otherwise have taken. But I do not believe this. The evidence shows that he was not trying to make any record passage or indeed any exceptionally quick passage. He was not trying to please anybody, but was exercising his own discretion in the way he thought best. He made a mistake, a very grievous mistake, but one in which, in face of the practice and of past experience, negligence cannot he said to have had any part; and in the absence of negligence it is, in my opinion, impossible to fix Captain Smith with blame. It is, however, to be hoped that the last has been heard of the practice and that for the future it will be abandoned for what we now know to be more prudent and wiser measures. What was a mistake in the case of the *Titanic* would without doubt be negligence in any similar case in the future.

British wreck commissioner's final report

Clearly, the wreck commissioner refused to blame Captain Smith under the circumstances, although he did suggest that a mistake had been made which, if repeated, would henceforth be regarded as negligence.

The US Senate inquiry made a series of recommendations to change maritime regulations to ensure that no repeat of the *Titanic* could occur.

RECOMMENDATIONS

The committee finds that this accident clearly indicates the necessity of additional legislation to secure safety of life at sea.

By statute the United States accepts reciprocally the inspection certificates of foreign countries having inspection laws approximating those of the United States. Unless there is early revision of inspection laws of foreign countries along the lines laid down hereinafter, the committee deems it proper that such reciprocal arrangements be terminated, and that no vessel shall be licensed to carry passengers from ports of the United States until all regulations and requirements of the laws of the United States have been fully complied with.

The committee recommends that sections 4481 and 4488, Revised Statutes, be so amended as to definitely require sufficient lifeboats to accommodate every passenger and every member of the crew. That the importance of this feature is recognized by the steamship lines is indicated by the fact that on many lines steps are being taken to provide lifeboat capacity for every person on board, including crew; and the fact of such equipment is being widely advertised. The president of the International Mercantile Marine Co., Mr. Ismay, definitely stated to the committee (p. 985):

'We have issued instructions that none of the ships of our lines shall leave any port carrying more passengers and crew than they have capacity for in the lifeboats.'

Not less than four members of the crew, skilled in handling boats, should be assigned to every boat. All members of the crew assigned to lifeboats should be drilled in lowering and rowing the boats, not less than twice each month and the fact of such drill or practice should be noted in the log.

The committee recommends the assignment of passengers and crew to lifeboats before sailing; that occupants of certain groups of staterooms and the stewards of such groups of rooms be assigned to certain boats most conveniently located with reference to the rooms in question; the assignment of boats and the shortest route from stateroom to boat to be posted in every stateroom.

The committee recommends that every ocean steamship carrying 100 or more passengers be required to carry 2 electric searchlights.

The committee finds that this catastrophe makes glaringly apparent the necessity for regulation of radiotelegraphy. There must be an operator on duty at all times, day and night, to insure the immediate receipt of all distress, warning, or other important calls. Direct communication either by clear-speaking telephone, voice tube, or messenger must be provided between the wireless room and the bridge, so that the operator does not have to leave his station. There must be definite legislation to prevent interference by amateurs, and to secure secrecy of radiograms or wireless messages. There must be some source of auxiliary power, either storage battery or oil engine, to insure the operation of the wireless installation until the wireless room is submerged.

The committee recommends the early passage of S. 6412, already passed by the Senate and favorably reported by the House.

The committee recommends that the firing of rockets or candles on the high seas for any other purpose than as a signal of distress be made a misdemeanor.

The committee recommends that the following additional structural requirements be required as regards ocean-going passenger steamers the construction of which is begun after this date:

All steel ocean and coastwise seagoing ships carrying 100 or more passengers should have a watertight skin inboard of the outside plating, extending not less than 10 percent of the load draft above the full-load waterline, either in the form of an inner bottom or of longitudinal watertight bulkheads, and this construction should extend from the forward collision bulkhead over not less than two-thirds of the length of the ship.

All steel ocean and coastwise seagoing ships carrying 100 or more passengers should have bulkheads so spaced that any two adjacent compartments of the ship may be flooded without destroying the flotability or stability of the ship. Watertight transverse bulkheads should extend from side to side of the ship, attaching to the outside shell. The transverse bulkheads forward and abaft the machinery spaces should be continued watertight vertically to the uppermost continuous structural deck. The uppermost continuous structural deck should be fitted watertight. Bulkheads within the limits of the machinery spaces should extend not less than 25 percent of the draft of the ship above the load waterline and should end at a watertight deck. All watertight bulkheads and decks should be proportioned to withstand, without material permanent deflection, a water pressure equal to 5 feet more than the full height of the bulkhead. Bulkheads of novel dimensions or scantlings should be tested by being subjected to actual water pressure.

US Senate board of inquiry final report

Here the focus clearly shifts to the speed with which the *Titanic*, once holed, began to sink and the way the bulkheads failed to prevent water from flooding the interior of the ship. The British report echoed many of these findings:

Recommendations

The following recommendations are made. They refer to foreign-going passenger and emigrant steamships.

Watertight Subdivision
1. That the newly appointed Bulkhead Committee should enquire and report, among other matters, on the desirability and prac-ticability of providing ships with (a) a double skin carried up above the waterline; or, as an alternative, with (b) a longitu-dinal, vertical, watertight bulkhead on each side of the ship, extending as far forward and as far aft as convenient; or (*c*) with a combination of (a) and (b). Any one of the three (a), (b) and (c) to be in addition to watertight transverse bulkheads.
2. That the Committee should also enquire and report as to the desirability and practicability of fitting ships with (a) a deck or decks at a convenient distance or distances above the water-line which shall be watertight throughout a part or the whole of the ship's length; and should in this connection report upon

(b) the means by which the necessary openings in such deck or decks should be made watertight, whether by watertight doors or watertight trunks or by any other and what means.

3. That the Committee should consider and report generally on the practicability of increasing the protection given by sub-division; the object being to secure that the ship shall remain afloat with the greatest practicable proportion of her length in free communication with the sea.

4. That when the Committee has reported upon the matters before mentioned, the Board of Trade should take the report into their consideration and to the extent to which they approve of it should seek Statutory powers to enforce it in all newly built ships, but with a discretion to relax the requirements in special cases where it may seem right to them to do so.

5. That the Board of Trade should be empowered by the Legislature to require the production of the designs and specifications of all ships in their early stages of construction and to direct such amendments of the same as may be thought necessary and practicable for the safety of life at sea in ships. (This should apply to all passenger-carrying ships.)

Lifeboats and Rafts

6. That the provision of lifeboat and raft accommodation on board such ships should be based on the number of persons intended to be carried in the ship and not upon tonnage.

7. That the question of such accommodation should be treated independently of the question of the subdivision of the ship into watertight compartments. (This involves the abolition of Rule 12 of the Life-Saving Appliances Rules of 1902.)

8. That the accommodation should be sufficient for all persons on board, with, however, the qualification that in special cases where, in the opinion of the Board of Trade, such provision is impracticable, the requirements may be modified as the Board may think right. (In order to give effect to this recommendation changes may be necessary in the sizes and types of

boats to be carried and in the method of stowing and floating them. It may also be necessary to set apart one or more of the boat decks exclusively for carrying boats and drilling the crew, and to consider the distribution of decks in relation to the passengers' quarters. These, however, are matters of detail to be settled with reference to the particular circumstance affecting the ship.)

9. That all boats should be fitted with a protective, continuous fender, to lessen the risk of damage when being lowered in a seaway.

10. That the Board of Trade should be empowered to direct that one or more of the boats be fitted with some form of mechanical propulsion.

11. That there should be a Board of Trade regulation requiring all boat equipment (under sections 5 and 6, page 15 of the Rules, dated February, 1902, made by the Board of Trade under section 427, Merchant Shipping Act, 1894) to be in the boats as soon as the ship leaves harbour. The sections quoted above should be amended so as to provide also that all boats and rafts should carry lamps and pyrotechnic lights for purposes of signalling. All boats should be provided with compasses and provisions, and should be very distinctly marked in such a way as to indicate plainly the number of adult persons each boat can carry when being lowered.

12. That the Board of Trade inspection of boats and life-saving appliances should be of a more searching character than hitherto.

Manning the Boats and Boat Drills

13. That in cases where the deck hands are not sufficient to man the boats enough other members of the crew should be men trained in boat work to make up the deficiency. These men should be required to pass a test in boat work.

14. That in view of the necessity of having on board men trained in boat work, steps should be taken to encourage the training of boys for the Merchant Service.

15. That the operation of Section 115 and Section 134 (a) of the Merchant Shipping Act, 1894, should be examined, with a view to amending the same so as to secure greater continuity of service than hitherto.

16. That the men who are to man the boats should have more frequent drills than hitherto. That in all ships a boat drill, a fire drill and a watertight door drill should be held as soon as possible after leaving the original port of departure and at convenient intervals of not less than once a week during the voyage. Such drills to be recorded in the official log.

17. That the Board of Trade should be satisfied in each case before the ship leaves port that a scheme has been devised and communicated to each officer of the ship for securing an efficient working of the boats.

General

18. That every man taking a look-out in such ships should undergo a sight test at reasonable intervals.

19. That in all such ships a police system should be organised so as to secure obedience to orders, and proper control and guidance of all on board in times of emergency.

20. That in all such ships there should be an installation of wireless telegraphy, and that such installation should be worked with a sufficient number of trained operators to secure a continuous service by night and day. In this connection regard should be had to the resolutions of the International Conference on Wireless Telegraphy recently held under the presidency of Sir H. Babington Smith. That where practicable a silent chamber for 'receiving' messages should form part of the installation.

21. That instruction should begin in all Steamship Companies' Regulations that when ice is reported in or near the track the ship should proceed in the dark hours at a moderate speed or alter her course so as to go well clear of the danger zone.

22. That the attention of Masters of vessels should be drawn by the Board of Trade to the effect that under the Maritime Conventions Act, 1911, it is a misdemeanour not to go to the relief of a vessel in distress when possible to do so.

23. That the same protection as to the safety of life in the event of casualties which is afforded to emigrant ships by means of supervision and inspection should be extended to all foreign-going passenger ships.

24. That (unless already done) steps should be taken to call an International Conference to consider and as far as possible to agree upon a common line of conduct in respect of (a) the subdivision of ships; (b) the provision and working of life-saving appliances; (c) the installation of wireless telegraphy and the method of working the same; (d) the reduction of speed or the alteration of course in the vicinity of ice; and (e) the use of searchlights.

MERSEY. Wreck Commissioner

We concur,
ARTHUR GOUGH-CALTHORPE,
A. W. CLARKE,
F. C. A. LYON,
J. H. BILES,
EDWARD C. CHASTON.
Assessors.

30th July, 1912.

British wreck commissioner's final report

Even before these recommendations were made public, there had been an immediate impact on the construction plans for the third of the intended three White Star Line vessels, the *Gigantic*, which was to be scaled down in terms of overall size and strengthened in key places. It was to be launched, as the *Britannic*, in 1914.

PLANS OF GIGANTIC WILL BE MODIFIED

London, Monday, April 22. It is understood that the plans of the White Star *Gigantic*, which is now being built at Belfast, and which was to have been 1,000 feet in length, will be modified. It is probable that the new plans will provide for a double-cellular bottom and sides, such as the *Mauretania* and *Lusitania* have, as a stipulated condition of receiving the government subsidy. The *Olympic* has been provided with forty collapsible boats and will carry sixteen additional lifeboats.

Seattle Daily Times, 22 April 1912,
Encyclopaedia Titanica member post

Despite the findings of the official inquiries, the causes of the sinking in the public mind remained excessive speed and inadequate care as the *Titanic* headed through the ice fields, due to the desire fuelled by Ismay's presence on board to arrive in New York ahead of schedule. These beliefs featured prominently in compensation claims brought against White Star over the next few years by families of victims and organisations that had suffered loss as a result of the tragedy. One line of reasoning was that Ismay's presence gave him executive authority over Captain Smith, and therefore any undue pressure exerted by Ismay to go too fast or ignore safety recommendations through a known place of danger constituted negligence. Ismay had denied exerting any pressure on Smith in the statement he released when arriving in New York; nevertheless, several witnesses came forward to claim that they had indeed seen or heard Ismay suggest that he was concerned about speed and had informed Captain Smith of these feelings.

For example, Mrs Emily Ryerson, who was on board the *Titanic*, is clear that Ismay was influential in disregarding warnings of floating ice.

Boston April 18 '13
79 Mt. Vernon Street

Dear Mr. Broen
They have asked for my testimony in regard to my conversation with

Ismay on board the Titanic & I feel there is no reason now to seem to want to hide it if it is any help in the steerage claims. This is the first time I have been asked directly to give this & it seems simpler & less public to voluntarily give it now than to wait for a subpoena which would involve an appearance in court.

As far as I can now recall all I could say would be that I was on deck in the afternoon of April 14 between 5–6 o'clock & Mr. Ismay came up & inquired if our staterooms were comfortable & the service satisfactory etc. & then thrust a Marconigram at me, saying, we were in among the icebergs. Something was said about speed & he said that the ship had not been going fast now that they were to start up extra boilers that afternoon or evening (I forget when). The telegram also spoke of the Deutschland, a ship out of coal & asking for a tow, & when I asked him what they were going to do about that he said they had no time for such matters, our ship wanted to do her best & something was said about getting in Tuesday night. I was not much interested & cannot remember the exact words & details but repeated the conversation immediately to my husband & to Miss Bowen when I went down to my cabin & she remembers it & the strong impression which was left on my mind & on hers was that they were speeding the ship up – to get away from the ice – & that we would probably get in late Tuesday night or early Wednesday morning – Mr. Ismay's manner was that of one in authority & the owner of the ship & that what he said was law.

If this can be of service to anyone I do not wish to be silent or seen to be protecting him,
   Yrs. Sincerely,
   Emily Borie Ryerson

Copy of letter, National Maritime
Museum, ref. LMQ/7/2/22

Similarly, Mrs Elizabeth Lines testified that she overheard a conversation the day before the disaster between Smith and Ismay in which she clearly heard Ismay encourage Smith to make good speed so that they might arrive in New York on Tuesday 16 April

Examiner: Would you be good enough to state when it was on Saturday April Thirteenth that this conversation occurred?

Mrs Lines: After the midday meal I went into the lounge to have my coffee – in the general reception room.

Examiner: Were the Captain and Mr. Ismay already there?

Mrs Lines: No, they came in after I was seated, and went to this same table which I had seen them occupy on the Friday.

Examiner: Could you estimate about what time it was that the Captain and Mr. Ismay entered the reception room or lounge?

Mrs Lines: Perhaps half past one.

Examiner: Do you recall what your luncheon hour was?

Mrs Lines: No, because it varied; it was a little later some days and a little earlier other days; but I should say that it was about one thirty when I went into the lounge.

Examiner: About how long, within your knowledge, did Mr. Ismay and Captain Smith remain in this reception room engaged in conversation?

Mrs Lines: At least two hours.

Examiner: Were you there all of that time?

Mrs Lines: I was there.

Examiner: Are you able to state from your recollection the words that you heard spoken between Mr. Ismay and Captain Smith on that occasion?

Mrs Lines: We had had a very good run. At first I did not pay any attention to what they were saying, they were simply talking and I was occupied, and then my attention was arrested by hearing the day's run discussed, which I already knew had been a very good one in the preceding twenty-four hours, and I heard Mr. Ismay – it was Mr. Ismay who did the talking – I heard him give the length of the run, and I heard him say 'Well, we did better to-day than we did yesterday, we made a better run to-day than we did yesterday, we will make a better run to-morrow. Things are working smoothly, the machinery is bearing the test, the boilers are working well.' They went on discussing it, and then I heard him make the statement: 'We will beat the *Olympic* and get in to New York on Tuesday.'

Examiner: In your last statement,

Mrs. Lines, were you giving the substance of the conversation or the exact words which were used?

Mrs Lines: I heard 'We will beat the *Olympic* and get in to New York on Tuesday' in those words.

Examiner: If there were any particular words spoken that you can remember, I should be glad to hear them.

Mrs Lines: Those words fixed themselves in my mind: 'We will beat the *Olympic* and get in to New York on Tuesday.'

Examiner: Do I understand you to say that the other things that you stated were the general substance of what you heard and not the exact things or words used?

Mrs Lines: No, I heard those statements.

Examiner: What was said by Mr. Ismay as regards the condition of the performances, of the engines, machinery and boilers?

Mrs Lines: He said they were doing well, they were bearing the extra pressure. The first day's run had been less, the second day's run had been a little greater. He said, 'You see they are standing the pressure, everything is going well, the boilers are working well, we can do better to-morrow, we will make a better run tomorrow.'

> Limitation of Liability Hearing,
> US National Archives, New York

However, other factors were advanced as contributing to the disaster. The following article, written in 1956 by E. Moore Ritchie, whose family were connected with the constructors Harland and Wolff, followed the conventional line that speed in a section of ocean where there was known to be floating ice was the main cause of the disaster; however, it also suggested that a head-on collision would have been preferable to the glancing blow the *Titanic* received, as the front section of the ship was stronger than the side:

GREATEST SEA DISASTER LINK WITH B.S.A. POLICE

In my youth my family was associated with the builders, Harland & Wolff, of Belfast, and while waiting for a promised opening on the press I secured through one of my family a job which made me secretary to Thomas Andrews for more than a year at a time when he had in hand the designing of the two ships whose yard numbers were: *Olympic*, No. 400, and *Titanic*, No. 401.

Contrary to popular belief, neither was an 'Atlantic racer'. The White Star Line had abandoned this practice as uneconomical nearly twenty years before. Good speed, size and luxury: these were the features of the company's policy, racing being left to the subsidised Cunard Company and the German companies of those days. The twin giants had a designed speed of 22 knots full out, their propulsive machinery (based on an early experiment in the White Star Canadian trade) being twin screw reciprocating engines with a third and smaller centre screw, driven by low pressure turbine.

Thomas Andrews was placed in charge of the designing by his uncle, Lord Pirrie, head of Harland's, whose working head then was A. M. Carlisle, a blend of organising genius and mountebank who ran the great shipyard with tyrannical discipline. Carlisle was hated as much as he was feared. Between him and the younger Andrews there was no love lost, and Andrews used to express to me with thinly disguised feeling what he thought of Carlisle.

It was never claimed by Andrews nor anyone connected with her builders that the *Titanic* was unsinkable, although in fact she was sunk by the only means she could have been – not a head-on collision, but a knife-edge cut that tore her inches-thick outer plating like cardboard.

Never again was any White Star liner dubbed with such a boastful description; too daring by far in the face of the mighty and unforgiving sea.

Steaming at full speed through ice-infested waters, and failure

[267]

to provide sufficient lifeboats were the blunders that led to the tragedy. Ship builders and others concerned had gradually been coming to feel that the provision of lifeboats in modern vessels was a matter of red tape, not a necessity – an illusion that the *Titanic* disaster corrected frightfully and for ever.

After joining the B.S.A. Police I kept in touch with Thomas Andrews. My last letter to him, written from the end room of the old staff kias [*sic*] at Bulawayo, was one of good wishes from his fellow Ulsterman and acting secretary on the completion of his long task and for the success of the great *Titanic*.

Andrews replied thanking me, and with best wishes, reciprocated.

His letter was dated 3rd April. I have it still. In those days it reached me many days later by sea – its writer by then gone for ever with his great ship in the chill Atlantic night.

Outpost, 5 September 1956, National
Maritime Museum, ref. LMQ/7/3/C

There would certainly appear to have been some design flaws that affected the ability of the *Titanic* to take evasive action, but the issue of glancing blow versus direct hit takes on more significance when modern forensic science is applied to the materials used in construction. An expedition to the wreck in 1998 was able to locate some of the original wrought-iron rivets used to hold together the steel plates that comprised the outer skin of the hull. Tests revealed that the rivets were not the 'best best' No. 4 rivets, made out of the purest and strongest wrought iron, but the cheaper No. 3 rivets that were of poorer quality since they containing a higher level of impurities. These made the rivets more brittle in colder water, particularly at their heads. The glancing blow from the iceberg meant that the rivet heads holding the outer plates together simply sheared off. As the water poured into the ship through the resulting hole in the hull it was able to move through the ship rapidly thanks to the fact that the original height of the bulkheads had been lowered to accommodate a more ornate staircase in the heart of the ship, with the result that the watertight compartments sat only ten feet above the waterline making them more vulnerable to flooding.

Another criticism levelled at the *Titanic* was that more lifeboats should have been installed. Alexander Carlisle appeared at the British inquiry to defend his decision to install the davits, and suggested that there should have been ample time – with proper use of the technology – to lower not just 32 lifeboats, but 48, namely three hung from each davit.

> I consider the whole of those boats ought to have been lowered into the water inside of an hour without any trouble. . . The 32 ought to be done in half-an-hour easily, because the one boat is in the tackles ready for lowering, and then you have to pull them up. I think with the present falls the greatest time would be lost in getting the blocks up again. That is really the complicated part of the lowering of boats. Of course since that was made, if it was used on a large scale like that, I think very likely wire ropes with gearing would be the proper thing, because there is a block invented and made that always hangs plumb. The difficulty with the ordinary block is that when you go to pull it up it turns round.
>
> British wreck commissioner's final report

Considerable blame for the high loss of life was also attached to the *Californian*, which failed to respond to the *Titanic*'s distress calls in time to help in the rescue. In a series of letters sent to Walter Lord, third officer Charles Groves reveals what really happened that night on board the *Californian*:

The Middle Watch April 15th, 1912

> *The* Californian *owned by the Leyland Line was a four-masted steamship with a gross tonnage of 6,223 and a maximum speed of about 14 knots. She had accommodation for 50 passengers and carried a crew of 55 all told. Leaving London on Good Friday April 5th 1912 bound for Boston, U.S.A. with a full cargo but no passengers, she*

was commanded by Captain Stanley Lord, a tall lean man who had spent some twenty years at sea much of which had been in the North Atlantic trade. He was an austere type, utterly devoid of humour and even more reserved than is usual with those who occupy similar positions. Owing to a certain concatenation of circumstances he had obtained command somewhat earlier than was usual.

The Chief Officer was G. F. Stewart a competent and experienced seaman nearing middle age who was well versed in the ways of the Western Ocean and was a certificated Master.

H. Stone, the Second Officer, had been some eight years at sea the whole of which period had been spent in the North Atlantic and West Indian trades. He was a stolid, unimaginative type and possessed little self confidence. He held a certificate as First Mate.

The Third Officer was C. V. Groves who had followed the sea as a career for six years and was in possession of a Second Mate's certificate. For three years his voyages had taken him mainly to South America and the Mediterranean. Latterly he had been engaged as a junior officer in the Indian and Colonial trades. Signalling was a strong point with him for which he held the Board of Trade's special certificate and he had made some progress as an amateur in wireless telegraphy.

Californian carried one Apprentice and this was J. Gibson who had completed three years of his indentures with the Leyland Line the whole of which time had been spent on the North Atlantic and West Indian run. He was a bright lad, keen on his profession and one who showed every sign that he would make headway in it.

The voyage proceeded normally until the afternoon of Sunday April 14th. when at a few minutes before 6.0 P.M. Mr. Groves went on to the bridge to relieve the Chief Officer for dinner. The sky was cloudless, the sea smooth and there was a light westerly breeze. Away to the southward and some five miles distant were three large flat topped icebergs. Nothing else was in sight and the ship was making eleven knots through the water. Captain Lord was on the bridge talking to the Chief Officer as they scanned the horizon. A few minutes later they both went below for their meal after which Mr. Stewart returned and relieved the Third Officer.

Mr. Groves went on watch again at eight o'clock to take over until midnight and was told by the Chief Officer that wireless messages had been received giving warning of ice ahead and shortly after went below. Almost immediately Captain Lord came up with similar information telling him to keep a sharp lookout for this ice. The night was dark, brilliantly clear with not a breeze of wind and the sea showed no sign of movement with the horizon only discernible by the fact that the stars could be seen disappearing below it. The lookout had been doubled there being a sailor on the forecastle head and another in the crow's nest. The Captain remained on the bridge with the ship proceeding at full speed when suddenly the Third Officer perceived several white patches in the water ahead which he took to be a school of porpoises crossing the bows. Captain Lord evidently saw this at the same moment and as he was standing alongside the engine room telegraph he at once ran the engines full speed astern. In a very short space of time and before the ship had run her way off she was surrounded by light field ice. This was about 10.30 P.M. Despite the clarity of the atmosphere this ice was not sighted at a distance of more than 400 yards nor was it seen by the lookouts before it was seen from the bridge.

Captain Lord went below shortly after the ship had lost her way through the water leaving instructions that he had to be called if anything was sighted. Absolute peace and quietness now prevailed save for brief snatches of 'Annie Laurie' from an Irish voice which floated up through a stokehold ventilator.

At 11.15 a light was observed three points abaft the starboard beam of which the Captain was immediately advised and his reply to the information that it was a passenger ship was, 'That will be the Titanic on her maiden voyage.' This light was some ten miles distant, but he did not go up to look at it. Mr. Groves kept the ship under close observation and at 11.40 he saw her stop and then her deck lights were extinguished, or so it appeared to him. The time of the stopping of the ship is accurately fixed by the fact that at that moment Californian's bell was struck once in order to call the men who were to take over the middle watch. The dowsing of the lights caused no surprise to the

Third Officer because for the two preceding years he had sailed in large ships where it was customary to put the lights out at midnight to discourage the passengers from staying on deck too late.

Captain Lord was told of the ship having stopped and at a few minutes before the close of the watch he went up on the bridge and after looking at the distant ship observed, 'That's not a passenger ship,' to which the Third Officer replied 'It is, Sir, when she stopped she put all her lights out.' The Captain then left the bridge saying that he must be told if that ship made a move or if anything else hove into sight. The ship remained stationary. The drama had commenced.

At midnight Mr. Groves was relieved by Mr. Stone to whom the Captain's orders were passed. The two young officers chatted for a while until the newcomer's eyes had got accustomed to the darkness when Mr. Groves bade him 'Good night' and then walked along the boat deck in order, as was his wont, to have a yarn with the sole Marconi Operator, Mr. Evans, before turning in. The Operator lay in his bunk asleep with a magazine in his hands. His visitor woke him with the query 'What ships have you got Sparks?' Dreamily he replied 'Only the Titanic. He was then told that she was in sight on the starboard beam. Almost mechanically the Third Officer picked up the wireless 'phones which lay on the operating table and placed them on his head to listen to what the ether might convey. He heard no sound for he had failed to notice that the clockwork of the magnetic detector had run down thus no signals could be received until it had been wound up. He could read wireless signals when sent slowly. Mr. Evans had dropped off to sleep again and the 'phones were replaced on the table. The Third Officer closed the door and went to his room to turn in. The time was then 12.25 A.M. and that was ten minutes after Titanic had commenced to send her messages of distress. Californian's operator slept peacefully. Titanic realised she was doomed and was lowering her lifeboats and twelve hundred souls had seen their last sunrise.

About 6.45 that Monday morning the Third Officer was awakened by hearing ropes being thrown onto the boat deck above his head and he realised that the boats were being prepared for swinging out.

Almost immediately Mr. Stewart came into his room to tell him to turn out as Titanic *has sunk and her passengers are in her boats ahead of us. Jumping from his bunk Mr. Groves went across the alleyway to the Second Officer's room and asked if the news was true and received the reply 'Yes, I saw her firing rockets in my watch.' Amazed at hearing this he went up on the bridge and found it to be a brilliantly fine morning with a light breeze and slight sea. There were more than fifty icebergs, large and small, in sight and the ship was making slow way through the water. Some five miles distant a four-masted steamship with one funnel was observed and she proved to be the Cunarder* Carpathia. *She lay motionless with her house flag flying at half mast.* Californian *arrived alongside her at about 7.30 and semaphore signals were exchanged when it was learned that* Titanic *had struck an iceberg at 11.40 the previous night and sunk two and a half hours later. Some 720 of her passengers had been rescued and* Carpathia *was returning to New York forthwith. Would* Californian *search the vicinity for further possible survivors?* Carpathia *then got under way by which time it was nine o'clock and less than twenty minutes later disappeared from view hidden by the icebergs.*

The sea was covered by a large number of deck chairs, planks and light wreckage. Californian *steamed close alongside all the lifeboats which* Carpathia *had left floating and it was particularly noted that they were empty. Scanning the sea with his binoculars the Third Officer noted a large icefloe a mile or so distant on which he saw figures moving and drawing Captain Lord's attention to it remarked that they might be human beings was told that they were seals.* Californian *now made one complete turn to starboard followed by one to port and then resumed her passage to Boston passing the Canadian Pacific steamship* Mount Temple *and another steamship of unknown nationality.*

Before noon Californian *had cleared all the ice and amongst many wireless messages she intercepted was one addressed to Mr. W. T. Stead, a passenger who was with those lost in* Titanic, *offering him a dollar a word for his story of the casualty [sic]. It was sent by a well-known New York newspaper.*

The New England coast was approached in a dense fog out of which loomed a tugboat containing a number of American newspaper men expecting to obtain a story. Their journey was a vain one.

What was the complete story of events aboard Californian *during the middle watch of that fateful morning of April 15th? The passage of time has not dulled the recollections of all who were in any way concerned.*

Mr. Stone and the apprentice Gibson saw the ship which Mr. Groves had reported as being a passenger ship fire eight rockets the first of which was seen at 1.10 A.M. This is the number which Titanic *is believed to have sent up between 1.0. and 2.0 A.M. and at 2.20 A.M. Mr Stone reported to Captain Lord that the distant ship had 'disappeared' and it is known that* Titanic *foundered at that time.*

Officers of Titanic *and many others aboard her reported having seen the lights of a ship which was stopped a few miles away from her and passengers on the ill-fated vessel were reassured on being told by the officers that this ship would soon come to their assistance.*

All that middle watch Californian *remained stationary for news of the rockets being seen did not stir her Captain into action and Mr. Stone lacked the necessary initiative to insist upon his coming to the bridge to investigate things for himself and it did not occur to him to call the Chief Officer when he realised the apathy of the Captain who apparently slept peacefully whilst this drama was being enacted.*

Mr. Stewart relieved the bridge at 4.0. A.M. when the events of the watch were related to him. Half an hour later he roused Captain Lord and when told about the rockets which had been fired he replied to the effect that he knew all about them. Shortly before 6.0. A.M. Mr. Stewart was instructed to call the wireless operator to see if any information could be obtained regarding the distress signals, when advice was received from several ships of the sinking of Titanic. *Slowly at first but eventually at full speed* Californian *got underway until she arrived at the scene of the disaster.*

Many questions will for ever remain unanswered concerning the failure of Californian *to render assistance to the stricken ship.*

Mr. Stone knew without a shadow of doubt that there was trouble aboard the vessel from which the distress signals had been fired but he failed to convince his Captain; but did Captain Lord need any convincing? Was Mr. Stone afraid that if he was too insistent he would arouse the wrath of his superior?

Why did Captain Lord take no efficient steps to render assistance before 6 o'clock? Did he consider problematical damage to his ship was of more importance than the saving of lives?

Many times the question of Captain Lord's sobriety on that occasion has been raised but it cannot be too strongly asserted that he was a most temperate man and that alcohol played no part in the matter.

Does an experienced shipmaster lay down fully clothed and in such circumstances sleep so heavily as he said he did on that night? Surely, surely that is open to the very gravest of doubts.

Probably it would not be far from the mark if it is stated that the fate of those twelve hundred lost souls hinged on the fact that Mr. Groves failed to notice that the magnetic detector was not functioning when he placed the 'phones on his head in the wireless office at which time the ether was being rent by calls of distress which he would have failed to recognize.

And what of those figures on the icefloe? Were they only seals as the Captain asserted? It has already been stated that all Titanic's lifeboats which were left afloat were closely examined and found to contain no occupants.

A month later in almost the same spot the White Star liner Majestic picked up one of these boats and in it were found the bodies of passengers who had evidently died of starvation for the ship's doctor who examined them reported the men's mouths contained fragments of cork from the lifebelts. Had these passengers escaped from the sea on to the icefloe and then eventually into the boat as it drifted past?

What is the probable explanation of her deck lights appearing to go out when it is beyond dispute that they burned right up to the moment when Titanic sank? She was approaching Californian obliquely and when she stopped she put her helm hard over and thus foreshortened her perspective thereby giving the appearance of the extinction of her lights.

The whole unfortunate occurrence was a combination of circum-stances the like of which may never again be seen and a middle watch which will not soon be forgotten.

Letter to Walter Lord, National Maritime
Museum LMQ/7/1/37

Pine Ridge.
Valley Road,
Ipswich. England.
July 17th 1955

Mr. Walter Lord.
25, East 38th. Street,
New York 16. N.Y.

Dear Mr. Lord.

Thank your for your letter of the 30th ultimo.
 I have never had the slightest doubt whatsoever that the ship which I saw on that evening in April 1912 whilst we were stopped in the ice was indeed the Titanic. *As a matter of fact when I pointed her out to Captain Lord when he came on the bridge he remarked 'That will be the* Titanic *on her maiden voyage.' Captain Lord certainly did not watch that ship from 11.0 P.M. onwards for he spent practically all hours in his cabin as although it was a breathless night it was bitterly cold with the temperature well below freezing. I watched the ship coming up on our starboard quarter in a blaze of deck lights and at 11.40 her lights seemed to me to go out suddenly and that did not surprise me as I had been for some time a junior officer in the Far Eastern trade where it was our custom to put the deck lights out at midnight to encourage the passengers to turn in and I concluded that* Titanic *had put her lights out for the same purpose. What however actually happened was that the iceberg had been sighted on the liner's starboard bow and she had immediately turned to port and thus foreshortened her view and accordingly shut out most if not all of her deck lights.*

Going over the events in the Marconi room with the Operator afterwards there is no doubt whatsoever that the distress call was actually being transmitted whilst I had the 'phones on my head but the whole tragedy was that 'Californian' was fitted with what was known as a magnetic detector worked by clockwork and this was not working as I had omitted to wind it up and as the Operator was lying in his bunk reading at the time he did not show any particular interest in the proceedings and as I could hear nothing I laid the 'phones down and that time would be about 12.30 A.M. Had that detector been working there is no doubt I would have heard the distress call as I took a great interest in wireless telegraphy and could read it moderately well.

I agree with you that probably Titanic was about ten miles distant at the time under discussion. She would certainly be no further. If you have read the summing up of Lord Mersey in the case of the Californian you will remember that he stated there could be no doubt that the ship we sighted was the Titanic.

Since my first letter to you I have recollected that the company with whom Captain Lord afterwards gained employment is that of Lawther, Latta of London. I believe their official name was Nitrate Producers' Company.

Let me know if I can be of any further assistance to you. I believe there is only one surviving officer of the Titanic and he lives in Australia. Lightoller died a few years ago.

Yours sincerely,
Charles T Groves

Letter to Walter Lord, National Maritime Museum LMQ/7/1/37

8

Life Goes On

Oh she is a comfort but she don't realise yet that her Daddy is in heaven. There are some dear children here who have loaded her with lovely toys but it's when I'm alone with her she will miss him.

For those that survived the sinking, life went on – even though it would never be the same again. Shattered families attempted to pick up the pieces, while the loss had huge implications for the future of long-distance marine trade. One of those most affected by the tragedy was Ismay himself, who would appear to have been genuinely distraught at the loss of life, and expressed guilt at his own survival when others perished. Whether this was because he had indeed encouraged Captain Smith to go faster will never be fully resolved. Ismay and Smith became the chief scapegoats for the tragedy, and one cannot help but feel some sympathy for both men – in Smith's case, because he lost his life with the ship and therefore never had a chance to defend his role; and for Ismay, because he survived and was roundly criticised for doing so.

Certainly he had the support of his family. A bundle of correspondence survives at the National Maritime Museum which shows how concerned his friends and relatives were at the adverse press he received after the accident, during the inquest and subsequently. It also shows that he wished to turn his back on the International Mercantile Marine Company and White Star, and drop out of the increasingly hostile public eye.

The first letter is from his son Tom.

Sandheys,
Mossley Hill,
Liverpool

Dearest Father,
This is just a line to let you know how sorry I am that I did not see more of you to-day, and to tell you that I quite realize what an ordeal you have had to go through and how deeply I feel for you. However, I very much hope that the worst is over now and that you will never again be misjudged and your words misinterpreted as they have been in the present inquiry. I hope you will be benefited by your stay at Dalnaspical and not be worried by any anonymous communication. . . I hope you did not meet too much rain on your run up to Carlisle and that you will not be recognised as I know how you must hate to be before the public eye especially under the present trying circumstances. I know that this letter is very badly expressed but I hope you will realize that the spirit in which it is written is none the less sincere for that. With hopes that your stay in Scotland will be a complete rest, I will close.
    I am
    Always your loving son,
    Tom

                    National Maritime Museum, ref. TRNISM/1/4

Yet not all public opinion was against Ismay, as the next piece of correspondence indicates.

Telephone 108X and Telegraph
Bryn Mawr

Gwedna
Bryn Mawr
Pennsylvania

May 24th [1912]

Dear Mr. Ismay,
I want to write you how glad I am that you are home safely, and also how pleased we were to read of the great ovation you had in England when you landed for no one realized more than Billy and I did, how much you had been through, and how wonderful you were through it all.

The notoriety we all got, and the dreadful things our press is allowed to say in this country is certainly revolting, and makes us sometimes ashamed that we live here, but fortunately, when they go to extremes, it is quickly over, and now it has completely died out, and no one even mentions it, and they are now criticising something else. I am enclosing a letter to you which Billy received in behalf of our chaffeur's widow (Mrs. Aldworth), he was with us. Would you send her name into the fund, it seems ridiculous to bother you about such a trifle, but I really don't exactly know how to help her there. There was quite a sum raised at our home, Rotherby, Leicester because the Chaffeur was the only one lost from there. I hope you are well and that your nerves haven't suffered. We are all quite well, and send you many kind wishes, and hope to see you next winter when we go back to Melton to hunt.

   Sincerely Yours,
   Lucile Carter

Mrs. Thayer is very well, and the boy splendid. You will be glad to hear.

National Maritime Museum, ref. TRNISM/1/4

Ismay also received support from within the International Mercantile Marine Company, especially from his vice president, Philip Franklin, who sought to robustly defend not just the position of the company at a time of criticism, but also the personal reputation of Ismay.

International Mercantile Marine Company
Office of the Vice President
9 Broadway
New York

Personal

May 7th 1912

My dear Mr. Ismay:
Your much appreciated telegram from the Adriatic *via Quarantine was duly received. I can only say that anything that I did for you was a pleasure or rather a comfort for me as I felt very keenly and deeply for you and many times I thought that I should have been more sympathetic, but I can only say that I did what ever I thought was best at the time and under the circumstances.*

The sentiment here has much improved and the papers have largely dropped the matter, barring the Halifax situation, except the 'yellow journals'. On all sides I hear that your actions on the Titanic *are most favourably commented upon and your leaving the steamer approved.*

As far as I am concerned I think that your bravery and conduct on the Titanic *were excellent and that you were absolutely right in leaving the steamer as you did and that any other course would have been deliberate suicide and that you cannot and should not in any way reproach yourself. If it was not for the terrible loss of life we could all say let us forget it and bend all our energies for the future, but we must deal with these poor people who have lost their loved ones for some time . . .*

Our friend Senator Smith spent three days last week in N.Y. trying to prove that we received a telegram early Monday, but could not do so and is not man enough to acknowledge it to the public and owing to his statements I gave the attached to the press on Friday after a telephone talk with him . . .

I do hope that you had a restful voyage on the Adriatic *and got out on deck and I am sure you got a hearty welcome at Liverpool.*

Please give my love to Mrs. Ismay and tell her how sorry I felt for her and I knew what an anxious and trying time she had and how delighted she must have been to see you at Queenstown.
With very kindest regards and deepest sympathy
I am
Most sincerely,
P. A. S. Franklin
(Vice President of the IMM Co.)

Statement attached released to the press by Franklin:

Referring to the statements that have appeared in the press during the last few days, based upon Mr. Dunn's testimony in Washington to the effect that we received a telegram between 7.45 and 8 o'clock Monday morning, April 15, officially advising us of the sinking of the *Titanic* and making some mention of reinsurance, I can only say that we most emphatically deny the receipt of any such telegram, and that I so testified before the Senate investigation committee in Washington.

I have requested the Senate investigating committee to sift this matter to the bottom, stating to them that we relieve the wireless and telegraph companies from any obligations which they might be under to us to withhold any information regarding any message sent or received by us.

Further than this, I most emphatically state that we did not withhold information, but had no idea that the *Titanic* had sunk or would sink until we received Captain Haddock's message from the *Olympic* about 6.20 p.m. on Monday, April 15, which information was promptly given to the press, and I defy anybody to prove to the contrary.

National Maritime Museum, ref. TRNISM/3/1

Ismay had decided to step down as president of the International Mercantile Marine Company before the *Titanic* tragedy, but despite the strain the entire episode had obviously caused him, his colleagues were still loath to see him go.

On board RMS Olympic
Aug. 8th 1912

My dear Mr. Ismay,

In a few minutes we will be in Queenstown but I did not want to leave without again endeavouring to express to you how deeply I appreciated your very frank & generous treatment of me & I am certainly very much indebted to you. You have always been most courteous & kind to me & it was always a great pleasure & honor to me to serve under you & whenever I was with you I learned something every minute & my deep regret always was that I did not have the opportunity of being more with you.

Before traveling on this steamer I had no idea what a splendid, comfortable, & marvelous steamer she is, but all the time I cannot help thinking of your good self – the man that had the nerve & ability to order & plan her & then of what has happened & it all seems too cruel, but I suppose there was some good reason for it . . .

I can only say that I <u>regret exceedingly</u> that you have decided to go out of the business & wish it were otherwise.

Your position regarding the Titanic *is improving every day & the more thinking people consider it the better it will be & you certainly have absolutely nothing to reproach yourself with. You were saved for some good purpose & must take advantage of it.*

Please give Mrs. Ismay my very kindest regards & accept the same & <u>many many</u> thanks for your good self.

Most sincerely yours,
P. Franklin

National Maritime Museum, ref. TRNISM/2/5

Three pieces of correspondence show that this departure was something Ismay had intended long before the *Titanic* sank, but that the tragedy clearly made him want to speed the process up from a proposed handover date of 30 June 1913 to as quickly as possible:

Tel. No. Gerrard 3745

Brook's
St. James's Street

15 Feb 1912

Dear Ismay,

In answer to your letter, let me explain my position. Six weeks ago <u>both you and Sanderson told me you wished to quit the I.M.M. Co. at the end of 1912.</u> I said how much I regretted that either of you should leave and that if both of you went, the Company's position would be most serious.

From that day I have heard nothing from <u>you</u> except for the letter you wrote to Sanderson suggesting most generously a way out of the difficulty. To-day, not having heard from you since your return from the U.S.A., I suggested having a talk with you and Sanderson on the subject. You gave me to understand that after a personal discussion with Sanderson, you would only feel inclined to report to Steele as representing J. P. M. & Co. with whom you had made your original arrangements.

It was at your suggestion that I succeeded Dawkins as Vice President and Chairman of the London committee.

Having no shipping experience, I can only be considered to hold my position as representative of Morgans. As such I consider myself entitled to know on their behalf if any vital changes in the executive are contemplated.

If you and Sanderson <u>are both leaving the I.M.M. Co.</u>, the loss will be so great that we must seriously and at once consider what is the best way of filling your places.

Let me here say how fully I recognise and admire your ability and your unique grasp of the great business you have built up. Further I appreciate the wrench it will be to you if you settle to give up the active conduct of affairs.

On my side it is due to my position in the city, to insist that if I am a high officer (nominally) of any company, I shall be treated <u>with confidence</u> by the heads of the executive.

I hope you will not mind this statement of what I conceive to be my position.

It is my earnest wish that there may be shortly a solution of the present difficulty satisfactory to you, Sanderson and the I.M.M. Co.

Yours sincerely,
E. C. Grenfill

National Maritime Museum, ref. TRNISM/3/1

Ismay's reply.

18 Feb.
Sandheys

My dear G,

Many thanks for your letter. I also am very glad indeed we had a talk as so far [as] I am concerned it has resulted in entirely clearing away the imaginable [sic] something there was between us and I am convinced it has done good. I am pleased you think the arrangement come to with Sanderson is a very fair one. As you say the 30 June 1913 is a long way off and many changes may take place ere then, but at the same time it is abundantly clear to me that Sanderson unless it is clearly understood that he is to be made President in July 1913 will retire on 31 Dec. 1912 and in his present frame of mind he would not think of remaining on any other condition. Of course things may change. I think it very likely that I will be in London more in the future and repeat what I said to you, viz., that I will be very pleased indeed to see you any time you care to look in at Cockspur Street and have a talk.

National Maritime Museum, ref. TRNISM/3/1

On hearing Ismay wanted to step down immediately Harold Sanderson wrote to encourage him to wait for the good of the company.

Oceanic House
1 Cockspur Street
London, S.W.

7 May '12

My dear Bruce
I received your Marconi to-day while in Court, requesting me to place your resignation in the hands of the Sea, Asiatic and Protection Boards, and also of the Committee of the Palatine and Exchange Clubs.

I feel very strongly that it would be a serious mistake to do anything of the kind, and I am taking upon myself the responsibility of disregarding your instructions . . .

You are I fear unduly depressed by what you have gone through, Bruce, and I don't wonder at it, but you will find the atmosphere here quite different to that in which you have lately been living and suffering.

Your friends are going to stand by you, and the splendid cable sent by our Insurance friends ought to reassure you about the views of your business associates.

I was never more sure of anything than I am that to act on your wire would be to make a false and damaging move. I have seen your Wife and told her of my decision and I think she agrees with me, but I told her I would not alter my decision unless she told me positively to do so.

You will find things will work out all right, and you must just keep a stiff upper lip and see it out.

<u>You</u> know what you did was right – <u>you</u> were on the spot, and could judge properly.

The criticism which existed here was attributable to misrepresentation and to ignorance of the real facts.

I am up to my neck in this wretched B of T Enquiry – it looks like going on for weeks. Furniss is coming to Queenstown to interview Titanic *officers, etc., coming up Channel. Good luck to us all and a stout heart for yourself is the sincere wish of*
Yrs sincerely,
Harold A. Sanderson

National Maritime Museum, ref. TRNISM/3/1

Ismay finally stepped down, as originally planned, on 30 June 1913. His son wrote to him two weeks beforehand, expressing concerns about the politicking surrounding the succession and their own financial position.

Telegrams: 'Mossley Hill'
Parcels: ALLERTON, L. & N.W. Ry.

Maryton,
Allerton,
Liverpool

June 16th 1913

Private.

My dear Father,

You will have seen all the news in the papers this morning, it will be curious to see how it all works out.
The letters from New York have already become rather aggressive and the President elect seems to lean towards consulting all sorts of people, so much so that I wonder whether the title of Manager conferred upon the triumvirate really carries all that the world and its congratulations imagines.
Financially it might have been better, ought to have been retrospective, or at any rate we might have touched some of

*Sanderson's unearned increment. He might also have made us direc-
tors, as others wanted us to be, but that it appears had difficulties which I cannot fathom, but is a bait which is to be dangled
before us.*

*Sanderson knows my ambition and that I shall stay and do all I
can to help him so long as life is agreeable and we receive proper
renumeration: there were some things I did not like in the new
arrangements but the air was too highly charged with electricity to
say much: the future may provide the chance.*

*Meantime I feel more than I can say the changes, out of
sentiment and affection for one who is about to go, whose word was
law, and who did not do certain things because it pleased others,
only because it was right. Sorry to miss you before you go to London.*

*Your affec. son
Tom*

National Maritime Museum, TRINSM/10

For the most part Ismay was able to slip away from public life, moving
to Ireland for a spell before returning to England during his last years.
He died in London on 17 October 1937. Many letters of condolence
were received by his widow, including this one, which shows he was
still considered someone of importance at the end of his life.

*24 Elm Hall Drive
Mossley Hill
Liverpool 18*

October 20th 1937

*Dear Mrs. Ismay,
It is with feelings of the deepest regret that I have heard of the death
of your dear husband.*

*Remembering your many kindnesses to me in the past I hasten to
express my heartfelt sympathy with you in this great bereavement.*

As I walked through the streets yesterday & saw the flags flying halfmast as a token of respect & to honour the passing of a great son of Liverpool I was deeply impressed at the thought that another link had been severed between the City & one of its greatest families.
    Trusting God will give you strength to bear the great trouble
I remain
Yours sincerely
Nannie Marshall

National Maritime Museum, TRNISM/10

Not all of the major players lived out the rest of their lives in relative peace. Fred Fleet, the lookout who spotted the iceberg, ended his own life in a state of depression after his wife passed away in 1965. Despite returning to the sea after the loss of the *Titanic,* his obituary shows that he was forever unable to escape its shadow.

TITANIC LOOKOUT IS DEAD BY HANGING AFTER WIFE'S DEATH
Southampton, England, Jan 11. (Reuters) Authorities today ordered an inquest into the death of Fred Fleet, a lookout on the liner *Titanic,* who hanged himself yesterday two weeks after his wife's death. The body of Mr. Fleet, who was 76 years old, was found hanging from a post in the garden of his Southampton home. The police said he had been depressed since the death of his wife, 74. Mr. Fleet was one of the principal witnesses at an inquiry on the sinking of the *Titanic . . .* He was part of the crew of one of the ship's lifeboats and was picked up three hours later by the liner *Carpathia.* The disaster did not deter him from going back to sea. He spent the next 24 years on various vessels before taking a job on shore during the depression. He preserved his seaman's discharge book, in which his *Titanic* experience was recorded in two terse sentences: 'Discharged at sea. Destination intended for New York.' Some criticism for the heavy loss of life among the

Titanic's passengers was aimed at Capt. Stanley Lord, master of the liner *Californian*, which was stopped in ice only a few miles away when the *Titanic* sank. Courts of inquiry, held in Britain and the United States, censured Captain Lord for failing to appreciate the nature of rocket signals reported to him. He contended that the *Californian* could not have reached the scene of the disaster ahead of the *Carpathia*, the first vessel to do so. Mr. Lord died in 1962 without gaining a rehearing on his role.

National Maritime Museum, LMQ/7/3/F

It is also worth remembering those who left England on the *Titanic* for a better life but had their plans destroyed that night. Charlotte Collyer lost her husband Harvey, though she was rescued in the *Carpathia* with her daughter Marjorie. However, she was left utterly destitute by the shipwreck, losing all the family's savings. The desperate plight she faced was recorded in a letter she sent back to her parents-in-law.

Brooklyn, New York
Sun April 21st

My dear Mother and all,

I don't know how to write to you or what to say, I feel I shall go mad sometimes but dear as much as my heart aches it aches for you too for he is your son and the best that ever lived. I had not given up hope till today that he might be found but I'm told all boats are accounted for. Oh mother, how can I live without him. I wish I'd gone with him if they had not wrenched Madge from me I should have stayed and gone with him. But they threw her into the boat and pulled me in too but he was so calm and I know he would rather I lived for her little sake otherwise she would have been an orphan. The agony of that night can never be told. Poor mite was frozen. I have been ill but have been taken care of by a rich New York doctor and feel better now. They are giving us every comfort and have collected quite a few pounds for us and loaded us with clothes and a gentleman on Monday is taking us to the White Star office and also to another office to get us some money from the funds that is being raised here. Oh mother there are some good kind hearts in New York, some want me to go back to England but I can't, I could never at least not yet go over the ground where my all is sleeping.

Sometimes I feel we lived too much for each other, that is why I've lost him. But mother we shall meet him in heaven. When that band played 'Nearer My God To Thee' I know he thought of you and me for we both loved that hymn and I feel that when I go to Payette I'm doing what he would wish me to, so I hope to do this at the end of next week where I shall have friends and work and I will work for his darling as long as she needs me. Oh she is a comfort but she don't realise yet that her Daddy is in heaven. There are some dear children here who have loaded her with lovely toys but it's when I'm alone with her she will miss him. Oh mother I haven't a thing in the world that was his only his rings. Everything we had went down. Will you, dear mother, send me on a last photo of us, get it copied? I will pay you later on. Mrs. Hallet's brother from Chicago is doing all he can for us in fact the night we landed in New York (in our nightgowns) he had engaged a room at a big hotel with food and every comfort waiting for us. He has been a father to us. I will send his address on a card (Mr. Horder) perhaps you might like to write to him some time.

God bless you dear mother and help and comfort you in this awful sorrow.
Your loving child Lot

Donald Hyslop, Alastair Forsyth, and Sheila Jemima
Titanic Voices: Memories from the Fateful Voyage
(Southampton: Sutton Publishing Ltd, 1997)

Charlotte Collyer sold her story to the *Semi-Monthly* magazine in May 1912 and received a further sum from both the American Relief Fund and the British Titanic Relief Fund.

> No. 83. (English)
> The husband was drowned. His wife and seven-year-old daughter were saved. He was a merchant in England and had been the parish clerk in the village where they lived. They were highly respected people in fair circumstances. The wife had contracted tuberculosis and they were coming to this country to buy a fruit farm in Idaho, where they hoped the climate would be beneficial. He was carrying $5,000 in cash; this was lost, and all their household belongings. Both the widow and her daughter suffered severely from shock and exposure. They were at first unwilling to return to England, feeling that the husband would have wished them to carry out his original plan. For emergent needs she was given $200 by this Committee, and $450 by other American relief funds. After a short residence in the West she decided to return to her family in England. Through interested friends in New York City, a fund of $2,000 was raised, and she received $300 for a magazine article describing the disaster. She returned to England in June and her circumstances were reported to the English Committee, which granted £50 outright and a pension of 23 shillings a week. ($200).
>
> www.encyclopedia-titanica.org

Charlotte Collyer remarried but in 1914 succumbed to the tuberculosis that had impelled her and her family to set foot on the *Titanic* in the first place.

Yet there were happy endings for some. Marion Wright met her fiancé Arthur Woolcott in New York. She wrote to her parents shortly after travelling on to Cottage Grove, Oregon, where his farm was located. They married, and stayed in America, where they raised three sons. She eventually died in 1965, aged 80.

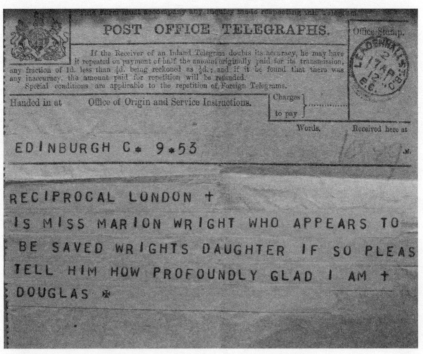

POST OFFICE TELEGRAPHS.

If the Receiver of an Inland Telegram doubts its accuracy, he may have it repeated on payment of half the amount originally paid for its transmission, any fraction of 1d. less than ½d. being reckoned as ½d.; and if it be found that there was any inaccuracy, the amount paid for repetition will be refunded.
Special conditions are applicable to the repetition of Foreign Telegrams.

Handed in at   Office of Origin and Service Instructions.

EDINBURGH C. 9.53

RECIPROCAL LONDON +
IS MISS MARION WRIGHT WHO APPEARS TO
BE SAVED WRIGHTS DAUGHTER IF SO PLEAS
TELL HIM HOW PROFOUNDLY GLAD I AM +
DOUGLAS *

Telegram from a family friend to Marion Wright's family.

Cottage Grove, Oregon
Sunday aft. May 3rd 1912

Dearest Dad & Mother,
This is my first letter to you from my new home. I wish you could see it. I am very happy & comfortable & feel already that I am going to like this country very much. It seems odd to think that while I write this, you are in bed, as tis 10pm with you now & only just after 2pm with us. Arthur & I arrived here i.e. Cottage Grove, on Thurs morning May 2nd at 6.30am & were met by a friend of his who lives about halfway between this house & Cottage Grove. This man Curtis Veatch seems very nice & his wife feel will be a friend. We had breakfast at their house, & then later drove up here. Arthur had written a neighbour here to come in & put to rights a bit, & she had got the place so beautifully clean & also cooked the dinner, we sat down to

our first meal with company, as Mr. Veatch & his wife & a close neighbour & her little girl were with us. We both felt very tired with the train journey & Arthur had almost lost his voice with having too much chiffy [sic] air in the train or car as they call them out here. It is alright now though & we both feel rested. Everybody says that I don't look much like anyone who has been through such a terrible experience. I can't very well say in a letter or even put into words quite what I feel about it all but the memory of it all will never go I'm sure. Everything was so sudden & my heart is full of thankfulness to God for having preserved me through all the great kindness shown by quite strangers right along from New York, still continues. We have about 20 fresh presents including doz silver spoons, silver cruet stand, a beautifully bound teacher's bible, prayer & hymn book, picture, damask table cloth, doz dinner napkins, a quart jug from a neighbour, 4 or 5 under garments for myself, £2 from a friend of Arthur's in Chicago, & about doz songs from various people, & yesterday we drove into town & called at the P.O. to see if there were any letters & found about doz, including Bertie, Marian, Balding, Blanche, Kate (a girl friend of Marian's) & also one from Alsie Woolcott containing £2 to get some blouses she says. All these latter were written after they had seen of the disaster to the Titanic. Poor old Bertie, in fact I feel more sorry for all my relations & friends in England than I do for myself, because the shock & anxiety must be pretty bad to all. That was what troubled us in the lifeboat. We knew the disaster would be in all the papers Monday morning the 15th April & you wouldn't know of our safety for some time. But all in our boat kept well right through & except for feeling a trifle weary, probably owing to the shock, I am none the worse thank God. The people round here are holding a reception in Cottage Grove next wed, May 8th in the evening to welcome me to the neighbourhood & they are giving us a handsome present. I will tell you later on what form it takes. At this reception they have asked me to say a few words about my 'experience' & although I don't care about it _at all_ yet as they are being so kind I feel I must make a slight return & so have said I will, although I have told them that such things are better not talked about as it all seems so terrible. I hope you have been able to send my letters to the boys & Ernie to read. I have written Ernie a separate account as you will see when the letter arrives at home. I wrote p.p.c's to most of my relations & friends (to whom I did not send letters) on the train. The journey also was a little wearying, but we had splendid nights on the train, the scenery is truly grand, especially along the Colombia river & down the Willamette Valley. For a day & a half we were crossing the Rockies, covered in snow & the prairie beneath them, a very wild part I can assure you! We were both very glad to get home & to find all going on well. I do so enjoy the milk & cream from Arthur's Jersey cow & hope next week to try my hand at butter making. I haven't had to do very much cooking in the pudding & cake line so far as friends & neighbours gave us all kinds of things. Several cakes & fruit & jellies etc. were here awaiting our arrival, so I have only had to cook meat. Next Sat. we most probably shall be asking our friends in, we were told people were coming to see us this week & Arthur thinks it would be better if we say we will be <u>at home</u> one day, & then I can prepare for them properly. It will be a wee bit strange acting the part of hostess, but all I have met so far, & that all includes a good number, have been very pleasant & exceedingly kind. Arthur drove us into Cottage Grove on Friday, to get our baggage, the latter was the result of shopping in Chicago from the money that the ladies of the relief committee gave me. I have a nice stock of underlinen, boots, shoes, coat & skirt, dresses (2 & cotton), mackintoch, then we got sheets, pillow cases, the latter I have to make up, we are sleeping in cotton blankets at present & they are so 'comfy', then household things such as jugs, table silver!, towels, quilt etc. & if we get our claim from the White Star Co., we will be able to get along very well indeed.

Monday aft! I wasn't able to finish this yesterday aft. as a friend came in to see us & before that I went up into the woods with Arthur to bring down the cow. She had got through the fencing some how, so it took us a considerable time to get her onto our own land. I picked a lovely bunch of flowers while up there, flowering currant iris & several other sorts. There are any quantity of flowers of varied kinds here, the colum vine, arum lily, large corn flowers etc. look so pretty in the field up Arthur's hill. The mountains are grand & today is such a lovely day, bright hot sun. I have been wearing a cotton dress ever since I arrived here & find it plenty warm enough (short sleeves and low neck). Arthur was off at 8am this morning & will be back at 6pm this evening. He has gone to put up new telephone poles on the line that he & 4 other neighbours own. He called me up on the phone just now & I had a talk with him, ours is 5 short rings, but we hear all the others, each has a different call! The first morning, while we were having breakfast, a humming bird came & hovered just outside one of the windows. They are sweet little birds, then that same morning I saw two flocks of geese flying north. They fly in curious form thus >. Arthur's trees look very well. The old ones of which he has a good number are very full of blossom, we have two large apple trees peeping into the kitchen windows & they are in full bloom & smell really lovely! I had my first lesson in driving the tram last Friday coming home from town & got on very well. I don't think it will take me very long to learn, anyway I hope not. I am going to be busy making up curtains, as soon as possible, we bought a good many yds of spotted muslin in Chicago then Mrs. Veatch is going to let me hem my sheets on her machine & anything else I like, till I get one of my own. I am writing Bertie a short letter, but would you mind letting Mrs. Woolcott see this when you have read it, & then send it to the boys & Evie. I cannot get much time for long letters to many people, especially just now, when so many people are continually dropping in to have a talk with us & later on I shall have got into a regular routine & then can write letters to everybody I trust. How are the three children, I have thought several times lately of one of Marjorie's remarks before I left England, do you remember she said 'she wouldn't like to go to sleep on the sea in case she got wrecked' & I told her I didn't think about such things as wrecks. I hope you are all quite well. I am exceedingly so, the air here is so refreshing, the smell of the grass blowing down from the mown lawn is lovely. Arthur & I join in love to all & hoping to hear from you

*soon (I went down to our letter box at the end of our lane & found
several for me this morning).*
   Your ever loving daughter,
   Marion Woolcott

National Maritime Museum, HSR/Z/30/1-17

The last word, however, has to belong to someone who lived the longest
and fullest life of all those who survived that terrible night – Elizabeth
Gladys 'Millvina' Dean. At nine weeks old, she had no recollections
of the event, and only found out that she had been on board several
years later when her mother eventually remarried. Millvina's mother
and brother also survived the disaster, and eventually returned to
England on board the *Adriatic*. As the youngest survivor, she naturally
attracted much attention from the other passengers on board. '[She]
was the pet of the liner during the voyage, and so keen was the rivalry
between women to nurse this lovable mite of humanity that one of
the officers decreed that first and second class passengers might hold
her in turn for no more than ten minutes' (*Daily Mirror*, 12 May 1912,
British Newspaper Library).

Millvina's parents Bertram and Eva ran a public house, but had
decided to uproot the family – they had an older son Bertram Vere,
born in 1910 – to Wichita, Kansas to start a new life in America with
friends and family. They had secured third-class passage on another
White Star liner, but were transferred to the *Titanic* due to the coal
strike. Millvina recalls her mother talking in devoted terms about her
husband, and in her view it was his quick thinking that had saved
their lives. Millvina recounted that 'he heard the collision, a bit like a
loud bang, and went out to investigate. He came back shortly afterwards and said he didn't like the look of things. He said to us, "Come
on, let's get up on deck just to be on the safe side." Mother got us
dressed and we followed him up.' During the pandemonium of the
evacuation, Bertram remained calm throughout, ushering his family
to the lifeboats so that they could get to safety. However, he was forced
to stay on deck as his wife and children were evacuated – although he

said he'd get into another lifeboat, he was unable to secure a place and went down with the ship. His body was never recovered. According to Millvina, the loss 'broke my mother's heart'.

Millvina recalls how she was placed in a mail sack, and lowered over the side into the waiting arms of fellow passengers already in the lifeboat. 'Mother had a moment of panic when she couldn't find my brother Bert – she started calling his name, and was close to panic, when another passenger said that she'd got him and we were reunited.'

In many ways, Millvina's recollections of the sinking of the *Titanic* do not add much in the way of detail to the overall story – they were memories passed to her by her mother and, as she admitted herself, became more fascinating as the number of survivors diminished. When conducting the interview, the way she told the story of her escape seemed polished, the result of telling the tale to reporters and journalists many times over the last few years. As she readily admitted, she did not feel that the disorder had affected her early life enormously, although of course she would have been brought up as an American and had no father until her mother remarried when Millvina was eight. The real fascination lay in the way the *Titanic* came to play an increasingly important role in her later life, as she happily recounted to me stories of how, from her seventies, she had suddenly been given the opportunity to visit places and meet people she simply would never have met. There were trips to America, VIP invitations to open exhibitions, and growing media interest.

Despite well-reported financial troubles at the end of her life, which forced her to sell some of her memorabilia, Millvina seemed happy and comfortable, and – in the nicest possible way – to enjoy her celebrity status, even though she could never fully understand the fascination of the *Titanic* nearly a century after it had sunk. Yet the ship that had changed her life and placed her in the media spotlight still cast a shadow over her. 'I can't help wondering what would have happened if my father had survived. I look at his picture and think of my mother, and the pain she felt at the time. It must have been so hard for her to bring us back to England, to her family and farm, and start again without him.' Perhaps it is no coincidence that she found it difficult to watch any film that dramatised events, and was equally uncomfort-able about the way the wreck was explored after its discovery in 1985, knowing that her father's was among the bodies still undiscovered down there. Hopefully, she would have approved of this attempt to give the memory of the *Titanic* back to those who were there at the time, and it is a great regret that I cannot now hand her a copy, as I promised her in February 2009.

Sources

National Maritime Museum, Greenwich

Ismay Files (TRNISM)

- TRNISM/1/1 – Transcripts of letters of support for J. B. Ismay in the aftermath of the *Titanic* disaster. Also includes transcripts of newspaper extracts relating to *Titanic* (1912 onwards)
- TRNISM/1/2 – Transcripts entitled 'Speed': correspondence and newspaper extracts relating to the proceedings of the *Titanic* inquiry (1912 onwards)
- TRNISM/1/4 – Transcripts of correspondence mainly to J. B. Ismay and also of newspaper cuttings regarding *Titanic* inquiry (1912 onwards)
- TRNISM/2/2 – Transcript of correspondence and agreement relating to presidency of International Mercantile Marine Company and Bruce Ismay's appointment. Also include copy of agreement between Oceanic Steam Navigation Company and Bruce Ismay, whereby Bruce is made Managing Director of the Company in England (1903–1906)
- TRNISM/2/3 – Transcripts of correspondence regarding Bruce Ismay's retirement, the directorship of White Star Line and the presidency of International Mercantile Marine Company (1911–12)
- TRNISM/2/4 – Transcripts of letters to Bruce Ismay on his resignation from presidency of International Mercantile Marine Company (1913 onwards)
- TRNISM/2/5 – Transcripts of correspondence and documents

relating to Bruce Ismay's resignation from International Mercantile Marine Company (1913 onwards)

- TRNISM/3/1 – Transcripts of miscellaneous correpondence relating to Ismay, Imrie and Co., International Mercantile Marine Company and subsidary companies, and various appointments to or resignations from their Boards of Directors. Also copies of newspaper extracts and correspondence relating to *Titanic* disaster (1855–1930)
- TRNISM/10 – Joseph Bruce Ismay obituaries: one volume of newspaper cuttings. Also copies typed up from newspapers and company minutes. Also includes letters of condolence to Mrs Florence Bruce Ismay on Bruce's death

Lord MacQuitty Files (LMQ)

- LMQ/1/12/1 – Original set of 12 photographs taken by Louis Mansfield Ogden of the scene of the *Titanic* disaster, taken from the deck of the CARPATHIA, 14 April 1912. Accompanying letter from Mr Ogden to Mrs H.A. Cassebeer, 2 May 1912
- LMQ/1/14/1 – Engineer's notebook with comments on *Titanic*, written by David Watson. Watson was employed at Harland & Wolff when *Titanic* was built. Includes comments on Thomas Andrews and shortcomings in the ship's design
- LMQ/1/14/2 – Letters from Bruce Ismay to Edith Russell and her mother, 14 October 1912
- LMQ/1/14/10 – Christmas card sent by *Titanic* 5th Officer Lowe to Renee Harris, survivor, 1935
- LMQ/4/1/11 – Front page of *The Daily Mail and Empire* Toronto, Sat, 20 April 1912
- LMQ/5/1 – Private wireless traffic to and from the *Carpathia*. Copies of messages sent and received by survivors of the *Titanic* from the *Carpathia*
- LMQ/7/1/1 – Typed account by Mrs J. W. Anderson, *Titanic* survivor, of her memories of the sinking
- LMQ/7/1/2 – Letter from Mr. W. H. Dobbyn to Robert Ferguson, both employees of the Astors, relating Mrs. Astor's account of the disaster, dated 15 May 1912

- LMQ/7/1/5 – Papers relating to *Titanic* survivor Karl H. Behr. Includes typed account of *Titanic* disaster from scrapbook of Karl H. Behr, and Chapter XIV – an excerpt from a book written by Behr for his family and friends. Also copy of journal article on Behr entitled 'Two Lawrentians who survived the *Titanic*' by Tracey Allen, Lawrentian, Spring 1998
- LMQ/7/1/7 – Letter from Mrs John Black (Lillian W. Bentham), *Titanic* survivor, to Geoffry G. Martin, Rank Film, dated 23 July 1958. Includes her experience on the lifeboat and being rescued
- LMQ/7/1/9 – Letter from Betty Bolling, *Titanic* survivor, dated 8 July 1958, recounting how experiences in the lifeboat after the sinking of the *Titanic*
- LMQ/7/1/12 – Copy of a letter from Harold Bride to W.R. Cross, 27 April 1912, providing a full account of his experiences of the sinking of the *Titanic*
- LMQ/7/1/16 – Letter from Mrs (Eleanor) Henry H. Cassebeer, Jr., *Titanic* survivor, to Walter Lord, 9 November 1955, recounting her memories of the disaster
- LMQ/7/1/15 – Photocopy of a letter from W.G. Browne to Mr Maxtone Graham, 3 October 1991, about Alex Carlisle, former Harland and Wolff yard manager
- LMQ/7/1/17 – Letters from Gus Cohen, *Titanic* survivor, to Walter Lord, June – July 1955, includes his account of the disaster
- LMQ/7/1/18 – Letter from Walter Lord to Mrs. Cooke, daughter of Capt. Smith, dated 26 June 1955, explaining what his book, *A Night To Remember* would be about
- LMQ/7/1/19 – Copy of a letter from Edwina Corrigan (nee Troutt), *Titanic* survivor, to William MacQuitty, 20 March 1958
- LMQ/7/1/20 – Copies of letters from Cunard and Bruce Ismay, including advice on how to avoid icebergs, 1912
- LMQ/7/1/23 – Article from *The Wiltshire Times* Sat, 20 April 1912, reading: 'To-days telegrams: The sinking of the *Titanic*, News at Last, Details of the Disaster, Captain Shot Himself Dead, The Sufferings of the Survivors'
- LMQ/7/1/24 – Letter from Mrs Celiney Decker (nee Yazbeck),

Titanic survivor, to Walter Lord, 15 June 1955, providing an account of her experiences on the night of the *Titanic* disaster

- LMQ/7/1/28 – Copy of a letter from Laura Mabel Francatelli, *Titanic* survivor, to Mary Ann Taylor, dated 28 April 1012. The letter gives a detailed account of her memories of the sinking of the *Titanic* and her rescue

- LMQ/7/1/29 – Letter from Marguerite Frolicher, *Titanic* survivor, to Walter Lord, dated 27 December 1955. Also includes abstract of interview Lord conducted with her on 13 July 1955, in which she mentions her experiences on the *Titanic* and her rescue

- LMQ/7/1/30 – Letter from Mrs (Lily) Jacques Futrelle, *Titanic* survivor, to Walter Lord, dated 20 November 1955, includes her account of the *Titanic* disaster

- LMQ/7/1/31 – Letter from Harry Giles to Walter Lord, dated 5 July 1955. Giles was a fireman on board the *Titanic* and survived the sinking

- LMQ/7/1/32 – Transcript of an interview between Walter Lord and Katherine Gilnagh, *Titanic* survivor, 1955. Includes her experiences as a steerage passenger on board *Titanic* and surviving the disaster

- LMQ/7/1/33 – Excerpts of correspondence by *Titanic* survivors about the disaster. Includes letters from Mrs Frank Goldsmith and Frank Goldsmith, a third-class passenger

- LMQ/7/1/34 – Letter from Frank Goldsmith, *Titanic* survivor, to Walter Lord, dated 7 March 1956

- LMQ/7/1/35&36 – Obituary for Lady Duff Gordon and Cosmo Gordon in *The New York Times* dated 21 April 1931 and 22 April 1935, and cuttings from the same paper about court cases for the bankruptcy of her business in 1919

- LMQ/7/1/37 – Third Officer of the Californian, Charles Groves, account of the night'

- LMQ/7/1/38 – Letter from George Harris, cook on the *Titanic* to William MacQuitty, dated 16 December 1956. Includes his account of the sinking of the *Titanic* and his time in the lifeboat

- LMQ/7/1/39 – Transcript of an interview between Walter Lord and

Mrs Henry B. Harris, First Class passenger and survivor of the *Titanic* disaster, dated 31 May 1964. Also includes typewritten account of the *Titanic* disaster

- LMQ/7/1/40 – Copy of a letter by Eva Hart to Mrs Bloomfied, written on RMS *Titanic* stationery whilst onboard the *Titanic*. Also includes an account of her survival in the lifeboat following the sinking
- LMQ/7/1/42 – Copy of a letter from Mary Hewlett, *Titanic* survivor, written aboard RMS *Laconia*, dated 30 May 1912. Includes her account of the *Titanic* disaster and the rescue by the *Carpathia*
- LMQ/7/1/44 – Letter from Walter Hurst to Walter Lord, n.d. Hurst worked in the engine room on *Titanic*. Provides account of the *Titanic* disaster and how Hurst survived
- LMQ/7/1/47 – Letter from Charles Joughin, chief baker on *Titanic*, to Walter Lord, n.d. Also includes letter from Capt J. J. Anderson to the editor of the Ladies Home Journal, about Charles Joughin
- LMQ/7/1/49 – Letter from George Kemish, boiler room worker on *Titanic*, to Walter Lord, 19 June 1955. Includes his memories of the *Titanic* disaster
- LMQ/7/1/51 – Copy of letter received by Gretchen Langley whilst a passenger on board *Titanic*, dated 10 April 1912. Includes note from Walter Lord on how Langley survived the *Titanic* disaster
- LMQ/7/2/1 – Copy of a letter from Alexander Macomb to his mother, USS FLORIDA, New York, 16 April 1912, on the reaction in New York to news of the *Titanic* disaster
- LMQ/7/2/5 – Correspondence between Walter Lord and Mrs Madeline V. Mann (nee Mellinger), *Titanic* survivor, dated 1955–69, includes detailed account of the *Titanic* disaster and her experience in the lifeboat
- LMQ/7/2/8 – Letters from Arthur Olsen, *Titanic* survivor, to Mr G. Martin, 26 July 1958 and 14 September 1959. Olsen was 9 years old when he sailed on *Titanic*. Second letter includes names and details of passengers he was acquainted with on *Titanic* and further details of his experience in the lifeboat

- LMQ/7/2/9 – Letter from Helen R. Ostby, *Titanic* survivor to Walter Lord, 7 March 1956, includes account of lifeboat 5 and being picked up by the Carpathia
- LMQ/7/2/11 – Letter from George Perkins to Walter Lord on behalf of his mother Victorine Perkins, *Titanic* survivor, 19 May 1955. Includes copy of newspaper article about Victorine's experience on *Titanic* entitled 'Woman almost locked in *Titanic* cabin'
- LMQ/7/2/12 – Letter from Richard Proffer, Second Class cabin waiter on *Titanic*, to Walter Lord, includes account of the *Titanic* disaster and his rescue
- LMQ/7/2/13 – Letter from A. Pugh (3rd class Steward), *Titanic* survivor, to Walter Lord, includes account of the *Titanic* disaster and his experience in the lifeboat, 20 Jul 1955
- LMQ/7/2/15 – Letters from L. Dent Ray, *Titanic* survivor, to Walter Lord, describing the sinking of the *Titanic* and his rescue, 14 July 1955. Second letter refers to items removed from *Titanic* in Ray's coat pocket
- LMQ/7/2/16 – Photocopy of letter from George Rheims, *Titanic* survivor, to his wife, in French, dated 19 April 1912. Includes account of the *Titanic* sinking and rescue of the survivors. Includes Engish translation
- LMQ/7/2/19 – Letter from Miss E. Rosenbaum (Edith Russell), *Titanic* survivor, to Walter Lord, 28 April 1956, mentioning her book about the *Titanic* disaster. Includes detailed account of her experiences on *Titanic*, dated 11 April 1934 and a copy of her memoirs 'A pig and a promise saved me from the *Titanic*'
- LMQ/7/2/20 – Letter from the Countess of Rothes, *Titanic* survivor, to Walter Lord, 7 Aug 1955. Includes detailed account of the *Titanic* disaster and her rescue in a lifeboat
- LMQ/7/2/21 – Letter from George J. Rowe, crewmember on *Titanic*, to Walter Lord, n.d. Includes account of *Titanic* disaster and his rescue in the same lifeboat as Bruce Ismay
- LMQ/7/2/22 – Copy of letter from Mrs Emily Ryerson, *Titanic* survivor, dated 18 April 1913, she was with Bruce Ismay on *Titanic* when he received telegram warning about icebergs

- LMQ/7/2/25 – Photocopies of wireless cable sent from the *Carpathia* by Spencer V. Silverthorne, *Titanic* survivor, giving news of his rescue. Includes transcript of his interview with Walter Lord, dated 14 July 1955
- LMQ/7/2/26 – Copy of letter from Dr Jack Simpson, Assistant Surgeon on *TITANIC*, to his mother, on RMS *Titanic* writing paper, dated 11 April 1912. Also correspondence to his family about Dr Simpson's last moments on *Titanic* before she sank
- LMQ/7/2/27 – Letters from Anna Sjoblom, Third Class passenger on *Titanic*, to Walter Lord, dated 24 June 1955 and 18 July 1955, recounting her experiences of the sinking and escape in a lifeboat
- LMQ/7/2/28 – Copy of letter from May Sloan, Stewardess on *Titanic*, to her sister Maggie, on board S.S. *Lapland*, 27 April 1912, about her experiences of the *Titanic* disaster
- LMQ/7/2/29 – Transcript and notes of interview with Maude Slocomb, first class Masseuse on *Titanic*, to Walter Lord, July 1955, recounting her experiences of the *Titanic* sinking
- LMQ/7/2/30 – Copy of letter by Mrs Isidor Strauss, written on board *Titanic* and posted before the ship sank, on RMS *Titanic* writing paper
- LMQ/7/2/32 – Copy of letter from Mrs J.B. Thayer, *Titanic* survivor, to President Taft, 21 Aprikl 1912, describing memories of Major Butt, aide to President Taft, who died in the *Titanic* disaster
- LMQ/7/2/33 – Copy of letter by Edwina Troutt, Second Class passenger on *Titanic*, to Mrs Milling, 5 June 1912, recounting memories of Mr Milling who died in the *Titanic* disaster. Includes letter from Geoffrey G. Martin to Walter Lord, 11 Nov 1958, about interview he conducted with Edwina Troutt
- LMQ/7/2/36 – Photocopy of account by Robert A. Vaughan, Steward on *Carpathia*, 'A memory of 15 April 1912: the rescue of the survivors of RMS *Titanic*'. Also includes two further accounts 'I remember', 20 Jan 1962 and 'I was there when the SOS came'
- LMQ/7/2/37 – Letter from Bertha Watt, *Titanic* survivor, to Walter Lord, 10 April 1963, includes account of *Titanic* disaster and how she took a menu from *Titanic*

- LMQ/7/2/38 – Letter from Mary Louise Wellman, *Titanic* survivor, to Walter Lord, account of *Titanic* disaster and return voyage to New York on *Carpathia*
- LMQ/7/2/39 – Letter from Frank Johnston to James MacQuitty, 20 November 1956, enclosing copy of letter from *Titanic* greaser Alfred White to brother-in-law of Mr Parr, Assistant Manager of Electrical Dept, Harland & Wolff, dated 21 June 1912
- LMQ/7/2/40 – Mrs. J. Stuart White (Ella Holmes White)'s Statement, a letter and a copy of her claim against the Oceanic Steam Navigation Co. for her losses
- LMQ/7/2/43 – Letter from Alice Cleaver (later Mrs. Williams), nurse to the Allison family, written to Walter Lord in 1955
- LMQ/7/2/44 – Correspondence between R. Norris Williams, *Titanic* survivor, and Walter Lord, April – May 1964. Includes typed account of *Titanic* disaster 'Some reminiscences ot R. Norris Williams II on April 14–15 1912' and notes taken by Walter Lord, dated 27 April 1962
- LMQ/7/2/45 – Letter from Mr J. Witter, Second Class Duty Smokeroom Steward on *Titanic*, to Walter Lord, 9 July 1955, includes account of disaster and copy of his paying off sheet from *Titanic*
- LMQ/7/2/46 – Hugh Woolner's letter home written aboard the Carpathia and published by the *New York Sun*
- LMQ/7/3/A – *Providence Evening Bulletin* 24 April 1912 article about Mrs. Rosa Abbott's escape from ship, but her two sons drowned
- LMQ/7/3/A – *The Tacoma Sunday News Tribune And Ledger* 2 December 1955, interview by Bob Merry with Ole Abelseth
- LMQ/7/3/A – 1992 article in *Canadian Connections: They Sailed Aboard Titanic* about the Allison Family
- LMQ/7/3/A – 1992 article in *Canadian Connections: They Sailed Aboard Titanic* about Molly Brown
- LMQ/7/3/B – Copies of letters from George Arthur Beedum to his mother and family while aboard the *Titanic*
- LMQ/7/3/B – Letter from Lawrence Beesley to Walter Lord analysing the noise of the people screaming in the water
- LMQ/7/3/B – Letter from Lawrence Beesley to his daughter Kit on

board the *Titanic*, 10 April 1912, and article in *The New York Times Magazine* 25 June 1995, written by Beesley's grandson Nicholas Wade

- LMQ/7/3/B – Newspaper article dated 19 April 1912 with interview with Karl H. Behr
- LMQ/7/3/C – Article in *Outpost* 5 September 1956, headed 'Greatest Sea Disaster Link with B.S.A. Police' by E. Moore Ritchie
- LMQ/7/3/CANDEE – File of Candee material for Hugh Brewseer compiled by Walter Lord
- LMQ/7/3/D – Newspaper interview with Margaret O'Neill (nee Devaney), 3 class Irish immigrant, in *The Herald-News* 5 Feb 1974
- LMQ/7/3/F – American Newspaper report about Fred Fleet's suicide, 1965
- LMQ/7/3/G – Article written by Elin Hakkarainen in *Yankee* September 1987
- LMQ/7/3/G – Newspaper clippings from *Niagara Falls Journal* about the loss of the 8 members of the Goodwin family, whose relatives were awaiting them in New York
- LMQ/7/3/GOLDSMITH – Water Lord's foreword for a book published in 1991 of Frank Goldsmith's memoirs, mainly made up of his mother's correspondence

Marion Woolcott Papers (HSR)

- HSR/Z/30/1-17 – Papers of Mrs Marion Woolcott (nee Wright), 1885–1965, *Titanic* survivor

Fred Hamilton's Diary (JOD)

- JOD/221/1,2 – Diary of Frederick A. Hamilton, cable engineer, whilst aboard the *Mackay Bennett*, recovering corpses after the loss of the *Titanic*, 17 Apr 1912 – 1 May 1912. Includes sketches and Transcripts of the diary of Frederick A. Hamilton, cable engineer, whilst aboard the *Mackay Bennett*, collecting bodies after the loss of the *Titanic*, 17 Apr 1912 – 1 May 1912

British Library

Newspaper Collection

* *Daily Mirror* Consortium Online Newspapers
* *The Times* Digital Archive
* Irish Newspaper Archive (Online)

Public Record Office of Northern Ireland

* D3655 – Andrews' Family Papers
* D2805 – Harland and Wolff Papers (the private ledgers of William James (Viscount Pirrie), the chairman of Harland and Wolff, 1896–1924)

Merseyside Maritime Museum

Correspondence

* DX/504 – Joseph Bruce Ismay, Papers, including correspondence relating to the *Titanic* enquiry (1909–1916)
* D/BRW/2 – Mildred Brown's letter written on board *Carpathia* to her mother
* DX/1549/R – Telegram sent by survivor Esther Hart to relatives, informing them of the loss of her husband and the return of herself and her daughter, Eva, on SS *Celtic*, 20 April 1912
* DX/1522 – Transcripts of survivor Gladys Cherry's three letters home, written on board the rescue ship SS *Carpathia*, describing the events of the sinking in graphic detail, 17–19 April 1912. Also two issues of the *Daily Mail*, 16 and 22 April 1912

Plans

* B/CUN/8/1911.1/1/11 – Original large filed plan of the Midship section
* B/CUN/8/1911.1/1/9 – *Olympic* Rough sketch of stern frame castings and rudder, 4 December 1909

- B/CUN/8/1911.1/1/1 – *Olympic* 2nd class smoke room window
- B/CUN/8/1911.1/1/7 – *Olympic* Function of dummy tunnel
- B/CUN/8/1911.1/1/5 – *Olympic* proposed arrangement of Murrays Nesting Lifeboats Accommodating all Persons on Board in Nests of 2 Lifeboats under each pair of davits' (*c.*1920)

Titanic Inquiry Project

- British and American Courts of Inquiry – http://www.Titanicinquiry.org/

Oral History Archives

- BBC *Titanic* Archive – http://www.bbc.co.uk/archive/Titanic/

Books

Barczewski, Stephanie, *Titanic: A Night Remembered* (Hambledon Continuum, 2004, 2007)

Gracie, Colonel Archibald, *The Illustrated Truth about the Titanic* (Amberley, 1913, 2009)

Gracie, Colonel Archibald, *The Truth About the Titanic* (Amberley, 1913)

Green, Rod, *Building The Titanic: An Epic Tale of Modern Engineering and Human Endeavour*

Hislop, Donald, Forsyth, Alastair and Jemima, Sheila (eds), *Titanic Voices: Memories from the Fateful Voyage* (Sutton Publishing Ltd, 1999)

Lord, Walter, *A Night to Remember* (Holt McDougal, 2008)

Marcus, Geoffrey, *The Maiden Voyage: A Complete and Documented Account of the Titanic* (Aberdeen University Press, 1969)

Mitchell, David, *Cloud Atlas* (Sceptre, 2004)

List of Illustrations

Plate Section Images

Plate Section 1:

Page 1: Harland and Wolff shipyard, © Ulster Folk and Transport Museum

Page 2: Sister ships *Titanic* and *Olympic* next to each other in the Harland and Wolff shipyard, © Ulster Folk and Transport Museum; A port main engine at Harland and Wolff, © Ulster Folk and Transport Museum

Page 3: Harland and Wolff workers fitting the starboard tail shaft, © Ulster Folk and Transport Museum

Page 4: A plan of the layout of the *Titanic*, © Father Browne Photographic Collection; Harland and Wolff workmen leaving the Queen's Island dockyard, © Ulster Folk and Transport Museum

Page 5: Harland and Wolff employees, © Ulster Folk and Transport Museum; *Titanic* as seen from the tender *America*, © Father Browne Photographic Collection; Second-class passengers promenading on the boat deck, first published in the *Daily Mirror*, 19 April 1912 © Mirrorpix

Page 6: Jacques Fotrell, © Father Browne Photographic Collection

Page 7: Second-class passengers, © Father Browne Photographic Collection; the bridge of the *Olympic*, © Father Browne Photographic Collection

Page 8: Port bow view of the *Titanic* prior to her launch, © Ulster Folk and Transport Museum; *Titanic* entering the water for the first time on launch day in Belfast, © Ulster Folk and Transport Museum

Plate section 2

Page 1: The Café Parisienne, © Ulster Folk and Transport Museum; The gymnasium, © Father Browne Photographic Collection,; The swimming pool, © Father Browne Photographic Collection

Page 2: First-class elevators, © Ulster Folk and Transport Museum; First-class suite, © Ulster Folk and Transport Museum; First-class en-suite bathroom, © Ulster Folk and Transport Museum; Second-class state room, © Ulster Folk and Transport Museum;

Page 3: Photo of the *Titanic*'s officers, © Ulster Folk and Transport Museum; *Titanic*'s two wireless officers, © Ulster Folk and Transport Museum

Page 4: Inspection of the hull prior to launch, © Ulster Folk and Transport Museum; Thomas Andrew, © Ulster Folk and Transport Museum; First-class passengers awaiting the departure of the boat train from London Waterloo, © Father Browne Photographic Collection

Page 5: Passengers on the White Star Wharf at Queenstown, Ireland, © Father Browne Photographic Collection; Passengers disembarking from the tender *America* at Queenstown, © Father Browne Photographic Collection; Mail being loaded onto *Titanic*, © Father Browne Photographic Collection

Page 6: Artist's impression of the *Titanic* sinking, image courtesy of Southampton City Council Arts and Heritage, published in *The Sphere*, 27 April 1912

Page 6–7: Father Browne's last photograph of the departing *Titanic*, © Father Browne Photographic Collection

Page 7: Survivors being rescued, image courtesy of Southampton City Arts and Heritage, printed in *The Deathless Story of the Titanic* by Philip Gibbs, published by Lloyd's Weekly News, 1912 and new edition Lloyds of London, 1985

Page 8: Anxious relatives awaiting news of survivors, © Southampton Council City Arts and Heritage; The first *Titanic* survivors photographed on their arrival back to Southampton Docks, © Southampton Council City Arts and Heritage

Text Images

All images © National Maritime Museum, Greenwich, London

Page 97: Letter from Marion Wright to her father

Pages 103, 104: Letter from Marion Wright to her father

Pages 136, 137, 138: Letter from George J. Rowe to Walter Lord

Page 148: Transcript of interview between Walter Lord and Mrs Henry B. Harris

Page 169: Letter from Bertha Watt to Walter Lord

Page 197: Letter from Alice Williams to Walter Lord

Pages 198, 200, 202: Photo of *Titanic* collapsible and accompanying letter from Mr Hill to Walter Lord

Page 231, 233: Diary of Frederick A. Hamilton

Page 293: Telegram to Marion Wright's family

About the Author

Dr Nick Barratt obtained a PhD in history from King's College London in 1996. He started work in television whilst working at the BBC as a specialist archive researcher. He is also in demand as a speaker on popular history and geneology following his work as a presenter, reviewer and commentator on all aspects of history, notably family history for the BBC on *Who Do You Think You Are?* Nick also wrote a weekly column in the *Daily Telegraph* called, 'The Family Detective'.

Index